The Path of Faith

Believing, Learning, Following, Resembling Jesus

The Path of Faith
Believing, Learning, Following, Resembling Jesus

2025년 04월 18일 초판 인쇄
2025년 04월 28일 초판 발행

지은이 서창원
펴낸이 정영오
펴낸곳 크리스천르네상스
출판등록 제2019-000004호(2019. 1. 31)
주소 경기도 안산시 단원구 와동로 5길 3, 301호(와동, 대명하이빌)
표지디자인 디자인집(02-521-1474)

ⓒ 서창원, 2025

* 신저작권법에 의하여 한국 내에서 보호받는 저작물이므로
  무단 전재와 무단 복제를 금합니다.
* 잘못된 책은 구입처에서 교환하여 드립니다.

ISBN 979-11-94012-10-8(03230)

값 20,000원

The Path of Faith

Believing, Learning, Following, Resembling Jesus

Rev. Prof. Dr Changwon Shu

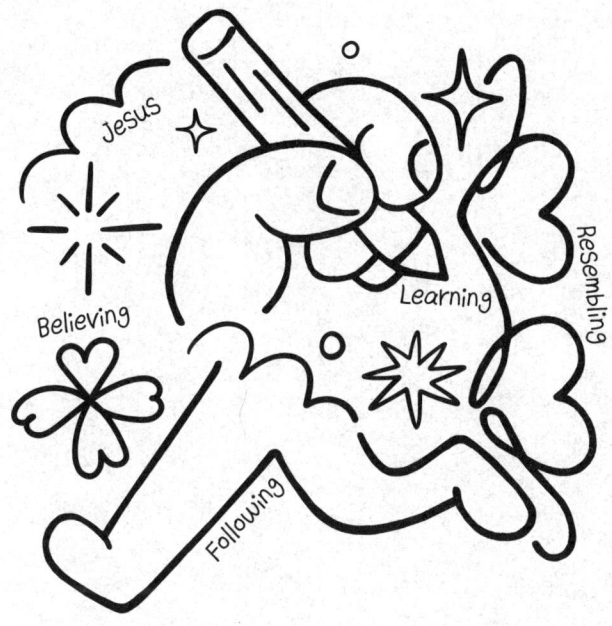

크리스천
르네상스

Contents _

Chapter 1
Believe in Jesus(believing) / 9

Why Jesus?	10
The Basis of Faith	14
Life with Jesus	19
A Life of Worshiping God	22
A Life of Serving the Believers	35
* Review of Learning Content	44

Chapter 2
Learning Jesus / 49

The Way of the New Creation	51
The Path of Learning	59
The Direct Path of Learning	64
The Indirect Path of Learning	67
The Content of Learning	72
The Knowledge of knowing God	76
Knowledge about Humanity	100
Can a Believer Accept Evolution?(By Gregg R. Allison)	103
What is humanity?	109
* Review of Learning Content	124

Chapter 3
Following Jesus / 127

What Does It Mean to Follow Jesus?	128
Entering Through the Narrow Gate	131
Above All, Guard Your Heart	137
Be Filled with the Holy Spirit	141
Take Up Your Cross	150
Take Up the Whole Armor of God	154
* Review of Learning Content	187

| Special Meditation |

1. War with the World	189
2. The Battle with the Flesh	200
3. The War with the Devil	212
4. The Temptation of Jesus Christ	232
5. The Accuser Satan	244

Chapter 4
Resembling Jesus / 255

Love the Lord with All Your Heart	257
Be Like the Gentleness and Humility of Christ	267
Obey Until Death	278
Forgive	281
The Way of Serving	284
Seek the Things Above	286
* Review of Learning Content	291

Chapter 1

Believe in Jesus (believing)

Believing

"Therefore, as you received Christ Jesus the Lord, so walk in him, rooted and built up in him and established in the faith, just as you were taught, abounding in thanksgiving."
(Col. 2:6-7, ESV)

• Chapter 1 •

Believe in Jesus(believing)[1]

'Believe in Jesus!' 'Believe in Jesus and be saved!' What kind of thoughts might come to the person hearing these words? Would they just brush it off as the cry of fanatic believers, dismissing it as nonsense? Or would they be so struck by these words that they begin to ponder and eventually find themselves in a church, a community of believers? As a Christian and an evangelist, naturally, I hope for the latter. However, in reality, much more often than not, evangelists are ignored, mocked, given suspicious glances, or even scorned and ridiculed. Despite this, why do evangelists continue to shout, 'Believe in Jesus'? Why do they sometimes sound like they're threatening people with phrases like, 'If you don't believe in Jesus, you'll fall into the fires of hell'? Is it just to earn an evangelism award from the church? What can those who

---

1   The book **Are You Truly a Christian?** by the author, published by Kingdom Books in 2015, will greatly help both new and existing believers establish their identity in relation to this book. In particular, the sections on the evidence of being a believer and receiving the guidance of the Holy Spirit will provide practical help in believing in Jesus, learning, following, and becoming more like Him.

evangelize actually say about what it means to believe in Jesus? What does it mean to believe in Jesus, and what does salvation truly mean?

The desire to answer these questions has existed since the early church. The writings of the church fathers primarily address who Jesus is, what it means to believe in Him, and what the path of the believer should look like. In particular, the Apostles' Creed, confessions of faith, and catechisms describe well what it means to believe in Jesus. Just as the church did in the past, today's churches, regardless of denomination, urgently need to reaffirm and instill in their congregations the confessions of faith and catechisms that have traditionally been accepted and upheld by the church. This will reveal the true value of unwavering faith and lay the foundation for the church to stand firm as believers who delight the Lord through faith alone, and as lights and salt in the world, bearing fruit that will have eternal impact."

Why Jesus?

Before exploring what it means to believe in Jesus, let's first ask: Why must it be Jesus? This is an important question to consider. The object of faith is not something created by social conventions or customs, nor is it a subjective belief shaped by progressive or conservative ideologies. When I say I believe in Jesus, I am confessing that He is the object of my faith. Just as one might seek an ideological shift, faith is not about progressing toward or switching to something better at any given time; it is about confessing an unchanging belief in Jesus.

The first time I heard the name "**Jesus**" was, of course, at church. As a child, I heard it during Christmas celebrations in the church, while celebrating the arrival of the Savior. However, I didn't even understand the basic meaning of the name at that time. My only interest back then was the gift packages handed out by the church. They weren't anything special, but in the rural area where getting even a crumb of candy was difficult, and buying new school supplies was not easy, the candy bags or school supplies given out by the church were enough of an attraction to draw me to church.

However, it wasn't until I received the grace of salvation that I started to think about the true meaning of the name "**Jesus.**" During my middle school years, when I had a curiosity about divine beings, I read both religious texts—such as the Bible and Buddhist scriptures—and eventually came to believe that the God in the Bible was the true God. This led me to attend church regularly, and through the gospel preached there, my thoughts about Jesus deepened, ultimately leading me to salvation. I found the answer to the question, "**Why Jesus?**" at that time: there is no other savior who can rescue a sinner from sin.

The name "**Jesus**" is understood by believers to be the same as the name "**Joshua**" in the Old Testament, meaning "**Savior.**" "**She will bear a son, and you shall call his name Jesus, for he will save his people from their sins**" (Matthew 1:21). The term "**Savior**" can only be used under the assumption that humanity is in need of salvation due to sin. Of course, saving someone from drowning, rescuing a person from a fire, a traffic accident, or a natural disaster can all be considered forms of salvation. However, people do not worship firefighters, police officers, or brave citizens who risk their lives to help others as saviors. While these individuals are undoubtedly admirable and heroic, they cannot act as saviors who can rescue everyone in the world from the ultimate danger. Just because someone rescues one person in a specific situation does not mean they can rescue others in the same circumstances.

Therefore, to believe in Jesus means to accept that He is the only universal Savior who offers salvation to all sinners through faith in Him. This begins with exploring the teachings of the Bible, which is filled with messages of salvation, to understand who Jesus is, what He did, and why we must believe in Him. These teachings provide undeniable reasons for our faith in Him.

Moreover, there is no one in the world who can save humanity from sin. The Bible clearly declares that only Jesus can save us from sin. His coming into the world was not due to human ecological nature. He was not conceived through the union of a man and a woman, but through the coming of the Most High, the baby Jesus was conceived in Mary's womb. At the appointed time, He was born into the world as a child who grew by nursing from His mother's breast. He was not a child conceived through an illicit affair, as some strange logic might suggest. He was the Son of God who came into this world through the body of a pure virgin. Confessing belief in this is true faith. 'What, you want me to believe this? It sounds absurd, but they're presenting it so convincingly. How can you ask me to believe it?' This is a natural response from those who have no knowledge of Jesus. The expression of disbelief is evident. They ask questions like, 'If there was a family photo of Jesus or if there were records of Mary's gynecological treatment, then maybe I'd believe,' uttering nonsense. This was a time when there were no moving pictures, no gynecological clinics, and no medical facilities. Religion is merely a fabrication of people, they argue, often presenting such reasoning with an air of superiority, but faith is not based on scientific facts.[2] Even if scientific facts are presented, some will

---

[2] Yuval Harari, 21 Lessons for the 21st Century, Translated by Byonggeun Kim, Kimyoungsa, 2018. This book is a representative type.

not believe, and those who have faith will believe even without scientific evidence.

None of the early Christian believers believed in Jesus based on scientific facts. Even though they did not see, they believed and possessed inexpressible joy. In fact, faith is not something for everyone (2 Thessalonians 3:2). This might be criticized as an extreme prejudice or dogmatism, but it is the truth. Despite being told to believe in Jesus, many still do not believe. Those who do not believe would mock Christians as fools who believe in a myth made by humans. On the other hand, I wonder what they think about the academic achievements, industrial progress, and scientific developments accomplished by those who believe in Jesus. Believers are not people with less brainpower or less developed mental and physical structures than non-believers. Conversely, they are not madmen who have been driven to insanity by too much learning. The believer has an undeniable and clear truth about the object of their faith, and because of this, even death, the thing that humans fear most, could not silence them. The phrase 'I believe in God' in English originally means 'I am believing into God.' The preposition 'into,' which is typically used to show direction, is different from 'in,' which usually denotes a location or state. Therefore, believing in God is not about veering to the left or right, nor about looking back while holding a plow in hand. It is about moving forward only toward God. Thus, belief is not a temporary religious practice or hobby, but a lifelong journey that continues until one finds complete rest in God.

The Basis of Faith

Interestingly, faith is a virtue that humans possess, but Christian faith is not something that originates from humans themselves; rather, it is a gift given to humanity by God, the object of faith. If all humans possessed it, it would be hard to call it a gift. When I give someone a gift, if I give it to everyone, then the gift loses its special meaning to the recipient. A gift must be something special for the person receiving it in order to have value. God's gift is given to those who are chosen according to His sovereign will and His good purpose. Therefore, believing in Jesus may seem like a decision made by human will, but it is actually a gift from God. Jesus Himself said: **"No one can come to me unless the Father who sent me draws them..."** (John 6:44). The Jews believed that they were all chosen by God because of their physical, natural birth. However, what Jesus was saying was that the inheritance of faith is not automatically achieved through lineage, physical desire, or human will; before they could come to God, God must first draw them. Belief in Jesus is from God (John 1:14). Anyone who responds to God the Father will also respond to the Son. Without this drawing, no one would feel the need for a Savior.

In this sense, to believe means to receive (believe), and to receive means to embrace (John 1:12, Colossians 2:6). We often like to feel that we are the ones **"leading"** in our relationship with God. However, the truth is that when He calls, we come. This understanding of God's initiative in salvation means that God is leading people, and those whom the Father leads will come to His Son, Jesus. Therefore, believers are compelled to preach the gospel. Even if the majority responds with opposition, mockery, and persecution, this cannot stop the preaching of the gospel, because the preacher, too, is led by God, and there are those who will be led to Christ by the preacher. No human wisdom, power, or coercive means can prevent, block, or hinder the Father's leading. Preaching is done because there will certainly be fruits. Although it may seem like the work of the evangelist, it is, in fact, the work of God. Jesus said in John 6:29, "**The work of God is to believe in the one he has sent.**" Therefore, believing in Jesus Christ means coming to Christ, and coming to Christ means that the Father leads us to Christ. Being led to Christ means that those who were chosen before the foundation of the world, who were predestined for eternal life, will come to receive Christ and become God's children.

However, God's choosing and leading are unseen to our eyes. Therefore, from a human perspective, coming to Jesus itself can be understood as the same as believing in Jesus. Of course, coming to Jesus is not the entirety of faith. It is merely the beginning, like taking the first steps of a child. But for the one who comes, it is an outward act of believing that Jesus is our Savior and our King. Coming to the Lord also means recognizing that it is the only true way to come to God the Father. When Jesus says, "**Let the little children come to me**" and that "**the kingdom of heaven belongs to such as these,**" He is declaring that He Himself is the only way to the kingdom of heaven. This is because He is the Way, the Truth, and the Life. Hearing this truth generates faith.

Therefore, those who criticize or mock evangelism may find it difficult to understand, but evangelism will always bear fruit, even if it takes time. This is because there is no mistake or regret in God's work. Whether the time is favorable or not, the reason for preaching is to call people to believe in Jesus. Through such proclamations, God creates faith in people, leads them to Jesus, and grants them the authority to become children of God. The Greek word for "**leading**" used by Jesus carries the same meaning as the word in Jeremiah 31:3 in the Old Testament, which says, "**I have loved you with an everlasting love; therefore I have continued my faithfulness to you.**" This "**leading**" is not an irresistible (unrejectable) grace. Even Augustine, a great supporter of the doctrine of grace, confessed this. If a person were to be dragged unwillingly, he might argue that it is a form of coercion contrary to his will. But consider this: if a person does not want to be led, they would not believe, and if they do not believe, then they have not truly come. It is not through the independent action of running to Christ with our own will, but only through God's leading and the reception of the truth He presents that we come to Christ by faith. It is not a physical submission to coercive power, but a voluntary movement of the heart and will. In this sense, we do not need to think that coming to the Lord is something we are dragged into against our will. This voluntary drawing is motivated by love. Thus, God leads His people with His everlasting love. The faith that follows is the willing submission of our will, moved by God's love. This could be described as the persuasion through the inner working of the Holy Spirit.

Therefore, the "**drawing**" here is not a pull caused by attraction, but rather a "**drawing**" by the inner inspiration of the Holy Spirit, or an understanding of it as being captivated or persuaded. In this sense, Chrysostom explains that "**coming to God is not a drawing that removes our role, but rather emphasizes the necessary help that draws us to God.**" This is understandable even when considering the issue of election. It is God who leads those chosen to receive His gift. It is not I who chose God, but God who chose me. How do we know this? Because those who were determined to receive eternal life are the ones who accept Jesus as their Savior (Acts 13:48). As evidence, through the call of the gospel, those who hear the call and are captivated by the gospel come to the Lord through voluntary obedience, believing in their hearts and confessing with their mouths. This drawing or attraction is the invisible work of the Holy Spirit. In other words, faith does not come by seeing, but by hearing (Romans 10:17, 2 Corinthians 4:18).[3]

In this way, to **"believe"** is the same as to **"receive"** or **"embrace."** The foundation of faith is belief. Without faith, one cannot be called a believer. A Christian is someone who receives and acknowledges Jesus Christ as the Lord and God. Jesus Christ is the only Savior who saves His people from their sins, and all things were made by Him, through Him, and for Him. He is the true God, and the one who is received and honored as the Savior. Jesus Christ is equal to the true God, who has existed from eternity, and in the fullness of time, He became human to save sinners. This is the complete belief that Jesus Christ bore all the sins of mankind, drank the cup of God's wrath, and surrendered to the power of death, which is the wage of sin. He took the punishment that sinners deserved, died, and on the third day, rose again. We believe that He overcame all the powers of sin and death and, having won the victory, grants eternal life to those who believe in Him, making them righteous and blameless before God, standing holy and without reproach. We acknowledge that He will return to judge the living and the dead, and that believing in Him means confessing this with our hearts and mouths.

This belief cannot exist without one essential premise. That is hu-

---

3   **"So then faith cometh by hearing, and hearing by the word of God,"** "While we look not at the things which are seen, but at the things which are not seen: for the things which are seen are temporal; but the things which are not seen are eternal!"

mans are sinners who are absolutely in need of salvation. The reason Jesus came to this earth was not to call the righteous but to call sinners, so that they might be saved from the power of sin and death. Just as a sick person needs a doctor, a sinner needs a Savior. Without a Savior, how could humanity ever resolve the problem of sin?

Therefore, determining whether one is a Christian or not is not simply about whether one is a registered church member or attends church regularly. It is not about attending every meeting without fail or being diligent in tithing. Nor is it about being born into a Christian family, receiving basic religious education, and growing up in that environment. Faith is not proven by becoming a member of a family. Faith begins with a personal encounter with the Lord Jesus Christ. It starts with the confession and declaration that Jesus is the Christ, the Son of the living God. Spiritual birth begins with the confession of faith in Jesus Christ. In other words, those who receive Him and believe in His name are believers and children of God. To them, the power to become children of God is granted.

This does not simply mean attending an event to welcome and receive a dignitary or prominent person at a ceremonial function. An usher at such an event can participate without having any relationship with the dignitary. However, the role of a believer is not merely to participate in ceremonial acts of worshiping God Almighty. To receive means to believe, and to believe means to fully entrust my entire existence to Him. Just as a child's life, growth, and activities are entirely dependent on the care of their mother, believing in Jesus means acknowledging that every aspect of my life, including my future, is completely in the hands of the Lord Jesus Christ. It means sharing in fellowship with Him, discussing all the challenges in my life with Him, entrusting my life to Him, and depending entirely on His guidance and providence. It is walking with Him, for Him, and toward Him. Previously, I could not see Him, nor did I know of His presence, but now I know that there is no other god like Him in all creation. I have come to believe in Him. I no longer chase after elusive illusions, but instead, I recognize and worship the true God revealed in the Bible. At the same time, whether I live or die, I live and die for the Lord, not hesitating to be His servant (Romans 14:8).

To believe in Him as Lord (Kyrios) means to affirm that He is the most trustworthy, the one worth believing and following. Therefore, since my ownership belongs entirely to Him, I fully entrust myself to the Lord according to His will. This is the reality of confessing faith in the Lord. This entrusting is not like storing all my wealth in a bank vault for safekeeping. The most important aspect of entrusting is the ongoing personal encounter and fellowship between myself and the Lord Jesus Christ. There are many human relationships that end after a single encounter, but believing in Jesus is having a relationship with Him that is like that of a husband and wife who walk together for a lifetime. Just as no one can separate what God has joined together, the fellowship with our Lord Jesus Christ is a life-giving bond that can never be broken or separated by tribulation, hardship, persecution, danger, sword, famine, nakedness, or anything else.

Life with Jesus

Then, our faith in believing in Jesus must be not just abstract, but practical. What kind of picture would that look like? Since an inseparable relationship has been formed with the Lord, it is shown by living a life with Him throughout one's life, demonstrating that my faith toward Him is not fictional, but real. As pointed out earlier, it is not about being satisfied with a temporary life, remaining in a mechanical role in a ceremonial event where one is involved in receiving the highest VIP as a reception committee. Nor is it about feeling satisfied or secure simply with a sense of belonging to the church, like a member of a particular political party. It is also not enough to feel content with my name being listed on the earthly church register, like an ID card, instead of the Book of Life in heaven. Like the recipients of the Epistle to the Hebrews, even if one has attended church for years, yet remains at a beginner level (Hebrews 5:12, 6:1), should we not feel any shame? Regardless of the reason, a truly normal person seeks to grow in their area of life. Faith involves growth. Otherwise, one is nothing but a spiritual infant with any progress. A normal person grows not only physically, but spiritually and mentally. This growth leads one to become a skilled professional. Of course, proficiency in functional roles is necessary, but maturity without familiarity with the spiritual world is impossible. The difference between the child and the adult mentioned in Hebrews will be explored in more detail later, but here I want to point out the difference between a self-centered person and one who is not. Before receiving Jesus as Lord, life was focused on self-satisfaction and gain. However, even after believing in Jesus, some still carry that mentality and remain in a spiritual child-like state. Those who are unable to overcome this, often cause crying, irritation, and quarrels, and sometimes even division. One of the serious issues facing the church today is this. There are too many spiritual infants within the church. Though time has passed, and they are no different in size from adults, they are not mature in speech, behavior, faith, or love. This is not just the problem of a few individuals but is also seen among church leaders. It's like the blind leading the blind. It is not easy to break free from the whirlpool of confusion and conflict that continues to arise.

However, the maturity of believing in Jesus is not proven by joining a religious group and becoming skilled in the various visible duties of that group. A significant number of church members take pleasure in and are satisfied with this appearance, even feeling pleased with the crumbs that occasionally fall from the table because of it. When one attains an honorary position in the church, they consider it a great success. I would like to ask such people: To what extent do you have intimacy with Jesus Christ, the object of our faith, and what knowledge do you have of Him? Is it just that knowing His name? Or do you barely cross the threshold? Or do you search every corner of the house, even reaching the floor by the fire? Can you explain who Jesus Christ is, as clearly as describing a popular soap opera? How does the knowledge that He is my Lord and King influence your life? How deeply do you feel His reign and sovereignty in your personal life? Do you experience the joy of continuous fellowship and communion with Him? Do the people around you see and recognize these truths from you? If these things are not happening, what is the reason? It is because there is no desire to know, learn, follow, or imitate Him. This issue will be examined in detail in the context of learning from Jesus.

However, the central role that makes all of this possible is firmly established only through the church that the Lord has set up, through the church, and because of the church. In this sense, as Calvin described the church as the "**mother of the faithful**" (Mater Fidelium), it is true that believing in Jesus is deeply linked with being part of the church. Through attending the church, nurturing and care are realized. However, attending church without believing in Jesus is meaningless. Of course, as pointed out earlier, attending church is not a temporary or impulsive activity. It is not just a part of leisure activities that one attends occasionally when needed. It is the entirety of life, and eternal. Since faith has the characteristic of growth, it is impossible without hearing. Hearing comes from the Word of Christ, and without attending a church community where the pure gospel truth is proclaimed, one cannot achieve the growth of faith. The church is the body of Christ, and the saints are the members connected to that body.

Therefore, believing in Jesus does not stop at the confession of the heart and the mouth. If there is faith, it leads to worship and service to the Lord of our faith and who perfects us. If the purpose of God's creation and human creation is to proclaim God's glory to the whole earth, the most natural means of fulfilling this is through the act of worship. The primary function of the church community, the gathering of believers, is worship. Therefore, living a life of faith with Jesus is marked by worshiping God above and serving fellow believers beside us.

A Life of Worshiping God

Worship is both a privilege and a duty that stems from God's principle of creation. When God placed Adam and Eve in the Garden of Eden, He told them they could eat from every tree in the garden, except the fruit of the tree of the knowledge of good and evil. There has been much debate over this, but the most certain point is that it made clear that humanity cannot exist without God. The unique privilege of walking with God in the garden, a privilege no other creature could enjoy, shows the special relationship between humanity and God. While all creatures, like humans, were created by God, not all were permitted to enjoy the same joy of walking and running with God. Of course, all of creation reflects God's glory (Psalm 19:1 and following), but only humans, made in the image of God, are the beings who reverently worship God as a personal being. Tragically, the highest created being, human beings, fell into the temptation of wanting to become like God and were expelled from Eden. The worst consequence of humanity's fall was not just the loss of eternal life, but the severing of fellowship with God. This led to the creation of false gods and the idolatry that ensnared humanity: **"They exchanged the glory of the immortal God for images made to look like mortal human beings and birds and animals and reptiles"** (Romans 1:23). Humans fell from being true worshipers of God to those who exalted falsehood.

In truth, God's purpose in creating humanity in His image in the Garden of Eden was so that humans would acknowledge His dignity and give worship and praise to Him alone: **"The people I formed for myself that they may proclaim my praise"** (Isaiah 43:21). This is the same purpose stated in Isaiah 43:7, where it is declared that humanity was created for God's glory. Of course, all of God's creation is meant to praise the Creator (Psalm 148:7-10), but the creature best equipped to sing His praise and give glory is humanity: **"Let them praise the name of the Lord, for his name alone is exalted; his glory is above the earth and the heavens"** (Psalm 148:13). The psalmist concludes by saying, **"He has raised up a horn for his people, the praise of all his faithful servants, of Israel, the people close to his heart. Praise the Lord!"** (Psalm 148:14). The apostle Paul also makes this clear in his letter to the

Ephesians: "**Praise be to the God and Father of our Lord Jesus Christ, who has blessed us in the heavenly realms with every spiritual blessing in Christ. For he chose us in him before the creation of the world to be holy and blameless in his sight. In love he predestined us for adoption to sonship through Jesus Christ, in accordance with his pleasure and will—to the praise of his glorious grace, which he has freely given us in the One he loves**" (Ephesians 1:3-6). In verse 14, Paul affirms that the purpose of salvation is to bring praise to God's glory. Thus, praise is the central element of true worship. God has made us His children, granting us the amazing privilege of calling Him "**Abba, Father**" by His immeasurable love and grace, despite our death in transgressions and sins. Therefore, singing praises to His glory is a clear sign of true faith. A faith life without worship is impossible, but worship without praise cannot be complete.

However, unfortunately, today, the worship in Protestant churches is strangely marked by idolatry and subtle mixture, all done in the name of the Triune God.[4] It produces more people who come to see the worship than those who actually worship God. To such people, a single bird in their hand is worth more than ten birds in the forest. However, true worship must be filled with reverence for God, which is expressed through complete obedience to the word of God that is heard, and respect for the God revealed in that word. There is no greater active act of faith than this in response to God's amazing grace of redemption. Worship is the act that best reveals the relationship that humanity must

---

4 As pointed out earlier, instead of proclaiming the faith that arises from the gospel, there is a rush to show it. For those who believe that faith is generated or stirred by visible things, the visible world is more valuable than the invisible world. It is natural that idolatry arises from this.

have with God—why God is worthy of worship and why humans must worship God alone. In that sense, worship is not passive; it is active, voluntary, and enthusiastic participation. Worship is an encounter with the Almighty Creator God, and it is a meeting and fellowship with God and His people. Therefore, avoiding this makes a life of faith impossible. Ascending to God's house to worship this God is the most certain way to fulfill the highest joy and expectation that a human being can have on earth (Psalm 122:1). What makes this possible is faith in the Lord Jesus Christ, who is the only way, truth, and life leading to the Father. A life with Jesus leads to acts of worshiping God.

In fact, the joy of worship cannot be obtained by the worshiper's own qualifications. Of course, it is clear that before God, the saints are set apart, holy, blameless, and without reproach (Colossians 1:22), but the basis of this grace is the redemption of the Lord Jesus Christ, who reconciled us to God through His bloodshed on the cross, even though we were once His enemies. Therefore, offering ourselves as holy living sacrifices to God, which is a spiritual worship, is a voluntary decision made by the worshiper, and this decision is a natural and normal response for those who believe in the infinite love that God has bestowed through His Son, Jesus Christ. The natural response of the faithful, who are compelled by that love, is to worship God with all their heart, soul, and strength, as a confession of love. It is a reverence accompanied by thorough self-submission and dedication. Such true worship cannot help but be filled with joy. In the modern church, where worship is often reduced to formality and habitual practices, and where it focuses on entertainment, no one can experience the joy of worship in God's presence. This is because worship that is not focused on God is nothing different from idolatry, devoid of God's presence.

After Solomon's death and the division of Israel into two kingdoms, Jeroboam, who exerted the most powerful leadership in the northern kingdom of Israel, led the people to worship a golden calf. This act is described as **"the prototype of all questionable religious practices introduced in the name of the true God."** The text sharply warns about the deviation of today's evangelical church worship practices, stating that **"religious acts are not necessarily acceptable to God just because they are instituted in God's name."** Worship, as a practice, may seek convenience and popularity, and while it may be conducted in the holy name of Jesus, it could still deceive people. The rejection of Jeroboam's worship by God serves as a lesson to all generations of faithful believers, encouraging them to continue worship as prescribed by Scripture and not to replace it with something else.[5] The author also diagnoses the spiritual poverty in the worship practices of modern churches, particularly the outwardly fervent worship, and satirizes this as a hollow form of worship. They raise key questions such as: **"Is the preaching message faithful and biblical according to the gospel of Jesus Christ, or is it contaminated by the hedonistic culture around us? Does our public worship lead believers to worship the true God, or is it just aesthetically pleasing and entertaining?"** The text asserts that Christianity can only apply cultural or social forms to itself while remaining faithful to God's word.[6]

However, the act of worshiping God is not limited to public worship in the church. Through public worship, believers receive God's grace, which enables them to express their faith in their homes, work-

---

5   John R. Thornbury, The Convenient Religion of Jeroboam I, The Banner of Truth in Korea, #188, 2024, August, 62.

6   *In the above, 63.*

places, and daily lives. Everything in life—whether eating, drinking, or any action—should be for the glory of God. This expresses the idea that our lives themselves are a continuous act of worship. Both communal worship and individual acts of worship are included in this. The appearance of one's life and devotion cannot be separated; rather, they are meant to run concurrently and become fully integrated into life. The grace received from the Lord, who loves the gates of Zion more than the houses of Jacob, has a profound impact on believers' homes, businesses, and social lives. Without this, faith becomes an accessory, used only when needed, rather than being the foundation of one's entire life. A believer's personal worship and daily life align with the written word when they become true worshipers whom God accepts. This highlights the repeated emphasis on the importance of public worship.[7]

Public worship, as part of the faith community, is the gathering of the entire church on the day set by the Lord, the Sabbath. It is God who established this principle first, not Adam and Eve who suggested it to please God. God set apart the Sabbath day as a day for worship and declared it **"My Sabbath."** Those who observe the Sabbath and rejoice in the Lord will receive a memorial and a name better than that of sons and will be given an eternal name that will never be cut off (Isaiah 56:4-5). Furthermore, even foreigners who **"join together to serve and love the name of the Lord, keeping the Sabbath and not defiling it, and holding fast to His covenant"** will be led to God's holy mountain and will find joy in His house of prayer. Their sacrifices will be gladly accepted on God's altar, for His house will be called a house

---

[7] For more information on the importance of public worship, the author recommends referring to pages 209 and onwards in *Puritan Theology and Faith* (Ji-pyeong Publishing, 2013).

of prayer for all nations (Isaiah 56:6-7).

This passage emphasizes the importance of the seventh day as the Lord's Day, which must be observed as a day of rest and worship. While humans are given dominion over the other six days, the seventh day is specifically the Lord's, and its ownership is not granted to Christians to use freely. The teachings passed down by the faith's ancestors, including the importance of keeping the Sabbath, are still relevant today. Not only did the Lord command a day of worship, but He also provided specific guidelines on how to worship. In this regard, Reformed churches emphasize the "**regulatory principle**" of worship and urge believers not to deviate from it.[8]

However, today's churches often cater to the preferences of congregants, even to the point of treating the Lord's Day as a day that belongs to the people, freely used as they wish. Worship styles are often tailored to meet the worshipers' desires, turning this foolish behavior into something that seems acceptable. The purpose of worship is to express the highest value, and the glory of worship directed to God is like placing the heaviest weight upon Him. In this sense, the Puritans worked hard during the other six days to properly observe the Lord's Day, ensuring it was kept holy. In contrast, we tend to view the Sabbath as a day to rest in order to work well during the other six days. The truth is, even the six days do not belong to us; they belong to the Lord, who created them. While we are given freedom to use the six days, we are not exempt from responsibility for how we use them. Therefore, we must remember

---

[8] The regulative principle of worship means that, unlike worship models, the order of worship must be based entirely on the Bible and should not be constructed using human imagination or any devised methods.

to use this freedom within the framework of discerning what is good, pleasing, and perfect according to the Lord's will.

There is one point to address here: Can observing the Sabbath be achieved with just one time worship service? Nowadays, many churches in Korea have made it the norm to hold only one service on Sundays, or an afternoon service instead of the traditional evening service. During my years of study in the 1980s in UK, I found it odd that Korean churches followed this pattern, but today, no one in Korea questions the practice of having only one Sunday service. Even when there is an afternoon service, the number of attendees is often less than a third of those who attend in the morning. I remember being challenged when I saw local churches abroad, particularly in the United States, where sometimes more people attended evening services. I assume that in the UK, local churches now also have significantly fewer attendees. In the past and even today, the practice of having two services on Sundays is disappearing, and even Reformed church members have internal doubts about whether it is absolutely necessary to have two services. Furthermore, the experience of the COVID-19 pandemic has led to a reality where both the head and the heart must be in sync. This raises the question: Can one service really be enough to observe the Sabbath without any issues? As someone who actively supports the traditional practice of holding two services, I first acknowledge that the Bible does not explicitly command that we must have two or three services. However, I believe that the practice of having morning and evening worship is rooted in Scripture. This is based on God's creation principle, where He structured the day to begin with evening and then morning ("**And there was evening, and there was morning**" - Genesis 1). In Numbers 28:1-10 and Exodus 29:38-39, God commands the Israelites to offer sacrifices in the morning and evening at the Tabernacle. This is why the Psalmist declares in Psalm 92, a psalm dedicated to the Sabbath, "**It is good to give thanks to the Lord, to sing praises to your name, O Most High; to declare your steadfast love in the morning, and your faithfulness by night**" (Psalm 92:1-2). There is no reason to reject the idea that this tradition continued among the early New Testament church members. In Acts 20, we see that the Apostle Paul gathered with believers on the first day of the week (Sunday) to break bread and continued to preach until midnight. He preached for such an extended period that a young man named Eutychus fell from a window and was injured, but was later revived. This experience may have served as the foundation for the early church's tradition of holding extended worship services.

In fact, holding an evening service is not only a great help for keeping the Sabbath holy, but also a means of grace that adds more devotion to the faith life of the congregation. Pastor Michael Brown said in his article Preserving the Evening Service: "**One of the great practical benefits of having both morning and evening services is that they provide an excellent structure to help families keep the Lord's Day holy. The two services are like the spine of the Sabbath, allowing Christians not only to make a few hours in the morning holy but also to keep the entire day holy, as commanded**' (unlike what is popular in our culture, it is still the Lord's Day, not just the Lord's morning). **Observing His day is a sign of the covenant community of God, distinguishing it as holy and reminding its members that they are pilgrims on the way to the eternal Sabbath. Therefore, the evening service provides a beautiful rhythm for the Lord's Day. For centuries, countless Christians have realized that the gap between the morning and evening services is the perfect time for food, fellowship, devout reading, family prayer, acts of mercy, or, most not** so importantly, a nap! **Christians, freed from the madness of the week, can enjoy a day of worship and rest."**

Is there a better way to end a holy day than gathering with the covenant community to engage in the Word, fellowship, the Lord's Supper, and prayer (referencing Acts 2:42)?[9] What do you think? If living by faith can be called living by worship, then shouldn't the practice of worshiping twice on Sundays be something we must observe? Moreover, in this time when the wave of secularization is stronger than ever, if we can make use of the means of grace that God has provided even once more, it is only natural that there would be great spiritual benefits.

Heidelberg Catechism, Question 65, asks, **"It is through faith alone that we share in Christ and all his benefits: where then does that faith come from?"** The answer is, **"The Holy Spirit produces it in our hearts by the preaching of the holy gospel, and confirms it by the use of the holy sacraments."** Of course, the problem lies with the preaching of pastors. As pointed out earlier, in places where it is difficult to hear biblical and faithful preaching of Christ's gospel, filled with the inspiration of grace and truth, worship rituals can degenerate into mere religious events. When I served as an associate pastor, I was in charge of the evening services. Originally, about 40 or 50 people attended, but many began to gather to hear the associate pastor's sermon, which lasted over an hour. I was preaching through the Shorter Catechism, and when I left after two years to become the senior pastor, more than 200 people were attending. Even when I was a senior pastor, I emphasized the evening service and encouraged at least two-thirds of the congregation who attended in the morning to participate. The congre-

---

9   Michael Brown, "Preservation of Evening Service" in the Banner of Truth, October, 2007.

gation cooperated well, and I have vivid memories of even children attending enthusiastically. The pastor's efforts should follow in helping the congregation experience how much more abundant the grace is in public gatherings than in small group meetings.

True faith, strictly speaking, would be far more useful if we worshiped not just twice, but three or four times a week. However, this is the same as answering the question of why Sunday is only one day a week. While it is clear that having worship every day would greatly nourish and strengthen our faith, God has granted us only one day a week. On my way to Kenya, I stopped in Doha, and it just so happened that it was Friday. In the Middle East, due to the Islamic tradition, they do not worship on Sunday but instead observe Friday as their holy day. Not knowing this, I had planned to spend the day sightseeing. However, everything came to a halt, and I ended up attending a Korean church service that day. Then, as I spent the following Sundays in Kenya, I experienced, for the first time in my life, two Sundays in one week. At that time, I was more deeply grateful not for having two Sundays, but for the grace of having just one Sunday each week. I truly realize, from a pastoral perspective, how beneficial it is to keep the Lord's Day holy by worshiping twice, in the morning and evening, as it strengthens our faith.

We must respond to God's call to worship with the joyful act of obedience to Him. Evening worship provides us with continuity with the historic Christian Church. Many Christians hesitate to attend evening services because it is not part of their custom. But what they need to understand is that if they are only accustomed to a single worship service on the Lord's Day, they are not familiar with the practices of the historic Christian Church, but rather with modern innovations.

When we look at church history, we see that morning and evening services were common on the Lord's Day. In the early 4th century, Eusebius of Caesarea, the church historian, described the universal practice of the church in the following way: **"At the rise of the morning sun and at the evening hour, hymns and praises and truly sacred joy are offered to God in the churches of the whole world. This is not a small sign of God's power. God's joy is, in fact, the praise that resounds in all His churches on earth, both in the morning and the evening."**[10]

After the Reformation, evening services were primarily focused on explaining and teaching Reformed doctrine, but these were heavily attacked by the Arminians. As a result, this issue was raised at the Synod of Dort, and after long discussions, it was concluded that evening worship should be protected and cherished as an opportunity for the continued flourishing of Reformed faith and for Christians to have a greater opportunity to deepen their understanding. For centuries, this practice continued as a major part of Reformed worship, and it was practiced in the Dutch Reformed Church, English Puritans, Scottish Presbyterianism, and even in the Anglican and early Lutheran traditions. Therefore, Protestant churches that completely abolished evening services must understand that they have greatly deviated from the historic practices of the Christian Church.

As a pastor entrusted with the responsibility of feeding the flock and caring for their souls, I encourage you to attend evening services.

---

10   Eusebius of Caesarea, 'Historia Ecclesiastica', in *Nicene and Post-Nicene Fathers*, Second Series, Volume 1, trs. by Arthur Cushman McGiffert, Harvard University Press, 359.

It is beneficial for your soul. Of course, some may find it difficult to attend evening services due to their circumstances. There are those who may be physically uncomfortable or in situations where it is practically impossible to attend. However, most people who do not attend evening services prioritize their physical comfort over their spiritual benefit. It is not wrong to seek to distinguish between Christians and non-Christians through the observance of the Lord's Day. The practice of keeping the Sabbath truly vitalizes the history of practical faith.

Moreover, worship has a powerful influence on all areas of the believer's life. Therefore, it is impossible to have a faith life without worship, just as worship without faith cannot be recognized as proper. Obedience from a heart full of devotion is better than a formal sacrifice that excludes the heart. Such worship does not become a heavy burden for anyone in the congregation. It is like a spring that overflows with joy, excitement, expectation, and love. Worship that focuses on the worshiper's interest and emotions becomes a burden because the performance of the worship director becomes the priority. While temporary pleasure may come from the fulfillment of performance, it does not lead to spiritual maturity. This is because the direction of the worship is tailored to people's preferences and reactions. As this repeats, it becomes a tiresome church life that feels like a burden. The faith life of such individuals is likely to be a beautiful but hollow appearance. **"As each has received a gift, use it to serve one another, as good stewards of God's varied grace: whoever speaks, as one who speaks oracles of God; whoever serves, as one who serves by the strength that God supplies— in order that in everything God may be glorified through Jesus Christ. To him belong glory and dominion forever and ever. Amen!"** (1 Peter 4:10-11).

I wonder if the worship directors frequently exposed in modern churches have received an extraordinary gift for worship direction from God. Did the priests of the Old Testament plan and direct worship rituals? Did the leaders of the New Testament church design and direct the way to approach God and rehearse it? If any of you find such things, I ask you to let me know immediately. Gifts of any kind are given by grace, and they are for building up the body of Christ, not for show or for the sake of performance. God has entrusted us with grace to open wide the door to the tremendous blessing of becoming children of God, so that in everything, through our Lord Jesus Christ, we may give glory to God. The Bible does not mention worship directors, nor is there any mention of worship directors receiving applause. In fact, there is no such thing as the "**glory applause to God**" which would be irreverent. Leading someone to exhaustion while claiming it is for the Lord is the work of the devil. Serving the Lord is not a continuous cycle of exhaustion that wears down the body. It is work done with joy and gratitude, sweating in thankfulness. Such people rejoice, considering it right to suffer and endure persecution and trials for the name of Jesus Christ (Acts 5:41).

A Life of Serving the Believers

Belief in Jesus is not just about worship, but also about loving and serving our neighbors as ourselves. The entire life of a believer is service to God and to others. Serving as the light and salt of the earth, performing good deeds as children of God, and reaching out with loving hands to those who are poor, needy, suffering, and in pain—if we do not do these things, our worship becomes a testimony of hypocrisy. The truth that faith without works is dead is self-evident. If you claim to be offering yourself to God but attempt to avoid honoring your parents, or if you claim to love the unseen God but do not love your visible brothers and sisters, there is no opportunity for absolution before God, who sees the heart. Service is not about giving what is unnecessary to others but about sharing what is precious to me. Though we know that it is more blessed to give than to receive, service is not an investment for personal gain. It is like throwing away our wealth into a flowing river for the sake of those in need. In such service, the Lord does not remain blind but remembers and rewards accordingly (Hebrews 6:10). There is a reward awaiting us in heaven. It is not to gain popularity with people, nor to satisfy a desire for showing off. Knowing that everything I have comes from the Lord (all good things come from the Father of lights), I willingly offer it for the glory of the Lord and for His church and people. Sharing and charity should first be directed to the members of the faith, but at the same time, through our good deeds, we should lead the Gentiles to give glory to God.

Serving is when the great help the small, the strong help the weak, those with wealth help those without, the wise help the ignorant, and those with worth help those without worth, so that all may share in the heavenly inheritance. When the small serve the great, it is likely to be a form of submission entangled with self-interest. However, the service of a Christian does not bring humiliation or shame. It should not give rise to feelings of superiority or inferiority. Serving is like a teacher washing the feet of a disciple. It is when those in higher positions care for those in lower positions with love. It involves understanding, considering, and instilling courage and confidence in others. It is not for the purpose of improving our own status or quality of life, but for the benefit of others. There is no room for domination, tyranny, oppression, or discrimination here. Only love, meekness, and humility, which give oneself, exist. Believing in Jesus considers serving, the path of the lowly, as one's crown. J. Cameron Fraser, who wrote about 'servant leadership,' defined it as 'sharing power, thinking of others' needs first, and helping people develop to achieve the best results.'[11] In this sense, we can say that the goal is to improve the satisfaction of those being served. This is not unrelated to how merchants in the past often used the phrase 'the customer is king' and worked hard to improve customer satisfaction.

In this sense, the service of church leaders should prioritize God's satisfaction above all else, while also striving to enhance the satisfaction (spiritual) of the congregation. Of course, it is impossible to make everyone happy or satisfied. Even God does not do so. Although He gives us the same gospel, some feel anger and express hostility rather than satisfaction. Wherever the true gospel of Christ goes, the same pattern emerges. In this sense, it is selfish for a pastor to try to please every member of the congregation. Rather, we should reflect on Paul's confession that if one tries to please people, they are not a servant of Christ (Galatians 1:10). Therefore, church leaders and congregants must remember that serving is not a stretch of authority, but being faithful to one's duty. As a husband to his wife, as a wife to her husband, as a child to parents, and as a parent to children, one must fulfill their responsibilities. As a student, being diligent in studying is serving the school and showing respect for the teachers. As a worker, being faithful in work is serving the company, and that leads to serving oneself and the family. It is about becoming a stepping stone for others, not a burden. Of

---

[11] J. Cameron Fraser, "the Servant Leadership" *The Banner of Truth* in Korea, #188, 2024, 47.

course, sometimes it is not always clearly separated. While being diligent at work, one may neglect family, and while being enthusiastic about church activities, one may neglect their work. In such times, there may be a desire to give up one thing. This is where wisdom is needed. Prayer for wisdom from the Lord becomes essential. We will experience that the wisdom to balance family, work, and church life comes from the Father of all comfort and mercy. Wise service, which uses one's time, wealth, and talents for the benefit of others, is necessary for all Christians. The value of that sacrifice leads to the hope of receiving the blessings that come from the self-emptying of God's Son, Jesus Christ. **"For God is not unjust; He will not forget your work and the love you have shown Him as you have helped His people and continue to help them. We want each of you to show this same diligence to the very end, so that what you hope for may be fully realized. We do not want you to become lazy, but to imitate those who through faith and patience inherit what has been promised"** (Hebrews 6:10-12). Since God Himself is our reward, serving Him is followed by a fitting gift. This leads to diligence, and such service is like cold water on a hot day. Just as Olympic athletes' determination and passion drive away the heat it brings refreshing results to the hearts of the Lord and His people. This can be the kind of service that all the saints recognize, and it becomes something that is respected in the presence of God and in love, making us noble.

Before concluding this chapter, there is one important point to note: being in a position of service does not mean becoming a servant to people. True service refers to serving as a servant of God. It involves striving to meet the needs of others through God's sacrificial love, as God's servant. We are called to love people, even our enemies, but we are not their servants. Our purpose is not to please people but to serve others as servants of the Lord who has called us and made us His children. In this service, the will and opinions of the people we serve should not take precedence. Instead, we must focus on discerning and practicing what God's good, pleasing, and perfect will is. This is the life of one who lives by faith. In the Bible, the concept of a "**servant**" always accompanies the idea of service. A servant does not lead, but follows the master's commands. In that sense, the service of the saints is essential in following the Lord of the faith in which the saints profess to believe and the Lord who perfects our faith. This following issue will be discussed in Chapter 3. When we follow the Lord fully, both worship and service become the most natural acts, and our faith grows even stronger. Even Jesus, Himself, did not act according to His own will, but fulfilled the will of God the Father who sent Him (John 6:38). Likewise, any believer must act according to the will of God, who called us and made us His children on this earth. This is the path to becoming a humble servant, which is the virtue that a servant should possess.

This is the way to be a model of good faith and humility. So, what does it mean to have good faith? It means never straying from the path of total obedience to God's will. How can we know God's will? It is through the written word that God has revealed to us. In this sense, faith comes from hearing, and hearing comes through the word of Christ. A common question that arises here is whether we must know in order to believe, or must we believe in order to know? Generally, we must know in order to believe. Ignorance is the main factor behind being deceived. No one can say they trust someone they know nothing about. Ignorance cannot discern deceit, making it easy to fall victim to fraud, which results in great loss. Of course, even if we know, we can still be deceived, especially when greed takes over. Nevertheless, it is clear that knowledge is power. Trust is solidified through knowledge. However, Christian faith does not operate like the general acquisition of knowledge and trust built upon it. This is because the divine can't be understood through human ability. No one has gone up to heaven and met God in heaven. Likewise, no one has lived throughout human history to recount the events of the beginning or show vivid recordings of that time. To know the divine being, who has existed from eternity to eternity, is beyond human intellectual capacity. This is why Christian faith is called a faith based on revelation. The self-existent God, who created the heavens and the earth, makes Himself known, and through this revelation, humans come to know of His existence, love Him, serve Him, and delight in Him. This is faith. In this sense, the common stance of those who practice Christianity has been that believing leads to knowledge. Of course, there are those who say that you must know before you believe, even within the church. However, even those who argue this eventually surrender, as human wisdom and power cannot fully grasp the divine. Our knowledge is limited to what has been revealed. The divine transcends the realm of human existence. In this way, having good faith means having a deep understanding of the divine and knowing that He is the rewarder of those who seek Him (Hebrews 11:6). Therefore, it is a joy to walk with the Lord. This was the blessing Adam and Eve enjoyed in the Garden of Eden before their fall. They walked and ran with their Creator; rejoicing in Him was their delight.

As some might claim, there isn't a person who is so extraordinarily superior to ordinary humans that they invented the Christian God. If such a person existed, they would have become God themselves, not left behind such a fictitious idea only to die in vain. Moreover, if that exceptional person created the concept of heaven and hell, why didn't they make the conditions for entering heaven based on themselves? Or why didn't they use the standards of their own devoted followers? It's impossible for a human mind to do such a thing. Additionally, the human authors of the Bible did not meet each other to teach the salvation history they had in mind. Each of these authors was born in different times and lived under different circumstances. Even the earlier figures did not direct the later ones to continue progressively revealing God's salvation plan until it was finally completed through Jesus Christ. There were no reference books available for writing such a work. It was purely through divine revelation from God that this knowledge was made known. As people listened to this and believed, the clear path to salvation set by God became evident. If they refused to believe, they would wander aimlessly throughout their lives and eventually die in ignorance, either from exhaustion or malnutrition. Thus, Christian faith, as previously quoted, is about **"faith coming from hearing, and hearing through the word of Christ"** (Romans 10:17). At that time, it was not an era like now where things happening in one corner of the world spread around the world in an instant through SNS or public media, so it was impossible to show or tell the story of the events that occurred in Jerusalem, the land of Judea 2,000 years ago. Even if someone lived in that era, they would not have known what happened in a village in the south unless someone from there came to inform them. There were no journalists from various countries arriving to broadcast news or the technology to transmit articles. Yet, the early Christians, as Peter confessed, believed and received salvation without seeing (1 Peter 1:8). He described the glorious joy that comes from faith for salvation. Therefore, the feet of those who preached the gospel of Jesus Christ were significant, and this method of salvation continues to be valuable to this day.

Faith is not born from sight, but remains possible only through hearing. Most people dismiss the gospel, considering it absurd, and many don't even want to listen. Yet, the gospel continues to be proclaimed, and it must be proclaimed. This is because, as the Apostle Paul wrote, **"For since, in the wisdom of God, the world did not know God through wisdom, it pleased God through the folly of what we preach to save those who believe"** (1 Corinthians 1:21). The most wise God, who created all things, did not fail to realize that there was no other way to save the dead in sin and transgression except through the path where His only Son, Jesus, was crucified. There was no other way. Jesus is the only name through which salvation can be found (Acts 4:12). By receiving revelation, one comes to believe in Jesus, and this revelation stirs a desire not just to acknowledge what has been revealed, but to know more. Belief leads to a deeper understanding and fuels the desire for further knowledge. In this sense, faith grows like a living organism. It matures, progressing from childhood to adulthood. It moves from drinking milk to digesting solid food. It moves from shallow waters to deep seas. Faith in Jesus grows in this way, reaching maturity as it is continually learned and understood, as we will explore in the next chapter. The path of true faith matures through the apostolic teachings. As we obey and stand firm in the faith, thanksgiving abounds in our lives. If faith were possible through sight alone, the Apostle Peter would not have written the following: **"For we did not follow cleverly devised myths when we made known to you the power and coming of our Lord Jesus Christ, but we were eyewitnesses of his majesty. For when he received honor and glory from God the Father, and the voice was borne to him by the Majestic Glory, 'This is my beloved Son, with whom I am well pleased,' we ourselves heard this very voice borne from heaven, for we were with him on the holy mountain. And we**

have the prophetic word more fully confirmed, to which you will do well to pay attention as to a lamp shining in a dark place, until the day dawns and the morning star rises in your hearts" (2 Peter 1:16-19). Peter is saying that there is a more certain revelation than the one he saw on the Mount of Transfiguration. That revelation is the written Word of God, the Bible. The foundation and rock of our faith is the Bible, and the Lord, the author of Scripture, is the one who perfects our faith. He does not reveal Himself apart from the written Word. Thus, the worship and service of believers can only be accepted as perfect when they are in accordance with the written Word.

The motto sola scriptura—the Scripture alone—must remain until the Lord's return. Faith not grounded in the Bible is superstition and fiction. Faith that does not submit to the teachings of Scripture is merely personal conviction, and when the self is shattered, everything falls apart. All service, care, and good deeds not rooted in Scripture only elevate one's own righteousness. Such actions seek personal glory over God's glory, and this leads to a futile and hopeless death, with no one to care for them. True faith, based on correct knowledge, continually yearns for more true knowledge.

Review of Learning Content

01. What is the starting point of Christian faith?
    * What does it mean to believe in Jesus? (Matthew 1:21)
    * The English phrase "I believe in God" originally means "I am believing into God."

02. Consider our response to the gift of faith from God. (believe, receive, embrace)
    * John 6:64
    * John 1:14
    * John 6:29

03. Are you part of a crowd gathered for a formal event to welcome a national leader or influential figure? Or not? How can this be proven?

04. A tree is known by its fruit: Evidence of a practical life of faith
    (1) What is the Church? "The Mother of Believers" (Mater Fidelium)

    (2) Worship (Psalm 19:1-, Romans 1:23)
    * Isaiah 43:21
    * Psalm 148:7-10
    * Psalm 148:11-14
    * Ephesians 1:3-6
    * Psalm 122:1
    * Colossians 1:22

(3) Observance of the Sabbath (Isaiah 56:4-7)
   a. Is it possible to have a "freedom pass" for Sabbath observance?

   b. Does the Sunday service need to be held twice?

(4) What do you think is the cause of spiritual poverty in the modern church?

(5) Loving Service
   a. The best evangelism is believing in Jesus most faithfully.
      * Christians of the church in Antioch (Acts 11:26)
      * The fragrance of Christ's life (2 Corinthians 2:15-17)

   b. Why should we serve even when people don't recognize it?
      * Hebrews 6:10-12
      * Galatians 6:9

Chapter 2

Learning Jesus

Learning

"For though by this time you ought to be teachers, you need someone to teach you again the basic principles of the oracles of God. You need milk, not solid food."
(Hebrews 5:12)

• Chapter 2 •

Learning Jesus

The quality of a teacher is acquired through learning. There is no teacher without learning. A teacher is someone who learns throughout their life. There is no end to learning. Those who stop learning are akin to the dead. Learning brings about change and promotes growth, especially in the spiritual realm. Yet, as the passage above indicates, although a considerable amount of time has passed since they began believing in Jesus, they have not yet changed or grown and should have already become teachers by now. This is a rebuke. It points to a life spent without growth and change. To believe in Jesus naturally leads to a desire to learn about Him. A lack of interest in learning means either a lack of concern or the belief that it does not benefit them. Likewise, those who have no heart for learning about Jesus may appear to be part of the faith community outwardly, but in reality, they are like outsiders. If they have any gain, it is simply serving as reception committee members for Christian events. Of course, some do come to possess true faith in such a state.

However, the characteristic of all those who possess true faith is a thirst to learn about Jesus. This thirst never disappears until the breath of life on earth ceases. In this sense, there is no place for ignorance among Christians. In the believer's vocabulary, there is no word for **"stop."** There is no phrase like **"I have learned enough."** They live each day in the joy of drawing fresh water from an endless, deep well. A vibrant and life-giving faith shapes their life on earth. Learning makes life richer, more dignified, more meaningful, and more nourishing, and it creates a sense of fulfillment. It is due to Christians lacking the desire to learn about Jesus that the church has been disregarded or ridiculed. To restore respect and reverence, the church must be a place of learning about Jesus, and the members must diligently learn about Him. It should not be knowledge of the humanities, science, philosophy, or economics, but knowledge of Jesus Christ of Nazareth. We must grow in His grace and in the knowledge of Him (2 Peter 3:18).

One day, Jesus asked His disciples, **"Who do people say the Son of Man is?"** After hearing the reports from the people, Jesus asked His disciples, **"But what about you? Who do you say I am?"** Peter replied, **"You are the Messiah, the Son of the living God"** (Matthew 16:16). Jesus, in His explanation, made it clear that it was God the Father in heaven who had revealed this to Peter. This was not knowledge gained through years of deep study in the academic world or from practicing deep philosophical or spiritual disciplines. The God who appeared to Abram, who was helping his father in the idol-making factory, revealed who God is. This is why Abram left his home, his birthplace, and his family, and boldly set off to the land that God directed him to, without any hesitation. Similarly, when God led Israel out of slavery in Egypt, He first revealed who He was when announcing the good news of their liberation. And when they were celebrating their deliverance, He forcefully reminded them, saying, **"I am the Lord your God who brought** you out of the land of Egypt, out of the house of bondage." This truth was recorded in the Ten Commandments and was continually brought to their remembrance at every opportunity. They were reminded of this truth every year during the Passover feast, as it was essential to recall that the God they served was entirely different from the idols worshiped by surrounding nations. Their independence did not come from their military strength, economic power, diplomacy, or organizational skills, but entirely by the power of the Lord God of hosts, who is mighty in battle. They must not forget, "**I am the Lord your God!**" Israel's liberation and freedom came entirely from God. This is the starting point of believing in Jesus. It is a natural desire to want to know more about the Lord who has given us this blessing. How is this desire fulfilled? This is the main topic of the chapter.

The Way of the New Creation

Egypt symbolizes the world. The world is also the domain of the ruler of the air. It is a place teeming with sinners who need salvation. They are those who "**follow the ways of this world and the ruler of the kingdom of the air**" (Ephesians 2:2). They "**live according to the desires of the flesh and the mind, and follow their cravings... by nature, children of wrath**" (Ephesians 2:3). For them, there is no possibility of being liberated from the power of sin and death. The undeniable truth is that humans were dead in transgressions and sins and by nature children of wrath, and the only way out of this is through another prophet like Moses. Our loving God accomplished this work. A believer begins their faith journey by confessing and declaring that through the blood of Jesus Christ, the sinless Son of God who came to this earth in the name of Jesus of Nazareth, their sins are washed away, and they are made free from the slavery of sin and death. Those in Christ Jesus walk the path of the new creation, where the old has passed away and everything has become new.

Let us honestly reflect on the days we have lived. Could we overcome the power of sin and death through our own strength? Have we found a way to escape the constant allure of sin that torments us from within? No. It was something initiated by God outside of us. It is through receiving the Lord, who completely freed us from sin through the death of Jesus Christ on the cross, acknowledging Him as our Savior and King, and relying solely on Him in worship and service, which faith begins. A person who possesses this faith in Jesus naturally becomes humble. No matter how much knowledge, courage, or wealth a person may have, they have nothing to boast about. It is like children who do not try to show off their abilities in front of their parents. Of course, a rebellious child might ask what their parents have done for them, but a wise child, grateful for being born and raised, behaves respectfully in front of their parents, who endured hardship for their well-being. When we think about what the Lord did for our salvation from sin, we have no words to say, and we cannot lift our heads with pride.

The most blessed person in the church, the one most respected in the world, is the humble one. Pride leads to destruction, but humility paves the way for grace. The proud are opposed by God, but the humble receive grace and are exalted. Most people who fall from their success do so because of pride and greed. Whether they are kings or commoners does not matter. Those saved by God's grace, who brought the dead to life from sin, live and die with the desire that only Christ be exalted in them. This is what it means to believe in Jesus. Is this Jesus your Lord and your God? If so, then the desire to be with the Lord, to draw closer to Him, will never leave you. You will want to seize every opportunity to meet with the Lord.

Among such people, there is no one who does not want to live with a distance from Jesus. The desire to know more about who He is rises up within them. Those who do not have this desire are neither Christians nor children of God. As children live with their physical parents who gave birth to them, they naturally want to know who their parents are. How much more so should we want to know the One who redeemed us and made us children of God—the One who has become **"wisdom, righteousness, sanctification, and redemption"** for us (1 Corinthians 1:30). If someone does not have the desire to know Him more, they are liars. Learning about Jesus is not something completed in a short stage or process. Completing a Bible study or doctrinal education offered by the church does not make someone complete. This is a lifelong endeavor. Even then, the knowledge we have about Him is only the tip of the iceberg. Theology may be regarded as an academic field, but there is a clear reason to consider it beyond the boundaries of academic knowledge. In the realm of general scholarship, there are experts in particular fields. In foreign religions, there are high monks and enlightened religious figures who have reached the state of liberation. However, in Christianity, even if someone believes they have attained spiritual mastery, they do not boast about it. In fact, they cannot boast. The apostle Paul, who devoted his entire life to knowing the Lord after meeting Him, ultimately confessed, **"Oh, the depth of the riches of the wisdom and knowledge of God! How unsearchable His judgments, and His paths beyond tracing out!"** (Romans 11:33). Those with less knowledge naturally have less intellectual capacity. Those who have learned more can pour out as much as they have learned. Learning about Jesus is infinite, full of boundless wisdom and knowledge, so no matter how much you learn, it is never finished. This learning never tires, bores, or frustrates you. Therefore, there is no quitting. It is like a miner who, upon discovering a gold vein, cannot stop being captivated by the task of mining gold, which is more precious than pure gold and sweeter than honey—so much so that they cannot take their eyes off it for even a moment. The biggest reason the churches in Korea are declining or collapsing is, without a doubt, the ignorance of our Lord Jesus Christ and the lack of passion to know Him more. The goal of learning about Jesus is to be filled with Him, to reach the full stature of Christ. There will be no rest until then.

In Hebrews 5, the writer points out that the recipients of the letter have been believers for a long time, yet they are still in the beginner stages of their faith. They should have become teachers by now, but instead, they are still at the level of elementary understanding. They have only spent time passing by. The problem is not with the message itself, but with their lack of willingness to learn. They have no spiritual desire to learn. Among us, there are those who quickly grasp what is being said and those who do not. "**Grasping words**" refers to understanding the meaning of what is being said. Some people seem to have no understanding at all, while others, with just one word, can quickly understand and act accordingly. The former is frustrating due to their inability to grasp what is being said, while the latter is straightforward and clear. This situation can be observed in Hebrews 5. In verse 11, the writer of Hebrews expresses a deep regret that although he has much to say about Melchizedek, he is finding it difficult to explain because the recipients' hearing is dull. Here, being "**dull**" does not refer to their inability to hear physically, but rather to their lack of spiritual desire to listen and learn. The issue was not with their ears but with their hearts. The recipients of Hebrews had no desire to listen to God's word or to learn from it, and this lack of desire kept them in a state of spiritual immaturity.

The spiritual desire to know Jesus Christ comes from a heart of love for Him. Those who are in love naturally desire to know the person they love more. They will find ways to meet with them, no matter the excuse. Similarly, those who are compelled by the love of Christ are eager to know Him more, driven by a desire to understand Him. Of course, there are some who learn merely out of intellectual curiosity. But as they continue learning, they often find themselves in a place where they cannot help but love Him. In the spiritual world, this is a frequent occurrence. I hope that we may be filled with knowledge as we eagerly pursue to know the Lord more.

In the world, knowledge and affection for a particular person have limits. There are people who seem fascinating the more you get to know them, but for most, the more you know, the more disappointing and frustrating they become. Even those who are very charming have limits to how much you can learn about them. Eventually, their flaws are exposed. Living with them reveals their true nature. However, learning about Jesus has no limit. No matter how much you learn, there is always more depth to discover. All the treasures of knowledge and wisdom are in Him. That is why the apostle Paul, who walked with Him for a lifetime, said that his greatest desire was to know Christ more and to be found in Him. He considered all the things that hindered him from obtaining that knowledge—worldly wisdom, favoritism toward education and lineage, and ascetic training for personal righteousness—as rubbish. His longing for Christ surpassed all else, yet he acknowledged that even the knowledge he had of Christ on earth was partial and dim. Therefore, those who are immersed in learning about Jesus are not affected by pride. Spiritual or intellectual pride is the greatest enemy of learning about Jesus. That is why we humbly bow before Him, believing that in due time, we will know Him fully (1 Corinthians 13). In this sense, once we enter into learning about Jesus, there is no turning back. Even when the process becomes more difficult and the more we learn, the more we realize how much we still need to learn, the temptation to quit may come, but we do not give up. Instead, the more we learn, the more joy fills our hearts. There is nothing boring or tiresome about it. Just as some who are unaware of the incoming tide while gathering clams in the mud flats get swept away, those who are excited about Jesus live with such enthusiasm.

In Acts 26, when Festus heard Paul, who was bound in chains and being questioned, he said to Paul, **"You are out of your mind! Your great learning is driving you insane."** Paul replied, **"I am not insane, most excellent Festus. What I am saying is true and reasonable."** King Agrippa then responded, **"Do you think that in such a short time you can persuade me to be a Christian?"** Paul replied to King Agrippa, **"Short time or long, I pray to God that not only you but all who are listening to me today may become what I am, except for these chains!"** (Acts 26:29). When one is caught up in worldly desires, the outcome is always the same. But those who draw from the deep well of truth and continue to draw from the living water are captivated by the unending joy of giving, a joy that never runs dry. Just as the Lord Himself said: **"Whoever drinks the water I give them will never thirst. Indeed, the water I give them will become in them a spring of water welling up to eternal life"** (John 4:14). Because of this, they will come to consider everything that offers only temporary satisfaction or is destined to fade away as rubbish.

What are we doing to learn about Jesus? It is a problem if we cannot understand, but if we lack the heart and passion to listen and learn, we really need to reexamine ourselves. Hebrews 5 does not say that it's okay to stay at a child's level. It is a warning to quickly move beyond that. In 6:2, it commands us not to lay again the foundation, but to move on to maturity. Whether my faith in Jesus is normal or not is closely related to my desire to learn about Jesus. If that desire is absent, my faith as a believer is abnormal. This affects my prayer life as well. It may seem like I pray a lot, but I experience little to no answers to prayer. Proverbs 18:9 says, **"If a man turns his ear from hearing the law, even his prayer is an abomination."** If you feel like your prayers are not being answered, while it's possible that you're asking with selfish motives, first examine your attitude towards the proclaimed Word of God. And consider whether you have a longing to hear again the words you've heard throughout your life. A faith without passion or earnest prayer falls into a state of lethargy.

Many churchgoers today are content with shallow faith, like playing around in shallow waters. They diligently attend Bible study classes, but the reason they do so is not to satisfy a desire to know the Lord more, but as a means to solidify their position in the church. It's neither more nor less than that. Once that goal is achieved, they no longer actively pursue learning. As a result, even though they may complete all the courses offered by the church, it is rare to find someone who has truly matured and become spiritually mature. Despite having solidified their position in the church, their knowledge of the Lord remains poor. In fact, when problems arise—such as suffering or persecution due to the Word, or the temptations and cares of the world—these individuals may hear the Word but never grow into genuine wheat, remaining like empty husks (Mark 4:17-18). In reality, they seem to always be learning but never actually reach the truth. This is because they are led by various desires (2 Timothy 3:6-7). However, the path to bearing the finest fruit is to receive the Word with a good heart. These are those who, not only listening, but also practice the Word, overcoming difficulties to make progress in their faith.

The path of learning about Jesus is obtained through observation, but it is solidified through practice. Knowledge that cannot be practiced is meaningless. Learning must include both the infusion of knowledge and the practice or application of that knowledge to become complete knowledge. Many people have a driver's license but it remains unused in a drawer. The problem is not with the license itself, but with the driver who does not practice. This makes the license, in effect, a useless piece of paper. Similarly, in faith, there are many who seem to have the license of believing in Jesus but do not make effective use of it. This is a serious issue because their faith, without action, has become dead. There are quite a few people in the church who have obtained membership but fail to fulfill their responsibilities and duties as members. The problem is not that they don't try to learn; the issue is that even when they do learn, it is ineffective, or they never use what they've learned, thus experiencing little to no practical power. The Bible says, **"Taste and see that the Lord is good,"** but for them, it's like reading to a deaf ear. To break free from this and truly experience spiritual fulfillment, we must abandon the stage of only drinking milk, as Hebrews suggests. If we remain dull of hearing, we will never taste the spiritual richness of the faith, even if we attend church for a lifetime. Salt is salt, but if it loses its saltiness, it is trampled underfoot. We should never doubt the truth that is proclaimed in the church. What we must continually check is the state of our hearts in receiving the preached Word.

The Path of Learning

So, how can we help those who want to know the Lord more to increase their true knowledge of Jesus? Every child begins life by drinking milk. Eventually, they move on to solid food. What we need to understand here is that the reasons why people like milk and why they begin to eat solid food are completely opposite. The former does not require chewing. So, they come to the church, sit comfortably in a chair, and swallow what is given to them. The latter, however, enjoys the taste of chewing, and savors the food. As you all know, there are few adults who avoid solid food, except for those with weak teeth. But spiritual solid food does not require strong teeth; it requires our hearts and minds. The desire to know and the practical will to live according to what we know are crucial. However, the reason why people's lives do not improve, and why there is no transition from the form of godliness to the power of godliness, or why families do not change despite attending church for years, is because there is no intentional decision or action to learn and practice. They remain at the foundational level of faith and have no desire to move into a deeper world. They only want to appear as though they do. So, they create outward forms. They know that drawing lines on a pumpkin doesn't make it a watermelon, but they still disguise it that way.

However, the common characteristic of those who wish to become world-class athletes, or those who want to rise to a better position than others, is learning and training. They mature into strong athletes by laying a solid foundation and practicing. A long-distance runner does not run long distances from the beginning. At first, they run 5km, then 10km, and as they continue to practice diligently, they run the full distance. Only those who complete the full course can taste and enjoy the results.

Likewise, just as the thirsty seek water, the typical characteristic of someone who is hungry is that they seek food. At first, they will consume milk or easily digestible food. But over time, they start eating solid foods. And as more time passes, they begin to consume adult food. This process is possible because they have the desire to eat. Occasionally, among athletes who have won a gold medal, there are some who say, "**I am still hungry.**" They are not satisfied with just one gold medal; they have a desire to achieve even more. A true believer is never content with staying at the first limit. They strive for deeper, broader, higher, and more abundant things. And so, they pray: "**I keep asking that the God of our Lord Jesus Christ, the glorious Father, may give you the Spirit of wisdom and revelation, so that you may know him better. I pray that the eyes of your heart may be enlightened in order that you may know the hope to which he has called you, the riches of his glorious inheritance in his holy people, and his incomparably great power for us who believe**" (Ephesians 1:17-19).

True believers have a definite intellectual desire to know about the divine being and spiritual realities. The vitality of this desire is persistent. "**To know Jesus more, to know the great and wide grace and the love that has redeemed me, is my lifelong wish, my lifelong wish, to know the love that has redeemed me**" (Hymn 453, Verse 1). They do not express this yearning with just their lips, but with their whole being. This desire persists as long as life is in them. The psalmist sang, "**One** thing I have asked of the Lord, that will I seek; that I may dwell in the house of the Lord all the days of my life, to gaze upon the beauty of the Lord and to inquire in his temple"** (Psalm 27:4). It is clear what they will desire throughout their entire life. Therefore, there is no upper limit to learning about Jesus. The desire does not give up until the day when what was once known in part is fully understood. This represents the true spiritual character of the believer. Those who know the taste of learning do not hesitate to grow until they reach the full stature of Christ.

Of course, this process is not smooth. In the world of secular academics, the path of learning is also difficult. One may even experience intentional harassment from their professors. While this is not always the case, it is generally intended to train the disciple in a positive way. Likewise, learning about Jesus involves trials. There are times when we must pass through the furnace of suffering. We go through water and fire. Think about the life of Paul, who desired to know Jesus more deeply: **"We are hard pressed on every side, but not crushed; perplexed, but not in despair; persecuted, but not abandoned; struck down, but not destroyed. We always carry around in our body the death of Jesus, so that the life of Jesus may also be revealed in our body"** (2 Corinthians 4:8-10). He describes his difficult and intense circumstances, which are hard for people like us to comprehend: **"Are they servants of Christ? (I am out of my mind to talk like this.) I am more. I have worked much harder, been in prison more frequently, been flogged more severely, and been exposed to death again and again. Five times I received from the Jews the forty lashes minus one. Three times I was beaten with rods, once I was pelted with stones, three times I was shipwrecked, I spent a night and a day in the open sea. I have been constantly on the move. I have been in danger from rivers, in danger from bandits, in danger from my fellow Jews, in danger from Gentiles; in danger in the city, in danger in the country, in danger at sea; and in danger from false believers. I have labored and toiled and have often gone without sleep; I have known hunger and thirst and have often gone without food; I have been cold and naked"** (2 Corinthians 11:23-27). This part will be discussed in more detail later, but no one can reach spiritual maturity without going through such trials and pain. Through suffering, we also learn God's statutes. By undergoing discipline, we become workers of refined gold. Thus, suffering can also be beneficial, and we confess this. If we do not practice our faith, there is no suffering, and without suffering, there is no maturity. There is a clear reason why we view suffering and trials as opportunities for learning.

Many successful people in the world are those who have graduated from the school of pain. Seneca said: **"In my view, there is no more unfortunate person than one who has never known adversity. They have never passed through trial."** It is not in the classroom, but in the field of life, where the secret of becoming a mature person is learned. Theory without practical experience is empty. Thus, the psalmist sings about God, who saves us from trouble, calms the storm, and guides us to the desired harbor (Psalm 107:28-30). He also confesses: **"You, God, tested us; you refined us like silver. You brought us into prison and laid burdens on our backs. You let people ride over our heads; we went through fire and water, but you brought us to a place of abundance"** (Psalm 66:10-12). Those who have tasted the bread and water of suffering can become excellent mentors.

Just as acquiring knowledge in a specific field is not sufficient by just reading books, and the experience of putting what you've learned into practice in the field is necessary, we must remember that the knowledge of the Lord is not for a laboratory setting. It is knowledge that can reveal its true value in the form of a product that is ready to be marketed to the public. For our knowledge to become complete—becoming living knowledge—it must be transformed through practical experience, where the knowledge in the mind becomes embodied knowledge. The phrase **"acting on animal instincts"** often refers to the fact that one has been faithful in self-discipline. No matter the situation, one responds appropriately without conscious effort. In the spiritual world, even those chosen by God are always under threat from the evil work of the devil, who seeks to devour them. The devil lurks around the saints, waiting for an opportunity to attack, through false teachings, heresy, economic loss, physical illness, or sometimes through the betrayal of friends or acquaintances. Many such threats attempt to shrink the faith learned in Jesus, even breaking the small faith that one has. At these moments, the distinction between genuine and false faith becomes clear. True faith clings even more to the Lord, striving not to depart from Him, while false faith shrinks away at the smallest obstacle. Of course, true faith does not mean being immune to the devil's attacks. One may endure many wounds and pains, but it is through the process of healing and refining those wounds that one becomes a polished pearl, overcoming all challenges.

The way to overcome immaturity is by listening to the Lord's word every day. It is not about the reactions or evaluations of those around you. It is about allowing the Lord's word to act as the standard for judgment rather than being overwhelmed by the circumstances. Even when mountains crumble and the seas threaten to engulf, you remain unshaken. Just as athletes practice and train faithfully according to basic manuals and instructions, they also listen to the coach's guidance.

If an athlete does not heed the coach's advice, they will never get a chance to demonstrate their skills in a game and may even lose their opportunity to participate. In the spiritual world, it is not only the sound of the written word but also the teachings of shepherds, who lead the sheep to green pastures and still waters, that help believers grow into superior Christians.

The Direct Path of Learning

Learning about Jesus has both direct and indirect aspects. The direct ways include studying the Bible, commentaries, and doctrinal explanations, as well as engaging with public means of grace. However, self-study alone does not satisfy the hunger for spiritual knowledge. Of course, for those who love God and are called according to His purpose, everything works together for good. If one has the opportunity to meet a good teacher or a mature elder, their guidance and experienced instruction will greatly help the learner reach deeper levels of understanding. Therefore, the author of Hebrews teaches this: **"Remember your leaders, who spoke the word of God to you. Consider the outcome of their way of life and imitate their faith"** (Hebrews 13:7). This encourages believers to look at the leadership of the church, the body of Christ, and observe how they faithfully adhere to God's Word and live a godly life, and to follow their example. In the church, it is not only necessary to have devout teachers who teach God's Word well, but also devout followers who receive and obey their teachings. A faithful person can raise up another faithful person. The consistency of a leader's words and actions leads not only themselves but also those who listen to them to a place of salvation (1 Timothy 4:16). Of course, a leader does not need to be perfect. They cannot be perfect. However, they must demonstrate through their life the real power of Jesus that impacts and transforms lives. This is what gives those who follow them the faith to truly follow. Therefore, devout believers should continuously pray for their pastors and elders in the church, because of the influence they have on the congregation.

God's ordinances for all saints are the means of public grace. These include the word, prayer, and sacraments. We learn by hearing the word, and by being taught the way of the word. More directly, it is important to spend time alone with the Lord. While meeting the Lord once a week is necessary, experiencing Him day and night is also crucial. The church is the pillar and foundation of truth. Through the church, the Lord feeds, clothes, and nurtures His people into mature Christians. For this reason, it is said that there is no salvation outside the church, as the church is the mother of the believers (Mater Fidelium). Learning about Jesus involves fully utilizing the public means of grace that have been established for the church, the body of Christ. The common saying **"food is the best medicine"** applies here: the means of public grace are the spiritual nourishment that God has prescribed for each believer. Those who wisely use these means of grace are the ones who grow in wisdom. Through them, we learn to better know and emulate the Lord, who is our righteousness, wisdom, holiness, and redemption.[12]

The public means of grace established by Jehovah are the places where fallen sinners discover and learn about Christ. Thomas Boston

---

12 *For the use of the means of grace, please refer to the author's* **The Dying Church, The Thriving Church** (Reformed Practical Theology, 2024), pages 181-214, and **Theology is Life** (Christian Renaissance, 2023), pages 263-284.

pointed out several practices that should be used for the saints to come to know, follow, and resemble Christ:[13] First, the practice of meditation as established by God (Haggai 1:5, Luke 15:17, Psalm 4:4, 58:5-6). Meditation on God's word day and night is the mark of a blessed person (Psalm 1:1-2). Second, spiritual fellowship with fellow believers (Malachi 3:16, Luke 24:32). Third, singing the Lord's praises (Ephesians 5:18-19, Acts 16:25-26). Fourth, prayer. Prayer is the highway to discovering God (Matthew 7:7). One should participate in public prayers (Acts 16:13-14), set aside time for personal prayer at home (Acts 10:30, 12:12, Matthew 18:19), and have secret prayer time (Genesis 32:24, Daniel 9:22). One should also make time for heartfelt prayers (Exodus 14:15, Nehemiah 2:4). Fifth, reading and listening to the word. This is the way to open heaven's doors wide. The Lord often uses this method to approach His people. Read the Bible (Revelation 1:3). Augustine, too, was converted after reading Romans 13:12-13. Pay attention to the preached word (1 Corinthians 1:21, Acts 2:41). Sixth, the use of the sacraments. These ordinances are the places where Christ has established for believers to meet and find Him (Exodus 20:24). The place of public worship is where sinners gather to meet Christ, and where the saints partake in spiritual nourishment (1 Peter 2:2-3). It is a space where they can experience the heavenly delicacies in advance (Ephesians 4:11-13, Revelation 21:22, Song of Songs 4:6). True Christians cannot neglect these means of grace. It is important to approach each ordinance with the intention of seeking and meeting Christ. Whether reading or listening to the word, carrying out secret duties, managing personal affairs, or participating in public ordinances, one must approach them with the attitude of going to the door of wisdom to meet the King's face. It is to come with the expec-

---

13 Thomas Boston, *The Collected works of Thomas Boston*, Richard Owen Roberts, Publishers, Wheaton, Illinois, 1980. Refer to page 465 and below.

tation of enjoying communion with Him, smelling the fragrance of His garments. Those who sincerely seek Him will meet the Lord (John 4:10, Proverbs 8:17).

The Indirect Path of Learning

Indirect teaching is also gained through the practice of direct learning. This leads to the understanding that practice is more powerful than theory. It can become a concrete and practical learning appropriate to the situation. Even if theory is lacking, through practical experience, one can become a far superior expert compared to someone who is merely familiar with the theory. Christian faith is thorough in its theory, but knowledge that is not experienced is meaningless. Do not misunderstand. This does not mean that one can experience everything deep in the Bible. It is impossible to know everything in the Bible, the only standard that defines what to believe and how to live. However, the teachings of the Bible are not theoretical ideas of an ideal world that cannot be practiced. The theology taught by the Bible is life itself. In the spiritual world, there are no innate geniuses from the beginning. All humans are dead in their trespasses and sins. However, those who are born again through water and the Spirit must undergo training that leads to godliness. That training takes place in the real world. Only such people can sing the victory anthem in spiritual battles. If there is a way to overcome the current reality where ministers fall, churches collapse, and believers stumble, it is through experiential training by learning more deeply about Jesus and making a willful decision to practice.

A very important part of the difference between a child and an adult mentioned in the passage from Hebrews is this: Whether a child or an adult, one must eat to live. But a child loves milk. They avoid solid food because they do not want to make the effort to chew. On the other hand, an adult trains themselves to eat and chew solid food repeatedly. In the sports world, athletes who are well-known for their skills practice things like kicking a ball or shooting arrows thousands or tens of thousands of times. Similarly, the way to become a spiritual master is to delight in the Lord's law and meditate on it day and night. Knowing that the Lord's words are the source of all energy and that heaven and earth will disappear but the Lord's words will not, they do not give up holding onto the Word until the end. This is the secret to winning a medal in a competition. They know that the only way to survive is to cling to the Lord (Deut. 4:5-6). Even if there is immediate loss, pain, and at times the threat of death, they will not waver but hold onto the Lord's promises. They know that this is the lifeline. Look at Hebrews 5:14: **"But solid food is for the mature, who by constant use have trained themselves to distinguish good from evil."** Here, we discover another difference between a child and an adult: it is using discernment and undergoing training. The result is the ability to distinguish good from evil. There is nothing more joyful than becoming a true child in Christ. However, there is nothing more heartbreaking and depressing than seeing someone who should mature still remain as a baby. Perhaps our faith life is unstable. Babies wander aimlessly without thinking. They are tossed to and fro by every wind of teaching (Eph. 4:14-16). They blindly idolize people like certain fanatical followers. They sleep too long and cry at every little thing. A baby who only drinks milk and barely survives cannot consume solid food, and thus cannot reveal their true worth.

Of course, there is no one who can digest solid food right from the start. As mentioned earlier, over time, one progresses from breast milk to solid food and eventually to rice and meat dishes. However, if someone avoids eating solid food because they don't want to chew, they cannot develop the necessary strength and will fall apart when the time comes to use that strength. On the other hand, a grown and mature person uses discernment in eating. They know how to apply what they have learned. They also learn much more through practical experience in the field. Athletes who display extraordinary skills have undergone countless hours of training, but their abilities are further enhanced by the experience they gain from participating in actual competitions, such as the Asian Games, World Cup qualifiers, and finals. Likewise, believers who are trained through public means of grace, whether in public or personal settings, and who do not make an effort to implement all the truths they hear and see in their everyday lives, live without experiencing any wounds or pain. This is like having a worthless driver's license without any real experience. No athlete is free from the risk of injury. Although Jesus loves born-again believers so much that it might seem He would take them directly to heaven as soon as they believe, He does not do that. He leaves them in a world where the devil, like a roaring lion, seeks someone to devour, so that they might know that the world has light. Through believers, God wants to make it known to the world that He alone is the true God, and Jesus alone is the true Savior. Through their actions, believers are to long for heaven more and live in that hope.

Living by faith in this world is a life prepared to face injuries, losses, and even the possibility of losing one's life. Whether these things happen in the home, at work, or in the broader social community, when one strives to implement what they have heard and learned, they will experience the power of God's Word and the care and protection He provides. Through this, they will make progress in their faith and experience the joy of bearing excellent fruit. The use of discernment in this passage means that the knowledge gained penetrates all the sensory functions, naturally fostering adaptability. In short, it refers to continuous effort to raise one's practical sense. The growth of skills will be dramatically evident. They will be refined like pure gold and be used as a skilled worker, sensitive, agile, and swift. The way to measure the increase in spiritual ability is none other than superior discernment through discernment. The discernment mentioned in this passage does not merely refer to distinguishing right from wrong, good from evil, righteousness from unrighteousness, or good from bad. Rather, it refers to being able to discern and reject doctrines that are spiritually unhealthy, corrupt, and polluted, striving to be a mature believer who presents oneself to God as a worker without shame. It is a Christian who has turned away from the desires of the heart and the eyes that follow the trends and customs of the world (Num. 15:39) and who discerns what is God's will, which is good, pleasing, and perfect, by following His Word (Rom. 12:2).

In this way, the ability to discern is a very important measure of spiritual maturity. Spiritual discernment actively engages spiritual senses. The words of a retired general, **"A soldier serves wearing a uniform as shrouds,"** deeply resonate. The Christian life is the life of one clothed in Jesus. It involves using all of one's senses—taste, smell, touch, hearing, and sight—to give off the fragrance of knowing Jesus Christ. It is about expanding opportunities for training to become a living letter of Christ. Spiritual taste is the delight in experiencing how gracious the Lord is and how sweet His goodness and kindness are (1 Peter 2:3, Psalm 34:8).

Spiritual hearing is about keenly listening to God's subtle voice. **"Listen, that your soul may live"** (Isaiah 55:3)! **"Let him who has ears hear what the Spirit says to the churches"** (Revelation 2:7). Those who belong to God listen to His words (John 8:47). Even while running on the field, athletes pay attention to their coach's words and gestures. Similarly, while living in this world, we attentively listen to the words of our supreme Commander, Christ, and actively obey His guidance. Spiritual sight exists as well— it is the longing to open one's eyes to see the wondrous things in God's law (Psalm 119:18). It is the desire to know the hope of His calling and the richness of the inheritance in the saints (Ephesians 1:18). There is also spiritual smell, the longing for the fragrance of knowing Christ (2 Corinthians 2:14). We strive to be a fragrant offering to God (Philippians 4:18). Spiritual touch is about having a discerning mind and the softness that restores a hardened heart (Ephesians 4:18-19, 2 Kings 22:19). These sensory faculties are activated in all areas of life. It is about growing in the knowledge of the Lord.

As this training continues and one anticipates and confronts every situation in life, they become a mature person, a skilled instructor, and a seasoned believer. Such a person can handle any situation well, overcome any trial, resist any deception, and exhibit outstanding faith that discerns. This requires faith assurance and patience. Satan always tries to make us doubt the written Word. He whispers, presenting the discrepancy between the Bible and reality, urging us to stray from the Word and be faithful only to the reality. Still, we firmly believe in the word of promise, and even if we are shaken by the blowing wind, we do not waver by holding on to the promise that God will help us reach the harbor of hope. Those who endure and persist through life's storms will receive the grace to arrive safely in the harbor. It is through the training of patience and accumulating experience that one gains a solid ability to discern right from wrong. The author of Hebrews teaches this: "**We desire that each of you show the same diligence to the full assurance of hope until the end, that you may not be sluggish, but imitate those who through faith and patience inherit the promises**" (Hebrews 6:11-12). This clearly shows the goal of believers' learning of Jesus.

The Content of Learning

Now, let us briefly examine what learning about Jesus entails, and the most fundamental nature of that knowledge. First, in the Bible, Jesus says the following: "**Come to me, all you who are weary and burdened, and I will give you rest. Take my yoke upon you and learn from me, for I am gentle and humble in heart, and you will find rest for your souls. For my yoke is easy and my burden is light**" (Matthew 11:28-30). No one in life is without hardship. Even if a person lives for 70 years, or 80 if strong, the boast of those years is nothing but toil and sorrow, as the Bible says (Psalm 90:10). There is no world without tears, and no life without pain. It is to this kind of life that the Lord calls us. He speaks to those who are burdened and weary, urging them to come to Him and find rest. To learn from Jesus means to come to Him. While Jesus does come to us, it is generally a call for us to come to Him. Why does He say to come? It is to free us from the burdens of toil and heavy loads. The heavy weight of sin, which would otherwise drag us down into the abyss of hell, is something the Lord understands, and He invites us to come to Him. The reason is that He alone can give us rest. Furthermore, He invites us to take His yoke upon us and learn from Him. This means He will teach us how to carry the weight of our burdens and be freed from the pressure they exert on us. One might respond: "**But my load is heavy, and my toil is hard. How can I take on your yoke? You want me to carry your burden as well?**" Some might object. However, if we carefully listen to what the Lord has said, we will see that He does not merely tell us to take His yoke and learn from Him. He explains who He is: "**I am gentle and humble in heart,**" and "**My yoke is easy and my burden is light.**"

In fact, among the Jewish people, there are many types of yokes. Typically, there are yokes related to God: the yoke of the Kingdom of God, the yoke of the Law, the yoke of commandments, the yoke of repentance, the yoke of faith, and other yokes that God requires us to bear. But now Jesus says, "**Do not suffer under all these yokes. Forget about them, and take my yoke upon you, and learn from me, for my yoke is easy, and my burden is light.**" Jesus is saying that His yoke is much easier and lighter compared to others. His yoke, if we choose to accept it, is indeed light and easy. There will be no worries or anxieties associated with His yoke. It will not add any extra burden on us. Because He is gentle and humble, Jesus promises that if we take His yoke, we will find rest. To believe in Jesus means to trust in His promises. Therefore, no one who believes in Jesus will refuse to take His yoke upon themselves. Moreover, this is the Lord's yoke and His burden. It is the Lord who bears it, and He carries it for us. He does not act arrogantly or impose harshness upon us, because He is gentle and humble. Even though His yoke is easy and His burden light, He does not expect us to bear it on our own. He Himself bears it with us. Some may doubt whether the Lord, who has promised to be with us until the end of the world, would leave us struggling and sweating while He watches from the sidelines. But no—when we trust in Him, we will realize just how light and easy His yoke is. We will feel as though it is lighter than a feather.

In fact, through taking on the Lord's yoke and bearing His burden with Him, we learn of His gentleness and humility. We will come to understand just how gentle and humble He truly is—how free from anger, how soft and kind He is. We, who are often proud and stiff-necked, will be transformed into humble followers, like little puppies who obediently follow their master. This transformation comes through training and learning. For example, when ancient farmers trained oxen to plow, they would often put the yoke on the more experienced and stronger ox, which would carry the burden and lead the younger ox through the learning process. Likewise, the gentle and humble Lord, by taking on the yoke Himself and bearing our burdens, trains us to follow Him on this path. At first, everything may seem new and difficult. But as we become accustomed to it, we will realize that nothing is as light as this. The process of becoming a master is not easy, but once we reach that level, we will enjoy the joy of being in a realm where no one else can touch us.

Moreover, the Greek word for "**easy**" here also means "**a perfect fit.**" It is literally "**just right.**" The Lord's yoke is perfectly suited for beginners like us. There is no room for laziness or indulgence. We will diligently learn and grow. Thus, we will become those who can joyfully run the path of suffering alongside the cross of Jesus Christ. Gentleness and humility are traits developed through patience and training. As we learn, we will be refined as human beings, gaining social skills and wisdom to overcome difficulties. Similarly, as we learn from the Lord, we experience the bitterness of patience, but we also come to taste the sweetness of its fruit. We will become humble human beings, bowing our heads like ripe grain. So, what specific practical knowledge do we gain from learning the Lord?

Of course, the easiest place to start for any Christian, or even for someone who has stepped into a church at least once, is the Apostles' Creed. It succinctly summarizes what a believer holds to be true. In reality, there is a contradiction in today's church where people, whether they truly believe or not, all recite it collectively. However, it is essential to learn and understand the content of the Apostles' Creed and confess it with one's heart. A confession of faith acts like a map, guiding a traveler not only to their current location but also showing the way to their intended destination. The Apostles' Creed, although not directly written by the apostles, clearly reflects the teachings that they spread. It outlines the core aspects of the Christian faith. The content primarily deals with the doctrine of the Trinity and reveals the nature and work of God. Each denomination has its own more detailed confession of faith, such as the Westminster Confession of Faith and the Larger and Shorter Catechisms in Presbyterianism, which express the beliefs upheld by that church. The term **"creed"** comes from the Latin Credo, meaning **"I believe,"** and signifies a formal declaration of belief or conviction. The confessions of faith, like the Apostles' Creed, are declarations of what Christians proclaim and believe with certainty. They function as a **"standard of faith"** that outlines what we must believe and how we should live as Christians. While the Apostles' Creed serves as a general map, the confessions and catechisms provide a detailed guide to the specifics. In this section, I want to introduce two fundamental principles of belief that relate to Jesus, based on the teachings of the Apostles' Creed. One is the knowledge of God, addressing the doctrine of the Trinity, and the other is human nature in relation to redemption, addressing the doctrine of salvation. Knowing God and understanding humanity are essential for discussing the entirety of the

Christian faith. However, the purpose of this book is not to aid theologians, but rather to help ordinary believers and church leaders who wish to teach foundational Christian beliefs so that the roots of their faith may deepen. Therefore, I will briefly introduce some references for specialists, and those who wish to learn more should explore more specialized texts.

The first doctrine is the knowledge of God. This involves learning about God the Father, who created, preserves, and governs the universe; about God the Son, Jesus Christ, who redeems sinners and makes them new creations; and about God the Holy Spirit, who sanctifies believers, bears spiritual fruit, and brings them into the presence of God's glory. We believe in one God who is the Creator and Ruler of all things, and this one God is distinct in three persons: God the Father, God the Son, and God the Holy Spirit. The Westminster Confession of Faith describes this in detail (the content excerpted here comes from the appendix in Calvin's Geneva Psalter).

The Knowledge of knowing God

1) Who is God?

God is the only true, living God, infinite in His existence and perfection (Deut. 4:4, 1 Cor. 8:4, 6, 1 Thess. 1:9, Jer. 10:10, Job 11:7-9, 26:14). He is the purest Spirit (John 4:24), invisible (1 Tim. 1:17), without body or parts (Deut. 4:15-16, John 4:24, Luke 24:39), and without any passions (Acts 14:11, 15). He is unchanging (James 1:17,

Mal. 3:6), immense (1 Kings 8:27, Jer. 23:23-24), eternal (Psalm 90:2, 1 Tim. 1:17), immeasurable (Psalm 145:3, Rom. 11:33), omnipotent (Gen. 17:1, Rev. 4:8), most wise (Rom. 16:27), most holy (Isa. 6:8, Rev. 4:8), most free (Psalm 115:3), and most absolute (Exod. 3:14, Isa. 44:6, Acts 17:24-25). He accomplishes everything for His own glory according to His unchangeable and most righteous will (Eph. 1:11, Prov. 16:4, Rom. 11:36). He is abundant in love (1 John 4:8, 16), gracious, merciful, long-suffering, and full of kindness and truth. He forgives iniquities, transgressions, and sins (Exod. 34:6-7), and rewards those who diligently seek Him (Heb. 11:6). His judgment is most righteous and fearsome (Neh. 9:32-33), and He hates all sin, never acquitting the guilty (Psalm 5:5-6, Neh. 1:2-3, Exod. 34:7).

God has all life, glory, goodness, and blessing in Himself and from Himself (John 5:26, Acts 7:2, Psalm 119:68, 1 Tim. 6:15, Rom. 9:5). He is completely self-sufficient and does not need the help of His created beings. He seeks no glory from them, but only displays His glory in them, through them, and to them (Acts 17:24-25, Job 22:2-3). He is the sole source of all existence, and all things come from Him, through Him, and return to Him (Rom. 11:36). He governs all things sovereignty and does whatever He pleases for the benefit of all creation (Rev. 4:11, 1 Tim. 6:15, Dan. 4:25, 35). All things are exposed and revealed before Him (Heb. 4:13). His knowledge is infinite, perfect, and independent of His creation (Rom. 11:33-34, Psalm 147:5). Nothing is uncertain before Him (Acts 15:18, Ezek. 11:5). He is holy in all His plans, works, and commandments (Psalm 145:17, Rom. 7:12). It is proper for all creation, including angels, humans, and all other creatures, to worship, serve, and obey Him (Rev. 4:12-14).

In the unity of the divine essence, there are three persons: God the Father, God the Son, and God the Holy Spirit, who are one in substance, power, and eternity (1 John 5:7, Matt. 3:16-17, 28:19, 2 Cor. 13:14). The Father is unbegotten, not made nor proceeding from anyone, but the Son is eternally begotten of the Father (John 1:14, 18), and the Holy Spirit eternally proceeds from the Father and the Son (John 15:26, Gal. 4:6).

(For a more detailed explanation, I recommend reading works on the Westminster Confession of Faith, including commentaries by scholars like Dr. Yun-Sun Park, Dr. Yong-Jo Song, Dr. Yo-Suk Jeong, Robert Shaw's "Exposition of the Westminster Confession of Faith," Thomas Watson's "Theological System," and Thomas Boston's "Commentary on the Shorter Catechism.")

In the above text, God is clearly affirmed as the one true and living God. He is the Creator of the heavens and the earth and is the sovereign ruler of all things. Furthermore, while the Father, Son, and Holy Spirit are distinct persons, they are not three gods but one God, teaching the doctrine of the unity of God.

The world is divided between those who fear God and those who worship idols, between those who believe in Jesus Christ and those who need to believe in Him, between those who live according to the guidance of the Holy Spirit and those who are led by evil spirits. This content is primarily for those who fear God, believe in Jesus Christ as their Savior, and live according to the guidance of the Holy Spirit. It aims to help believers deepen their understanding of who Jesus is, who God is, and who the Holy Spirit is. Of course, this can also serve as a tool for apologetics to share with unbelievers. However, the primary audience for this book is Christian believers. The goal is to help believers grow in their knowledge of God, Jesus, and the Holy Spirit so that they may become rooted in their faith. The essence of God, as Calvin pointed out, is 'not an object for meticulous inquiry but an object for praise.'[14] Our meditation on the divine being revealed in the Bible only leads us to further praise the great and mighty Lord even more. This is because we cannot help but be overwhelmed by His greatness. This is also the fundamental purpose of the knowledge of God.

2) Almighty God

In the Apostles' Creed, the saints confess, **"I believe in God the Father Almighty, Creator of heaven and earth."** This is the first sentence recited during public worship. It is a confession that everything we see and do not see, everything on the earth, in the sky, beneath the earth, in the water, and all living creatures and microorganisms, came into existence through the Creator God. It means that God is the ultimate cause and driving force of all beings, including humans. Every created being is absolutely dependent on the Creator. This Creator God is called our Father because He is the Father (origin) of all created things. This confession leads us to acknowledge that He alone is worthy of worship and praise: **"...Bless the LORD, your God, who has been your refuge from generation to generation, for He is the Lord of heaven and the earth, the Creator and Preserver of all things, and all the heavenly hosts worship Him"** (Nehemiah 9:5-6). The prophet Malachi speaks of God's Fatherhood: **"Have we not all one Father?**

---

14 John Calvin, *Institutes of the Christian Religion*, translated by Won Gwang-yeon, Christian Digest, 2003, Volume 1, p. 69.

Has not one God created us?" (Malachi 2:10). All Christians and non-Christians are created by God. That is why when the Apostle Paul preached in Athens, he declared, **"In Him we live and move and have our being... as some of your own poets have said, 'We are His offspring'"** (Acts 17:28). Because we are God's children, it is natural for us, as created beings, to honor, seek, obey, and follow Him. However, as we know, humans have strayed from the original purpose of their creation, each going their own way, turning away from God, and foolishly worshiping idols. In His immeasurable love, God saved us, and those who believe in Jesus are given the right to become children of God. Having been redeemed by the precious blood of His only Son, Jesus, and made citizens of the heavenly kingdom, we are naturally called to worship, honor, and live to glorify Him. The desire to understand who this God is, as the created beings we are, is completely natural. Exploring what God has done to save us—sinners, weak beings, and enemies of God—is the way to repay the grace we have received. Whether we live or die, we do so for the Lord, because we are His people. Listening to what He speaks to us and obeying His will becomes our spiritual sustenance.

Some people argue for universal salvation, using God's Fatherhood as their basis. They claim that everyone will eventually be saved. However, even though all creation was made in God's image, in this world, there are those whose father is the devil and those whose Father is God. Only those whom God has given to His Son Jesus are redeemed as His people. The grace of Jesus Christ's redemption is foolishness to the children of the devil, but to the true children of God, it is the power of salvation (1 Corinthians 1:18). While some store up God's wrath, others experience His grace. Those who enjoy God's grace always desire to be with Him. They do not forsake the privilege of spiritual intimacy with God.

Moreover, is He not the Almighty God? The term **"Almighty"** fundamentally expresses that God is the sovereign Lord and King of all, omniscient, and the powerful God who rules over the entire universe. It signifies that there is no other being in existence that can compare to Him, highlighting His uniqueness as the supreme and only sovereign. As mentioned earlier, this is why we sing praises, honor, and glory to Him forever, as He is the most deserving of these. The more we come to know this God, the more we are overwhelmed by His majesty and His character, compelling us to continually offer praises, worship, and thanks (Psalms 93, 96, 97, 99:1-5, 100, 103). As Packer rightly pointed out, **"The issue of God's absolute sovereignty is a subject of debate, but in the Bible, it is a matter of worship."**[15] A detailed explanation of this can be found in Chapter 2 of the Westminster Confession of Faith, dealing with theology. The attributes of God, as well as the divinity and humanity of Jesus Christ and the workings of the Holy Spirit, are addressed in depth in systematic theology books, but I will make only basic references here.

There is one thing we must not misunderstand concerning God's omnipotence. The idea that God can do anything is not to be taken literally. Of course, God can do whatever He desires according to His will (Psalm 135:6). However, there are things that God cannot do. Can God do things that are impossible for Him? Yes, there are things He cannot do. First and foremost, He cannot do anything that is self-contradictory. He cannot lie. He cannot sin. These are things that are entirely contrary to His nature. They are unrelated to God's holiness, righteousness, truth, goodness, love, and immutable attributes. Therefore,

---

15   J. I Packer, *I want to be a Christian*, Kingsway Publications, Eastbourne, 1977, 29.

He cannot engage in any action or utter any words that would deny His own being. Good and evil, righteousness and unrighteousness, holiness and defilement, purity and impurity, truth and falsehood—God is perfectly capable of distinguishing them, but He cannot perform evil, unrighteousness, or deceit. The Bible says: "**God is not man, that He should lie, nor a son of man, that He should repent. Has He said, and will He not do it? Or has He spoken, and will He not fulfill it?**" (Numbers 23:19). "**But He is unchangeable, and who can turn Him? What He desires, that He does**" (Job 23:13). God is not fickle. He is not someone to be described as lacking love, being unpredictable, inconsistent, or unjust. He cannot forgive sins without redemption because that would be unjust. God forgives the sins we confess in faith, and He does not turn away from His promises. He is faithful to keep His word, and there is no possibility of failure in this regard. His omnipotence serves as a guarantee that we can place our complete trust in Him.

Of course, sometimes God hides His face from us (Psalm 13, Isaiah 59:2). Often, even His faithful people are led into darkness (Isaiah 40:27, 50:10), experiencing the bitterness of failure and defeat without receiving any help from Him. Some even experience the despair of feeling utterly forsaken (Psalm 22:1). The Church too can go through periods of great suffering, feeling abandoned (Psalm 74:1). However, these trials are for our sanctification, to make us more faithful servants of God. Ultimately, He will never forsake or abandon us (Joshua 1:5, Hebrews 13:5). The will of God for our salvation is irrevocable. His love will never drift away from us until we stand before His glory without blemish. Although humans may slip between the cup and the lips, God is entirely faithful and trustworthy. He will faithfully complete the salvation of His people (1 Peter 1:5). If this were not the case, He could not be the object of our faith. God loves us, and He will be with us until the end of the age. How glorious and proud it is to have this God as our God and our Lord. Rejoicing in Him is our strength.

Furthermore, God's omnipotence is most clearly demonstrated through His acts of creation, providence, and redemption, but what we experience most closely in our daily lives are the miracles and signs that the Bible frequently mentions. These are not merely additional occurrences to His redemptive providence but certainly distinct events that draw special attention. There are three main terms used in the Bible to describe miracles. According to Donald MacLeod[16], the first term is terata (τερατα), which refers to marvelous or inexplicable events. This term is defined by the emotional impact it has on those who witness it. Witnesses are often overwhelmed by amazement and awe because these supernatural events are completely different from anything they have previously encountered. The second term is semeia (σεμεια), which means "**signs.**" These were signs of God's presence, approval, and mission through those performing them. They were clear indicators that our Lord Jesus Christ was the Son of God and the Savior sent by God, and they affirmed that His prophets and apostles had been sent by God. These signs also indicated that the Kingdom of God had come. They were a form of encouragement and motivation for the labor and effort of God's servants. The third term is dunameis (δυναμεις), meaning "**powerful deeds**" or "**mighty works.**" Miracles are the effects of God's power. They involve divine intervention to rescue people from distress, demonstrating God's power in a way that cannot be explained apart from Him. These mighty works are characteristic of God's power. Without God's power, these events cannot be explained. In the Bible, supernatural events such as the Exodus, the raising of Lazarus, and the

---

16 Donald Macleod, *Behold Your God*, Christian Focus Publication, 1990, 60.

casting out of demons are examples of such acts. Not only in the creation of the heavens and the earth from nothing by His word, but also in these mighty works, we believe in an omniscient and omnipotent God who is capable of performing such miraculous acts.

3) The Father and the Son

However, believers become children of God because of God's Son, Jesus Christ. It is those who believe in Him as their Savior who are made children of God. The reason that believers call God "**Father**" is not because of the perspective that He is the Creator of all things. In reality, it is deeply connected to His only begotten Son, Jesus Christ. It can be said that the expression used to describe this relationship is meant to assist our finite understanding in relation to the essence of the Father, Son, and Holy Spirit. Jesus referred to the One who sent Him into this world as "**Father**," and when teaching the Lord's Prayer, He instructed His followers to address God as "**Our Father in heaven.**" The Apostle Paul testifies that by the Spirit of God, we are children of God, and as evidence of this, we call God "**Abba, Father**" (Romans 8:15-16). We are called children of God, and therefore, we call God "**Abba, Father**" (Galatians 4:6). The word "**Abba**" in Aramaic conveys a sense of closeness and respect, meaning "**Daddy.**" In fact, God declared about Jesus, "**This is my beloved Son, with whom I am well pleased**" (Matthew 3:17). Jesus loved the Father and always did what pleased Him (John 14:31, 8:29). From the moment He was sent to earth to save sinners, He never once acted on His own will, but completely depended on the Father who sent Him, from beginning to end. Paul teaches that although He was equal to God, He "**emptied Himself, taking the form of a servant, being made in the likeness of men. And being found in human form,**

He humbled Himself by becoming obedient to the point of death, even death on a cross" (Philippians 2:7-8). Jesus willingly took the cup the Father had given Him (John 18:11). It wasn't only the Son who acted in this way.

The Father also deeply loved His Son, Jesus (John 3:35). **"The Father loves the Son and shows Him all that He Himself is doing. And greater works than these will He show Him, so that you may marvel"** (John 5:20). Although Jesus was treated as a sinner for the salvation of sinners, His rejection ultimately led to His receiving the name above every name, and every knee bowing before Him. This glorified Him and led to the recognition of Him as Lord. J.I. Packer said, **"God the Father's eternal love for the Son is the archetype of the gracious relationship He has established with His redeemed people, and it is the pattern of the parental relationship He has created within the human family.[17]"** Believers enjoy all the spiritual blessings in the heavenly places because of Jesus Christ, God's beloved Son. God's people, redeemed by the blood of His Son, have entered into a new relationship as children of the Father and the Son, and God is generous in blessing His children. Therefore, His children pray in the name of His Son, Jesus Christ. Hence, Paul prays, **"For this reason I bow my knees before the Father, from whom every family in heaven and on earth is named, that according to the riches of His glory He may grant you to be strengthened with power through His Spirit in your inner being, so that Christ may dwell in your hearts through faith—that you, being rooted and grounded in love, may have strength to comprehend with all the saints what is the breadth and length and height**

---

17 J. I Packer, *I want to be a Christian*, Kingsway Publications, Eastbourne, 1977, 27.

and depth, and to know the love of Christ that surpasses knowledge, that you may be filled with all the fullness of God" (Ephesians 3:14-19). Oh, how amazing is this grace!

Let us reflect on the term **"only begotten"** used by God the Father. What does it mean? Typically, when someone is introduced as the **"only son"** of a particular person, the relationship between father and son is one of deep affection. The son is regarded as a treasure, so precious that you wouldn't feel any pain even if you placed him in your eyes. He is considered as dear as one's own self, a part of the father. This is how God relates to Jesus Christ. Jesus is the Father's most beloved Son. Jesus is fully and completely God. Historically, groups like the Unitarians, Arians, and even Jehovah's Witnesses today deny His divinity, but the Bible clearly testifies to the truth that He is equal with God in power, glory, and being. All things were made through Him, and all things were created for Him; He is eternal, existing as God from the beginning (John 1:1-3). Jesus is the Son of God, and He has eternally existed as the Son. The relationship between God the Father and Jesus is unique and unparalleled. Jesus is not merely a son but the only Son . The term **"only begotten"** does not refer to a created or born being, as in a mere created being, but rather indicates a divine and eternal existence that is not dependent on creation. Jesus is not a created being but is the eternal Son who exists by the Father's will. Jesus Himself said: **"As the living Father sent Me, and I live because of the Father, so whoever feeds on Me, he also will live because of Me"** (John 6:57). **"All things have been handed over to Me by My Father, and no one knows the Son except the Father, and no one knows the Father except the Son and anyone to whom the Son chooses to reveal Him"** (Matthew 11:27).

This does not mean that the Father existed first and the Son came from the Father, nor does it suggest that the Son is inferior to the Father. Just as we exist in the course of time in creation, Jesus is not merely a creation of the Father but is a divine being who existed before time itself. If Jesus were simply a product of time, He would be no different from any created being bound by time. However, Jesus transcends time and space as the Creator. He is God who exists from eternity to eternity. Therefore, as J.I. Packer suggests, the **"begetting"** of the Son is not a temporal or metaphorical event like the coronation of a king described in Psalm 2:7, applied to Christ in Acts13:33 and Hebrews 1:5. Rather, it represents an eternal relationship: the first person is always the Father to the Son, and the second person is always the Son to the Father.[18] The Father and the Son have an eternal relationship that spans from eternity to eternity. Though we may not fully comprehend the mystery of the Trinity from our limited perspective, we receive the teachings of Scripture by faith and teach others that it is true as the Bible instructs. Faith enables us to see what is unseen. Thus, our confession of faith describes it as follows: **"In the unity of the Godhead, there are three persons—God the Father, God the Son, and God the Holy Spirit—who are one in essence, power, and eternity (1 John 5:7; Matthew 3:16-17, 28:19; 2 Corinthians 13:14). The Father is unbegotten and does not proceed from anyone; the Son is eternally begotten of the Father (John 1:14, 18); the Holy Spirit eternally proceeds from the Father and the Son (John 15:26, Galatians 4:6)."**[19]

---

18 J. I Packer, Ibid, 40.

19 I would like to introduce books related to theology and the doctrine of the Trinity, written by my mentor, Professor Donald Macleod. These include *Behold Your God* (Christian Focus Publications, 1990), *The Person of Christ* (IVP, 1998), and *A Faith to Live By* (Mentor, 1998). The first book deals with the-

4) The Incarnate Jesus Christ

I would like to offer a more doctrinal explanation about how Jesus achieved the salvation of sinners in relation to learning about Him. Let's first reflect on what the Apostles' Creed states: **"We believe in Jesus Christ, our Lord, who was conceived by the Holy Spirit, born of the Virgin Mary, suffered under Pontius Pilate, was crucified, died, and was buried. On the third day, He rose again from the dead, He ascended into heaven, and is seated at the right hand of God the Father Almighty. From there He will come to judge the living and the dead!"**

The one who was incarnate was the Word of God (John 1:14). The Shorter Catechism Question 22 summarizes this as follows: **"Christ, the Son of God, became man by taking on a true human body and a rational soul, being conceived by the Holy Spirit and born of the Virgin Mary, but without sin."** The incarnation of Christ literally means that He was born in the flesh, or that the Savior was born as a human. This presupposes that He preexisted, and that He is God with divine nature. Since this has already been addressed earlier, it will not be discussed further, but His incarnation is a clear declaration of both His humanity and divinity. It was not the Father or the Holy Spirit who incarnated, but the Son, Jesus. He is God who came from heaven and took on human flesh. This does not mean that His divinity merged into His humanity to make Him a human. He was God, and He did

---

ology and the saving love of God, while the second focuses on the person of Christ as outlined in the Nicene Creed. The last book provides a practical description of living the Christian faith with theological assurance. I highly recommend these books to the readers.

not become God. The Apostle John uses the imperfect tense in the Greek phrase that describes His becoming man, signifying that He has always been the eternal Son of God. However, in John 1:14, the word **"became"** uses a simple past tense, not an imperfect, indicating that He became flesh at a specific, decisive moment, not that He was always flesh. It means He was always divine, but at a particular moment, He became flesh. He became flesh in a situation marked by the curse and lowly, sinful human condition. Hebrews describes Him this way: **"For we do not have a high priest who is unable to sympathize with our weaknesses, but one who in every respect has been tempted as we are, yet without sin"** (Hebrews 4:15). His suffering was like the confession of the prophet Isaiah: **"Surely He has borne our griefs and carried our sorrows; yet we esteemed Him stricken, smitten by God, and afflicted. But He was pierced for our transgressions; He was crushed for our iniquities; upon Him was the chastisement that brought us peace, and with His wounds, we are healed"** (Isaiah 53:4-5).

His death was not an accident. It was not the result of God's malicious action, but a sacrificial offering for sinners. He was the Lamb of God who took away the sin of the world (John 1:29). This explains the doctrine of atonement, which states that without the shedding of blood, there is no forgiveness of sins. The Apostle Peter declares that **"we have been made holy, blameless, and above reproach before God"** by the **"precious blood of Christ, like that of a lamb without blemish or spot"** (1 Peter 1:19). Our sins were transferred to the Lamb of God, Jesus Christ. His resurrection brought us justification: **"He was delivered up for our trespasses and raised for our justification"** (Romans 4:25). Why did the Apostle Paul confess this? **"For I decided to know nothing among you except Jesus Christ and Him crucified"** (1 Corinthians 2:2). It is because of the great blessings that the event of Christ's atonement brought to sinners. Although this work is not focused on systematic theology and cannot include every detail, this chapter specifically emphasizes that knowing only the cross of Christ is all we need to boast about (Galatians 6:14).

God, being unchanging, has undoubtedly affirmed who He is through the redemptive work of His Son, Jesus Christ. Jesus, through His atoning death on the cross, glorified God, and as a result, He received the name above all names. How can the holy and righteous God be the One who justifies the ungodly? The answer is presented in the gospel of the cross of Christ: "**It was to show His righteousness at the present time, so that He might be just and the justifier of the one who has faith in Jesus**" (Romans 3:26). In short, God's wrath against sin was satisfied, His justice was revealed, and at the same time, God's immense love for His people was demonstrated at the cross. This contains crucial theological lessons.

❶ Sacrificial Atonement

"**And walk in love, as Christ loved us and gave Himself up for us, a fragrant offering and sacrifice to God**" (Ephesians 5:2). The central concept of this doctrine is substitutionary atonement. This means sacrificing oneself in place of others, paying the penalty for sinners. Christ, standing in the place of His people, took upon Himself their penalty as their penal substitute. This atonement involves two important terms: expiation and propitiation. Expiation emphasizes the removal or cleansing of sin, specifically the removal of guilt from sin. "**To Him who loves us and has freed us from our sins by His blood**" (Revelation 1:5). But atonement also includes propitiation, which means satisfying God's justice and appeasing His wrath. "**But God shows His love for us in that while we were still sinners, Christ died for us. Since, therefore,** we have now been justified by His blood, much more shall we be saved by Him from the wrath of God" (Romans 5:8-9). As a righteous and just God, He must express His wrath toward all sin. That wrath was satisfied through the death of Christ, thus fulfilling His justice. "**In this is love, not that we have loved God, but that He loved us and sent His Son to be the propitiation for our sins**" (1 John 4:10).

❷ Reconciliation

"**We were reconciled to God through the death of His Son when we were God's enemies, much more, having been reconciled, we shall be saved by His life. Not only that, but we also rejoice in God through our Lord Jesus Christ, through whom we have now received reconciliation**" (Romans 5:9-10). Reconciliation is the removal of hostility between God and us. Christ's atonement removes the alienation that sin causes between humanity and God and restores the friendship and fellowship with Him. This is truly good news and should be proclaimed as the gospel, being an important part of preaching. Paul explains it as follows: "**All this is from God, who reconciled us to Himself through Christ and gave us the ministry of reconciliation: that God was reconciling the world to Himself in Christ, not counting people's sins against them. And He has committed to us the message of reconciliation. We are therefore Christ's ambassadors, as though God were making His appeal through us. We implore you on Christ's behalf: Be reconciled to God**" (2 Corinthians 5:18-20).

The idea that humans become new creations and enjoy eternal life is not something that can be achieved or obtained by human effort; it is entirely from God. God initiated this work of reconciliation, but He is the innocent party in this desired relationship. He reconciled us to Himself, not that we reconciled with Him. The key point is that God did this through Jesus Christ. God did not reconcile us to Himself by neglecting His holy justice or by **"submitting"** to sinful and rebellious humanity. Rather, He did this through the amazing and righteous sacrifice of love. The justice and righteousness that God demands from humanity were fulfilled through Jesus Christ.

The fact that God reconciled the world to Himself in Christ is an incredibly astonishing thing when viewed in light of what happened on the cross. At some point before Jesus died, before the temple veil was torn in two, and before Jesus cried out, **"It is finished,"** a miraculous spiritual transaction occurred. The Father placed upon the Son all the guilt and wrath that our sins deserved, and Jesus perfectly bore it in Himself, completely satisfying God's justice on our behalf. The Father and the Son worked together on the cross. The cup that Jesus drank was the cup of God's righteous wrath, and He trembled as He drank it (Luke 22:39-46, Psalm 75:8, Isaiah 51:17, Jeremiah 25:15). Because Jesus, as though He were God's enemy, bore the judgment and drank the cup of the Father's wrath, we do not have to drink it. In Jesus, we have been reconciled to God.

❸ Redemption

"In Him we have redemption through His blood, the forgiveness of sins, in accordance with the riches of God's grace" (Ephesians 1:7). Redemption refers to the payment of a price for our salvation, buying us back to live again for God. It is the concept of a ransom. The prominent concept in the Old Testament is established through Christ's atoning grace. The entire Exodus event was about redemption. This includes the idea of Christ as our guarantor. As a guarantor, He took on the responsibility of paying the debt of sin for His people. The New Testament also clearly reveals that Christ is the ransom. The price He paid for our redemption was the shedding of His own blood. Christ said, **"For even the Son of Man did not come to be served, but to serve, and to give His life as a ransom for many"** (Mark 10:45), referring to Himself.

To explain more specifically, Christians are redeemed from spiritual bondage, particularly from the bondage of sin, guilt, defilement, and the power of sin. **"Who gave Himself for us to redeem us from all wickedness and to purify for Himself a people that are His very own, eager to do what is good"** (Titus 2:14). Also, God's children are redeemed from the curse of the law. **"Christ redeemed us from the curse of the law by becoming a curse for us, for it is written: 'Cursed is everyone who is hung on a pole'"** (Galatians 3:13). Furthermore, Christians are redeemed from the works of the devil (1 John 3:8) and from the power of death. Through Christ's death, He destroyed the one who holds the power of death (Hebrews 2:14). The resurrection chapter of 1 Corinthians 15 clearly declares that the power of death is utterly defeated before the authority of Christ.

All of this has been accomplished through God's Son, Jesus Christ. For those who receive it (the scope of atonement is not for every sinner, but for those predestined to eternal life, those who believe in Jesus as their Savior)[20], they walk the

---

[20] The debate about who benefits from Christ's atonement was the main point of contention between Arminianism and Calvinism. Calvinism, or Reformed theology, which holds the Bible as the inerrant word of God, adheres to the five points of Calvinism. Those whom the Father draws to the Son, those who trust in the Lord Jesus Christ, are the ones who enjoy all the blessings of Christ's atonement. For a detailed discussion on this, refer to the author's *What Do Reformed Churches Believe?* (Flag of Truth, 2009). Also, see *The Collected Writings of John Murray*, The Banner of Truth, 1976, vol. 1, 29-39. I will introduce writings by John Owen: The Father poured out His wrath, and the Son received the punishment for: 1) all the sins of all people, 2) all the sins of some people, or 3) some sins of all people. In the first case, "if the latter is true," that

path of life, while those who reject it will face the resurrection of death. The one who confirms this great redemption in us is the Holy Spirit, who came as the Spirit of the Son.

❹ The Holy Spirit, the Spirit of Truth, the Other Helper

Let me once again quote from Chapter 2, Section 3 of the Westminster Confession of Faith regarding the Trinity: "**In the unity of the Godhead, there are three persons, the Father, the Son, and the Holy Spirit, each of whom is God, equal in substance, and co-eternal in power and glory. The Father is not begotten nor proceeding, the Son is eternally begotten of the Father, and the Holy Spirit eternally proceeds from the Father and the Son**" (1 John 5:7; Matthew 3:16-17; 28:19; 2 Corinthians 13:14). The phrase "**I believe in the Holy Spirit**" in the Apostles' Creed uses "**Holy Ghost**" instead of "**Holy Spirit**" in English. The word "**Ghost**," which is often found in English translations of the Bible, actually means "**spirit**" in some contexts, but its association with ghosts in modern English can give it a negative or unsettling connota-

---

is, if Christ bore the punishment for the sins of all people, "then every person has sins they must answer for, and no one can be saved." This can be excluded from the list. Secondly, "if the second is true," that is, if Christ died for all the sins of some people, "then Christ suffered for all the sins of the elect from the entire world. This is the true position." However, the third position is the Arminian view, which says, "If the first is true," that is, if Christ died for all the sins of all people, "then why are not all people free from the punishment of their sins? You would answer, 'Because of unbelief.'" Owen asks, "Then, I ask, is this unbelief sin or not? If it is, it is sin, and Christ either bore the punishment for it or He did not. If He did, then why should this sin be more hindering to them than the other sins for which He died? But if He did not die for that sin, then He did not die for all their sins." *The Works of John Owen, The Death of Christ*, vol. 10, The Banner of Truth, 1978, 248-249.

tion. J.I. Packer suggests that it is more appropriate to call the third person of the Trinity the **"Holy Spirit."** The reason is that the Hebrew word ruach and the Greek word pneuma refer to spiritual energy or breath, which is both divine and human, and therefore, the term **"Spirit"** is better suited to convey the idea of the Holy Spirit as a person.[21] The Apostles' Creed, after mentioning the creation work of the Father and the redeeming work of the Son, then confesses the renewing work of the Holy Spirit. Through the Holy Spirit, sinners are renewed in Jesus Christ, and through Jesus Christ, the new community, the Church, is formed. Those who are reconciled with God, having received forgiveness of sins, experience the great work of salvation, which includes eternal life.

Although the Westminster Confession does not have a separate section specifically about the Holy Spirit, it clearly describes the primary role of the Holy Spirit as the eternal God who proceeds from the Father and the Son. The primary role of the Holy Spirit is to testify of Jesus Christ, who saved sinners. Through the work of the Holy Spirit, the grace of Christ's redemption is applied to all believers (WCF 8:8, 11:4). The calling, the work of faith, repentance, and the imparting of the grace of salvation are all the work of the Holy Spirit (WCF 13:1). The growth of the saints in the grace of the Spirit is also the work of the Holy Spirit (WCF 13:3), and the Spirit works sovereignly to make the means of grace effective in individuals (WCF 7:5, 6). The Spirit enables the saints to pray (WCF 21:3), to have assurance of salvation (WCF 18:8), and to live in obedience to God's will (WCF 16:3). The Spirit leads believers to live holy lives (WCF 17:1) and, through His work and testimony, keeps believers on the path of salvation by faith (WCF 17:2). The Holy

---

21 J. I Packer, ibid, 60.

Spirit bears witness with our spirit that we are children of God (WCF 18:2). The lack of a specific section on the Holy Spirit in the Confession may be related to the fact that the Spirit's primary work is to testify to Christ. As Jesus said in the Gospel of John: **"But when He, the Spirit of truth, comes, He will guide you into all the truth"** (John 16:13). Nevertheless, the Holy Spirit is certainly worthy of worship, for He is God, the third person of the Trinity (WCF 21:2). The Church, through faith in the Holy Spirit, is united to Christ, the Head, and through union with Christ by the Holy Spirit, the Church is united in love, sharing in the gifts and grace of the Spirit (WCF 25:1). The Confession also addresses the work of the Holy Spirit in the sacraments (WCF 27:3) and the outpouring of promised grace by the Holy Spirit (WCF 28:6).

This section on learning about Jesus emphasizes that, just as the second person of the Trinity, Jesus, cannot be separated from the Father and the Holy Spirit, so too the person and work of the Holy Spirit must be addressed. Just as the Father and the Son work interdependently, so too the Holy Spirit does not work independently. The Holy Spirit served throughout Jesus' earthly ministry, from the conception of Jesus by the Holy Spirit (Matthew 1:20, Luke 1:35) to every aspect of His ministry. When Jesus was baptized, the Holy Spirit descended like a dove, indicating that Jesus was both the giver of the Spirit and the one who was filled with the Spirit (Luke 4:1, 14, 18). Jesus offered Himself as a sacrifice through the eternal Spirit (Hebrews 9:14). The Holy Spirit, guiding the people of God in truth, applies the salvation that Christ accomplished through His death and resurrection, preparing the faithful for their inheritance in God's kingdom (Romans 8:14, 17; John 16:13). Therefore, learning about Jesus is impossible without the presence of the Holy Spirit. Furthermore, the Holy Spirit glorifies not Himself but Jesus (John 16:14) and reminds believers of everything that Jesus taught. Through the Spirit's illumination, believers experience the work of salvation that the Father planned and the Son accomplished. As the **"Other Helper"** and representative of Jesus Christ, the Holy Spirit comforts, aids, supports, advocates, and encourages believers, helping them fight the good fight of faith and finish their race in this world, full of the world's trials and temptations. The Holy Spirit, the Spirit of Truth, leads believers to follow and become more like Jesus. This is the work He will continue until Jesus returns. For those who desire to know more deeply about the person, work, and gifts of the Holy Spirit, there are many resources available on the topic of pneumatology.[22] However, one key point to emphasize is that to rightly understand the Holy Spirit, we should not only study Acts and John 14-16, but also evaluate the work of the Holy Spirit in light of the teachings of Jesus in the Gospel of John. This will help ensure that our understanding of the Spirit is in line with Scripture.

First, the Holy Spirit, sent by God, came upon Jesus Christ without measure from His birth throughout His entire ministry, empowering Him to accomplish His work (Luke 1:35, John 3:34, Isaiah 11:2). Everything that Jesus did on earth was done through, by, and with the Holy Spir-

---

[22] George S. Hendry, *The Holy Spirit in Christian Theology*, SCM Press LTD, London, 1957. Abraham Kuyper, *The Work of the Holy Spirit*, John W. Mongomary Christian Today, 1975. J. I . Parker, *Keep in Step With the Spirit*, IVP. 1984, A. W. Tozer, Holy Spirit, *translated by Lee YoungBok, Kyujang*, 2006, James S. Stewart, *The Wind of the Spirit*, Hodder and Stoughton,1969, George Smeaton, *The Doctrine of the Holy Spirit*, The Banner of the Truth, 1882, Benjamin B. Warfield, *the Person and the Work of the Holy Spirit*, Cavary Press Publishing,1997. William Fitch, The Ministry of the Holy Spirit, Pickering & Inglis, 1977, Geoffry Thomas, The Holy Spirit, Reformation Heritage Books, 2011, Donald Macleod, The Spirit of Promise, Chrostoan Focus Publications, 1986. Sinclair Ferguson, *The Holy Spirit*, IVP, *translated by Kim Jaesung*, 1999. In addition to this, there are many books on the theory of the Holy Spirit.

it who came upon Him. Moreover, when Christ suffered His sacrificial death on the cross, the Holy Spirit supported Him (Hebrews 9:14). Just as the Holy Spirit conceived Christ, He also preserved Christ's body in the tomb, preventing it from decaying. The Holy Spirit played a significant role in His resurrection (Romans 8:11). [23]The same Spirit who raised Christ from the dead also gives life to the mortal bodies of believers.

Second, even after Christ's ascension, the Holy Spirit continues His Christ-centered work. Jesus said, **"When the Helper comes, whom I will send to you from the Father, the Spirit of truth who proceeds from the Father, He will bear witness about me"** (John 15:26). The outpouring of the Holy Spirit on Pentecost, described as a mighty wind from heaven, served the purpose of making all who received the Spirit witnesses of Christ, as testified in Acts 1:8. The work of the Holy Spirit is to testify of Christ. The Holy Spirit focuses entirely on Christ, glorifying Him alone. Just as Christ did not seek His own glory while on earth, the Holy Spirit does not seek to glorify Himself but to glorify Christ. The coming of the Spirit is completely Christ-centered, to reveal, make known, cause people to believe in, and lead them to follow the work of salvation accomplished by Christ. For this purpose, the Holy Spirit is sent by the Father and the Son.

Third, the Holy Spirit is the Helper who accompanies Christians from spiritual rebirth all the way to the end of time. The Holy Spirit regenerates those who are dead in trespasses and sins through the proclamation of the gospel, and by indwelling them, He transfers them from death to life. The Holy Spirit applies all that Christ accomplished for

---

23 "And if the Spirit of him who raised Jesus from the dead is living in you, he who raised Christ from the dead will also give life to your mortal bodies because of his Spirit who lives in you!"

the salvation of His people. Without the Holy Spirit's work, believers and the church are spiritually lifeless. They become tools of the enemy, even a den for the devil.

Lastly, the Holy Spirit always works in conjunction with the Scriptures. Without the work of the Holy Spirit, the proclamation of the Word can fall into the error of rationalism, while the absence of the Word in the Holy Spirit's work leads to the pitfall of mysticism. Believers and the church must be filled with the Word of Christ through the indwelling Holy Spirit. The primary work of church leaders is to clearly explain and proclaim God's Word with the help of the Holy Spirit, so that believers may be richly enlightened (Colossians 1:25, 3:16). This is why the apostles committed themselves to prayer and the ministry of the Word (Acts 6:4). We must note the order here. The work of the Holy Spirit is most active in the ministry of the Word, which is supported by prayer. The church, as a holy temple in which God's Spirit dwells, requires the gifts of the Holy Spirit for its proper building up. Each believer is a member of the body of Christ, and each member is placed in the body according to the will of the Holy Spirit, not according to the desires of the individual (1 Corinthians 12:11, 18). In this sense, we must reject any unbiblical teachings on the gifts of the Spirit. The Holy Spirit does not lead us beyond the written Word. Instead, He works within it, guiding us to live holy lives through it. His illuminating, enabling, and guiding work leads us to experience the righteous Word and helps perfect our faith, so that we may grow in our knowledge of Jesus Christ, the Author and Finisher of our faith.

Knowledge about Humanity

In fact, those who come to know who God is cannot help but be deeply interested in what God has done for humanity. When they learn that God sent His Son, and that the Son obeyed unto death to complete the salvation of sinners, the common reaction is to sing praises and testify about this incredible work. To understand how and through whom this work was accomplished, we must first understand who human beings are, the very objects of salvation. Knowing who humans are influences our responsibilities and daily actions. Thus, it is crucial to have a general understanding of humanity, but more importantly, to consider it according to the teachings of Scripture.[24] Moreover, many of the problems we face today are not solely due to ignorance of God and Jesus Christ, but can often be traced back to a lack of understanding of humanity itself. It is a foundational belief that all human beings have fallen into sin, and that all of their faculties are thoroughly corrupted. As a result, humans cannot know God by their own efforts, their thoughts are continually evil, and they are hostile to God, unable to avoid His wrath. Therefore, they need to be redeemed by the blood of Christ. The teachings of this are also reflected in the Westminster Confession of Faith:

---

[24] The most outstanding book on the doctrine of humanity is *Human Nature in its Fourfold State* by Thomas Boston, a pastor and theologian from 18th-century Scotland (published by Revival and Reformation). In this book, one can find the most Reformed and biblical teachings on the four states of humanity: the created human, the fallen human, the redeemed human, and the glorified human.

Chapter 6:
Of the Fall of Man, of Sin, and of the Punishment Thereof

1. Our first parents, being seduced by the subtlety and temptation of Satan, sinned in eating the forbidden fruit. This was their sin, and although God, according to His wise and holy plan, permitted it, He did so in order to manifest His glory (Rom. 5:19-21, 11:32).
2. As a result of this sin, they were cut off from their original righteousness and communion with God (Gen. 3:6-8, Eccl. 7:29, Rom. 3:23). They became spiritually dead (Gen. 2:17, Eph. 2:1), and all their faculties and members were thoroughly polluted (Tit. 1:15, Gen. 6:5, Jer. 17:9, Rom. 3:10-18).
3. Since they are the progenitors of the entire human race, the guilt of this sin is passed down to all of their descendants (Gen. 1:27-28, 2:16-17, Acts 17:26, Rom. 5:12, 15-19, 1 Cor. 15:21, 22, 49). Furthermore, due to this sin, the same death and corrupted nature are transmitted from the first parents to all of their descendants through natural birth (Ps. 51:5, Gen. 5:3, Job 14:4, 15:14).
4. Because of this original corruption, we are totally unable to desire or perform any good. We are opposed to all that is good, inclined towards evil, and inevitably commit sin (Rom. 5:6, 8:7, 7:18, Col. 1:21, Gen. 6:5, 8:21, Rom. 3:10-12, James 1:14-15, Eph. 2:2-3, Matt. 15:19).
5. This corruption remains even in those who are regenerated during their earthly life (1 John 1:8, 10, Rom. 7:14, 17-18, 23, James 3:2, Prov. 20:9, Eccl. 7:20). Although it is forgiven and restrained through Christ, the nature itself and all actions stemming from it are truly and accurately sin (Rom. 7:5, 7-8, 25, Gal. 5:17).
6. Original sin, actual sin, and all sin are violations of God's righteous

law, opposed to that law, and by their very nature bring guilt upon sinners. As a result, sinners are bound to God's wrath and the curse of the law (1 John 3:4, Rom. 2:15, 3:9, 19, Eph. 2:3, Gal. 3:10). This results in spiritual misery, and sinners are spiritually and eternally subject to death (Rom. 6:23, Eph. 4:18, Rom. 8:20, Lam. 3:39, Matt. 25:41, 2 Thess. 1:9).

What has been quoted above concerns the fall of humanity and redemption. God created man and woman in His own image and likeness (Gen. 1:26). Humans were not created by God's spontaneous thoughts but by a decision made within the Trinity, where they deliberated together. The creation of humanity was not an act of creation ex nihilo (out of nothing), but rather, God used pre-existing dust, and created Eve from Adam's rib (Gen. 2:7, 22). Of course, this act of creation is distinctly different from the creation of other creatures. The creation of humanity reflects God's artistic ability and His intricate design. The word **"formed"** captures this, indicating the detailed and intentional craftsmanship involved. Professor McCloud explains that it expresses God's **"love and care"** in creating humans.[25] In other words, God put immense effort into making humanity a beautiful and loving creation. While other creatures were spoken into existence by God's word, humanity was formed with God's own hands from the dust and created in His image, making them the pinnacle of His creative work. Thus, humanity was given the cultural mandate to rule, subdue, and multiply the earth. **"Then the Lord God formed the man of dust from the ground and breathed into his nostrils the breath of life, and the man**

---

25 Donald Macleod, *A Faith to Live By*, Mentor, 1998, 67.

became a living creature" (Gen. 2:7). "This reveals that God did not simply leave the universe to naturally produce humans through a process of deistic evolution or a self-sustaining, self-monitoring evolutionary process."[26] Instead, humans were created directly by God's hand and finished with His breath, completing them as the highest form of creation. There is no place for theistic evolution in God's creation. God's creation was not intended to evolve through time and environment, but from the very beginning, humans were created as complete, perfect beings.

Can a Believer Accept Evolution? (By Gregg R. Allison)

"The Church must continually read the biblical account of divine creation, faithfully adhering to the historical position, praising the Creator God who created from nothing to something, and praising all specific kinds of creation, including all living and non-living things. We are familiar with the term 'evolution.' When I majored in science in college, every subject I studied—biology, botany, ecology, microbiology—was taught from the perspective of evolution. In this context, evolution refers to 'the theory that all living things originated from inanimate matter, and that random mutations, over billions of years, caused changes without purpose or design, and developed through natural selection and speciation' (Baker Compact Dictionary of Theological Terms, 76).

Imagine elements like oxygen, hydrogen, nitrogen, and carbon

---

26 Donald Macleod, ibid, 67.

coming together to form inanimate substances like air, water, and metals, and living things like trees, grass, insects, birds, elephants, and humans. At an invisible level, changes occurred by chance. Random mutations in DNA provided slight advantages for survival, leading to the development of these unique kinds (species) of plants and animals. As these kinds evolved with survival advantages, they ultimately created the present diversity of all non-living and living things. What's crucial here is that this entire process occurred without God, without direction or purpose.

Theistic evolution is a subset of evolution with at least two versions. One version holds that theistic evolution is the theory that all living things evolved according to a process of evolution, with God occasionally intervening 'to achieve His purpose.' This version affirms both divine action ('theistic') and evolution (Baker Compact Dictionary of Theological Terms, 77). According to this version, the key difference between evolution and theistic evolution is that the former denies God's role in the evolutionary process that brought about all living and non-living things, whereas the latter retains some role for God in that process. For example, theistic evolution can be viewed as 'the view that after God created matter, He did not cause or induce any empirically detectable change in the natural behavior of matter until all life evolved purely through natural processes' (Theistic Evolution, 946). Thus, after God created the world separate from Himself, He did not continue to play a role in the evolutionary process He initiated.

The second version, represented by the organization BioLogos, defines theistic evolution as 'the view that God created all life through Christ, created humanity in His image, and actively employs the intentionally designed and ongoing natural processes that scientists today research as evolution' ("**The Faulty Mirror**"). In this version, God not only acted initially to create the world but is actively involved throughout the entire development of all things. He supervises evolutionary processes like natural selection, speciation, and random mutations, and through His divine design, He creates both living and non-living things. Do both versions of theistic evolution align with the Bible? To answer that, we need to examine church history and historical Christian doctrine.

The Church has believed throughout most of history that God created everything from nothing. This doctrine has been affirmed primarily based on the first verse of the Bible: 'In the beginning, God created the heavens and the earth' (Genesis 1:1). God, eternally existing as Father, Son, and Holy Spirit, created the universe with a purpose, and He truly created it. Other verses also support this belief. For example, the psalmist attributes creation to God's Word and breath: 'By the word of the LORD the heavens were made, their starry host by the breath of His mouth... For He spoke, and it came to be; He commanded, and it stood firm' (Psalm 33:6, 9). According to traditional understanding, God the Father created the universe through His Word (God the Son) and His breath (God the Holy Spirit). Creation was the powerful act of the Triune God.

Moreover, the Bible itself denies that God used pre-existing materials in His creation. 'By faith we understand that the universe was formed at God's command, so that what is seen was not made out of what was visible' (Hebrews 11:3). For example, God did not take two existing hydrogen (H) atoms and one oxygen (O) atom and fuse them to create water (H_2O). Rather, He created both the hydrogen and oxygen atoms, and He also created water. God's creation came from nothing! According to the rest of the creation account in Genesis 1, the Church also believes that God created all kinds of things that existed, such as light, water, air, earth, plants, the sun, moon, and stars, sea creatures, winged birds, land animals, and ultimately humanity in His image. The important point is that the Church has never accepted the idea that all non-living and living things came to exist and evolved through processes like natural selection, speciation, and random mutations. In fact, the early Church thoroughly condemned the 'atom' theory, which suggested that everything began from random collisions of small elements ('atoms') and developed by chance. The Church rejected randomness, preferring to praise the Creator as Origen did: 'But we Christians who worship the one God who created these things, give thanks to Him who made them' (Against Celsus, 4.75)."

The Church began to waver on its doctrine of creation in the 19th century as it faced many attacks on the authority and veracity of the Bible. With the publication of Charles Darwin's On the Origin of Species (1859), a new, comprehensive worldview emerged that denied the creation of life from nothing, the divine design and development of various kinds of inanimate and living beings, and the special creation of humans in the divine image. This evolutionary worldview now dominates most areas of modern Western society. Tragically, it presents one of the most intense challenges to biblical and historical Christianity today.

Simply put, the Church has always affirmed the creation doctrine presented above. One of the earliest statements of faith, the Nicene-Constantinopolitan Creed (381 AD), affirmed, **"We believe in one God, the Father Almighty, Maker of heaven and earth, and of all things visible and invisible."** In later theological developments, Thomas Aquinas rejected the idea that **"creation itself has the power to create or develop other living entities."** He reasoned, **"Only God, as an absolute** being, has the ability to create, and it is impossible for creation to possess such power" (Theistic Evolution, 935-936). His stance is in opposition to theistic evolution, which attributes creative power to material and purely natural processes. Similarly, Protestant theology has continued to affirm the traditional doctrine of creation.

Therefore, Christians who accept theistic evolution, besides contradicting the biblical account of creation, stand outside the historical position of the Church. While they may believe that God created matter, they cannot affirm that God created not just inanimate matter but also everything visible (e.g., oak trees and horses) and invisible (e.g., angels). "**Therefore, God's creation was not the creation of general material, but the creation of specific kinds and species of creatures**" (Theistic Evolution, 946). When applied to the second version of theistic evolution, BioLogos's theistic evolutionists (or "**evolutionary creationists**" as they prefer) affirm the principle of common ancestry. Using humans and chimpanzees (our closest relatives) as an example, they argue that a common ancestor existed about 300,000 generations ago, and this common ancestor "**was neither human nor chimpanzee but an ancient group that split into two groups, which eventually became reproductively isolated... and the characteristics of each group became sufficiently different that scientists recognized them as different species.**" The key point for evolutionary creationists is that "**the same story could be told about the ancestral line of the two species that lived earlier**" ("What is Evolution?").

This perspective on the origin and development of species, especially humanity, is at odds with the biblical account, even if it incorporates appeals to God's guidance and purpose. Evolutionary creationists reject the account in Genesis 1, where God directly created fish, birds, land animals, and ultimately humans without natural processes. Instead, they propose that God created these life forms through natural mechanisms over long periods of time. Their position also inherently denies the biblical explanation of the fall, as such an evolutionary process leaves no room for the historical Adam and Eve. For these reasons (and others), the Church must continue to read the biblical account of creation and remain faithful to the historical position. The Church should praise the Creator God, who created from nothing, and praise the purposeful creation of all specific kinds of living and non-living things.

Though somewhat lengthy, this discussion is particularly relevant today due to the heated debate surrounding theistic evolution. I believe that the creation account in Genesis 1 is not a myth but a historical fact. The Bible affirms this, as God incarnate gave humans the creation account in a language and manner that they could understand. When it says, **"There was evening, and there was morning, the first day,"** it is written in a way that readers can understand, and not with a higher-level meaning suggesting a day could span a thousand years or more. Furthermore, since God is eternal, the same yesterday, today, and forever, He would not have expressed the creation of things over six days as something that would later evolve into completed creatures. God's choice for human salvation was not made in anticipation of what people would believe, just as His actions in creation were not intended to evolve. Attempts to make the Bible conform to science often distort it. Moreover, the Bible is not a book teaching science.

What is humanity?

As a direct creation of God, humanity is a psychosomatic union consisting of both spirit and body. In short, this means that the soul and body do not function as separate entities, but are intimately united. A human cannot exist without the spirit. The body, without the spirit, is merely material destined to decay and return to the earth, possessing biochemical characteristics. There is nothing inherently evil or contemptible about the body. Since God Himself formed the body, it bears the dignity of being His creation. However, what makes a human being truly human is the spirit of life that God breathed into their nostrils—this is the work of the spirit. When God, who is Spirit, incarnated, He took on human flesh. The body became a precious vessel for His spirit. **"For in Him the fullness of the Deity lives in bodily form"** (Colossians 2:9). Among all the creatures in the universe, a human body, as the Son of God, has become a unique entity. It is a being suited for serving God. In this sense, we do not have the right to excessively cherish or indulge our bodies, nor do we have the right to misuse or exhaust them. However, since the salvation of fallen humanity includes not only the soul but also the body, it is the duty of believers to give glory to God with their bodies. **"Do you not know that your bodies are temples of the Holy Spirit, who is in you, whom you have received from God? You are not your own; you were bought at a price. Therefore honor God with your bodies"** (1 Corinthians 6:19-20).

Humans are not only material beings but also spiritual beings because they possess a spirit. The ability to think, decide, and feel belongs to the spirit. This is why humans are described as emotional creatures. Of course, other animals also have thoughts, decisions, and feelings, but what sets humans apart as the pinnacle of creation is the breath of life given to them by God. It is because of this breath that Adam, with his body, was called a "**living soul**" (Genesis 2:7). Humans are creatures who experience emotions like joy, sadness, fear, anxiety, hope, joy, and disappointment. They are beings who love and are loved. The ultimate dignity of humanity is its communion with God, the giver of life. As Professor McCloud points out, the human soul is "**not something that is attached or owned by his character, nor is it some external accessory to his nature.**"[27] Humans are, therefore, a union of flesh and spirit.

The characteristics of humans do not end here. That God created mankind as male and female (Genesis 1:27) speaks of the existence of sexual distinctions, just as there are distinctions between the Father, Son, and Holy Spirit. This is a fact that cannot be denied or altered. The sexual distinction of male and female is a principle and intention of God's creation. From this perspective, artificial gender transitions are not in line with God's will. They go against the order of creation established by God. The Bible says: "**Therefore God gave them over in the sinful desires of their hearts to sexual impurity for the degrading of their bodies with one another... Because of this, God gave them over to shameful lusts. Even their women exchanged natural sexual relations for unnatural ones. In the same way the men also abandoned natural relations with women and were inflamed with lust for one another. Men committed shameful acts with other men, and received in themselves the due penalty for their error**" (Romans 1:24, 26-27). Those who are born eunuchs or those who are sexually impaired due to accidents, such as castration, may not have an interest in the opposite sex.

---

27 Donald Macleod, ibid, 71.

However, the issue with homosexuality arises when there is no sexual desire for the opposite sex, and instead, a person seeks to satisfy those desires with someone of the same sex, justifying homosexual acts as a way to fulfill these desires. There is no genetic predisposition to homosexuality.[28] The Bible teachings on homosexuality can be found not only in Romans but also in Leviticus 18:22, 20:13, 1 Corinthians 6:9-10, and 1 Timothy 1:9-10. These passages clearly teach that homosexuality is a sinful act that goes against God's law and teaching. However, as Christians, instead of condemning and criticizing homosexuals, we must show the love and kindness of Christ, leading them with wisdom and gentleness to form normal human relationships.

The appearance of such evil phenomena is a result of humanity's fall. When humans ate the forbidden fruit of the tree of the knowledge of good and evil and were cast out of the Garden of Eden, they became fallen beings, cut off from the life of God. This is what is called "**Total Depravity**" in theological terms. Total Depravity is the doctrine that as a result of the original sin committed by Adam and Eve, every part of human nature (mind, will, emotions, body) has been corrupted by sin. It means

---

28 *Some studies suggest that there may be a genetic component to sexual orientation.* For example, twin studies have shown that identical twins are more likely to share the same sexual orientation compared to fraternal twins. However, this suggests a genetic influence but does not imply that it is decisive. In other words, genetics alone cannot fully explain sexual orientation. Today, most scientists and researchers believe that sexual orientation results from a combination of genetic, hormonal, developmental, and environmental factors. It is not purely genetic or purely environmental, but rather an interaction of multiple influences that shape an individual's sexual identity. The social acceptance of homosexuality, as well as its depiction in drama, films, literature, and the arts, tends to further spread this phenomenon. Therefore, Christianity should be able to provide a clear message on this matter.

that sin affects every aspect of human beings and, as a result, humans are incapable of doing what God expects as good, and without God's grace, they cannot choose or seek God on their own (Romans 3:10-12). In other words, all of humanity's cognitive, emotional, and volitional faculties have become incapable of enjoying a relationship with God. Therefore, every thought of the heart was wicked (Genesis 6:5), and the heart of humanity became the most corrupt of all creation (Jeremiah 17:9). This does not mean that humans have become entirely wicked or that they are demons or possessed by evil spirits. As McCloud explains, **"'Total depravity' means that, even considering all changes, the general grace constraints, and all the adornments of personality found in our human condition, still every aspect of human existence is influenced by sin."** [29]

People tend to think that human intellect retains some inherent goodness and that humans, compared to other creatures, naturally express and define moral superiority according to their standards. However, Total Depravity, according to Professor McCloud, means this: **"The human mind is so full of sin that it cannot think correctly. It cannot draw proper conclusions, nor can it pursue sound reasoning. In the process of collecting, organizing, and logically inferring information, its intellect is tainted by sin. It works in opposition to God. This is what Paul meant when he said, 'The mind governed by the flesh is hostile to God' (Romans 8:7). Human thinking, premises, assumptions, and logic all oppose God. To think that human rationality is not impaired is completely wrong. The distortion of sin, the bias against God, has already infiltrated even our level of understanding and intellect. We think in distorted ways. We think in ungodly**

---

29 Donald Macleod, *A Faith to Live By*, 83.

ways."[30]

The fall of humanity affects not only the intellect but also the emotions. Human emotions are corrupted as well. Things that are wrong bring happiness, while things that are wrong also bring sadness. Evil emotions such as depression, worry, dissatisfaction, envy, disorder, confusion, and anger arise in human life because of the influence of sin. For example, the feeling of love (eros) is truly one of the most beautiful and noble things, but this emotion, in a moral world, can also be the most destructive, dangerous, and harmful. This is because it is tainted by sin. Human will is likewise corrupted. The will itself is a slave to sin. Jesus said: **"Jerusalem, Jerusalem, you who kill the prophets and stone those sent to you, how often I have longed to gather your children together, as a hen gathers her chicks under her wings, but you were not willing"** (Matthew 23:37). The Apostle Paul also personally experienced human incapacity. He, who claimed to be blameless under the law, went as far as persecuting the Son of God, who is the most righteous, holy, and good. This is because humans, dead in their trespasses and sins, are **"darkened in their understanding and separated from the life of God because of the ignorance that is in them due to the hardening of their hearts"** (Ephesians 4:18).

What is sin? The Westminster Shorter Catechism, question 24, states: **"Sin is any want of conformity unto, or transgression of, the law of God, given as a rule to the reasonable creature."** And question 25 asks: **"What is the sinfulness of that state wherein man fell?"** The answer is: **"The sinfulness of that state wherein man fell consists of the guilt of Adam's first sin, the loss of original righteousness, and the corruption of his nature, which is conveyed to all his posterity,**

---

30   Ibid, 83.

and the nature of every one of his descendants is utterly bent on sinning against God, and it is totally inclined to evil, continually, and without end. All actual transgressions of God's law proceed from this sinful nature."

Let's listen further to Professor McCloud's explanation on sin: "**The Bible does not depict sin as a mere defect. Sin is corruption, it is decay, and it is the cancer of human life. It is pervasive, productive, lively, multiplying, and spreading on its own. Sin is violent. Sin is fire. Sin is alive. It is power, and an immensely powerful one at that.**"[31] Sin destroys everything that was good in God's sight. It drags all creation into the pit of groaning. Sin ultimately leads to death. The wages of sin is death (Romans 6:23). Just as God said, "**you will surely die**" the day you eat of it (Genesis 2:17), fallen Adam and Eve could no longer enter into the life-giving fellowship in the Garden of Eden with God. Even between Adam and Eve, who were once said to be "**bone of my bones,**" there became a broken relationship (Genesis 3:12). Not only that, but the relationship between humanity and the environment was also completely altered. The ground was cursed (Genesis 3:17). The influence of sin is pervasive and ever-increasing. There is no place where the effects of sin cannot be seen. Yet, there is no one seeking or desiring atonement for their sins. Even in places where justice should be most manifest and where laws of fairness and honesty are most prominent, there is no hope of solving the problem of sin. Unforgiving judgment runs rampant, guilt without atonement piles up, and corruption without purification overwhelms the senses. This world is not only one ruled by unbelievers.

Even those who believe in Jesus and are born again still have sin remaining within them. Although it is clear that they have been freed

---

31   Ibid, 85

from sin, in reality, the lives of believers cannot be lived without encountering sin. Sin still stirs within the hearts of believers. Living a life without the temptation of sin is impossible. Sin is irregular, cruel, and cunning to an unimaginable extent. There is no greater mistake than forgetting the reality of sin that is prevalent in our lives. Because of this, our spiritual strategy must be established in our Lord Jesus Christ, who has broken the power of sin and death and triumphed. As long as remnants of sin remain in us, we must remember that we are spiritually prone to easily fall into the flames of sin. Therefore, Christ, who poured out all of God's wrath against sin, has shed His blood and water to make our scarlet sins as white as snow, and though they are as red as crimson, He has made them as wool (Isaiah 1:18). Believers who confess Jesus as Lord will not face judgment due to their sins but will be disciplined by the Holy Spirit to live holier lives. They will experience the blessing of being transferred from death to life (John 5:24). For this, we must observe the works of Christ, who has defeated all the powers of sin and keeps, protects, and leads His people in the eternal kingdom where they will rest completely. Those addicted to drugs, alcohol, gambling, or games cannot escape from the chains of sin by their own will. They need help from others. No one can live a life free from the illegal temptations of sin just because they do not transgress the boundaries of the law. The only solution to all sin is Jesus Christ. He is the vine, and we are the branches, and without Him, we can do nothing. Therefore, the total depravity of mankind and the work of redemption naturally lead us to meditate more deeply on the grace of Jesus Christ's redemption.

Can a sinner judge a judge? Even in a world filled with the wicked, such a court does not exist. The God we believe in is not only the Creator of the world but also the Judge of the world. What awaits those who have strayed from the path God has set is His righteous judgment. At the same time, the mysterious way in which His justice and love meet is that He punishes the sinner while simultaneously saving them—a great mystery. This was accomplished by Jesus Christ, the only begotten Son, who received death on the cross and rose again on the third day to justify sinners. Therefore, anyone who believes in Him will not perish but have eternal life. This is the gospel. In fact, the gospel within the gospel, John 3:16, declares that all humanity is perishing in the sea of destruction, and it reveals the way to salvation from that sea. Otherwise, there would be no reason for God to send His only Son. Every human is conceived and born in sin, lives in sin, and dies because of sin. The path to salvation, presented to save such miserable sinners, is through Jesus Christ, the only begotten Son, whom God sent to us. There is no room for religious pluralism. The reason we are called to believe in Him is that without the Nazareth Jesus Christ sent by God, there is no way for anyone (regardless of race, gender, or social status) to be redeemed from destruction. By believing in Jesus Christ, who drank the full cup of God's wrath on the cross, took on the curse with His whole body, and poured out His precious blood for the salvation of sinners, we are given eternal life, not destruction. This is the core of Christian faith. We must deeply realize that we are sinners, corrupt, and fallen, unable to save ourselves, far from God, and living hopelessly outside of His kingdom. Faith involves firmly holding on to the rope of salvation that has been sent from heaven.

However, the problem is that humans are not given unlimited opportunities for salvation. On the human side, we are only given a short time to live on earth. As long as the earth exists, there will be an opportunity. The issue is that no one knows when that day and hour will come. Therefore, the time when salvation is offered lasts only until the second coming of Jesus Christ. Jesus, who ascended to heaven, is preparing a place for His people and praying for them. He will return to the world for the complete salvation of those whom God has chosen. That day will be the day He comes to judge the living and the dead. The judges who condemned the sinless Christ as a criminal and crucified Him will face eternal judgment from Christ, experiencing disgrace and failure, and will be locked in a place from which they will never return.

In fact, the remarkable aspect of the Apostles' Creed is that it comprehensively describes the past, present, and future works of Jesus Christ. It declares clearly His birth, His death, His resurrection, His ascension, His current reign, and His future return. The purpose of His return is to judge the living and the dead. The day will come when the final eternal legal judgment on finite human life will be pronounced. No one knows when that day will be, but what is certain is that it will surely come. In this way, the works of Jesus in the past, present, and future are closely related to the salvation of sinners. Without the work of Jesus, there would be no discussion about human salvation.

In reality, modern humans live lives without hope. Nihilism and pessimism due to sin are rampant. What people see and hear are all about wars, bankruptcies, strikes, aging, fear of loneliness, and not just rapid population decline, but also crimes enabled by AI, leaving no time to think clearly. Even though it seems urgent, the issue of human sin continues to give birth to problems without any hope of resolution. Since it cannot be solved by human power, God, in His infinite love, leads sinners away from the attachment to the fleeting things of the earth and urges them to live, longing for the better city that God Himself created and governs. Not only for ourselves but also when we look at those around us, there is no one to put our hope in. Only the Lord, who created the heavens and the earth and did not spare His only Son to save fallen humanity, is our hope, joy, and satisfaction. Anyone who promises a utopia on earth is a false teacher, and those who are deceived by their words, obsessed with satisfying fleshly, demonic, and worldly desires, are not true Christians. True Christians store treasures in heaven, where they will live forever with the Lord. That hope helps them endure present suffering and adversity while walking the path toward heaven.

Jesus' righteous judgment is a perfect verdict, with no reason for any moral objections or appeals. Those who deny God, the unbelievers, boast that the final judgment will never happen, but the Bible clearly speaks against this. Scientists and environmentalists warn that the destruction of the earth will come through environmental disasters like nuclear bombs or global warming, but the Bible says it will happen when the risen Christ returns. However, as previously mentioned, no one knows when He will come, and because He will come like a thief (1 Thess. 5:2), we must always be prepared to meet Him. That day will clearly divide the wise five virgins and the foolish five virgins. This leads us to live by faith in the world. He will return in the same manner as witnessed by those who saw His ascension in Acts 1 (v. 11), but no one knows how He will come. Apostle Paul, in speaking of the day of the Lord, says that when people say, **"Peace and safety,"** they will be living as they did in the days of Noah, buying and selling, eating and drinking, marrying and giving in marriage in a carefree way. But he declares, **"Destruction will come suddenly upon them, and they will not escape"** (1 Thess. 5:3). However, this destruction will fall on those who belong to darkness, while the children of light—those who stay awake, remain sober, and live with the breastplate of faith and love, and the helmet of the hope of salvation—will walk the holy path. The Bible says, "**The Lord Himself will descend from heaven with a shout, with the voice of an archangel and with the trumpet of God**" (1 Thess. 4:16).[32] His coming will be a day of joy and glory for the Lord's people, but for the wicked, it will be a day of terror and destruction.

This helps us walk the path of faith, relying on the Lord until the end, clinging to Him and never departing. And true Christians will be like Jesus Christ. For "**we shall see Him as He is**" (1 John 3:2). Therefore, we cry out, "**O Jesus, come quickly!**" (Rev. 22:20). This is a facet of the faith in the end times. Although we cannot predict the day or hour, the time appointed by God for His coming is steadily approaching without deviation. Perhaps for a true Christian, every day of life should be lived with the thought that it is like the last day of life.

However, a redeemed Christian, even living in a world filled with sin, is not a person belonging to the world, but a citizen of heaven. They live not in a fallen state, but under grace. They are those who have the privilege of regularly approaching the throne of grace to obtain mercy and find grace to help in time of need (Heb. 4:15). Having the right to use the means of grace already discussed, they remain in the

---

[32] The Bible mentions the second coming of the Lord more than 300 times. This is roughly once every 13 verses, indicating the significance of this promise. Because God is a faithful keeper of His promises, we believe that the return of the Lord, which is one of the unfulfilled prophecies in the Bible, will certainly come to pass at the time He has ordained. However, the lack of anticipation for the Lord's return can be attributed to several factors: the false teachings of certain heresies regarding the second coming, the fact that the expectation of Christ's return has been present since the early church but there has been no clear sign of His coming after 2000 years, and the material prosperity that has led to a diminished longing for heaven. Nonetheless, just as the Apostle Peter confessed (2 Peter 3), we firmly believe that He will certainly return.

place where they are protected by the power of the Holy Spirit. **"You are being protected by the power of God through faith for a salvation ready to be revealed in the last time"** (1 Peter 1:5). One cannot help but think of the perseverance of the saints, the last of the five points of Calvinism. This doctrine teaches that those who are saved by faith through God's grace are kept in faith until the end and are never in danger of losing their salvation. Once a person is truly born again and united with Christ through faith, they are securely protected by God's power and will not stray from their path until they reach eternal glory. This is not because of the believer's flawless, righteous life, but because of Christ's flawless grace of redemption that holds them.

❶ Salvation is the work of the Triune God from start to finish. It is God who chose, called, justified, sanctified, and will ultimately lead believers to eternal glory. Salvation is entirely and perfectly God's work, and because God is faithful, gracious, and omnipotent, He will not abandon those whom He has purchased with the blood of His Son. The Bible says, **"Being confident of this, that he who began a good work in you will carry it on to completion until the day of Christ Jesus"** (Phil. 1:6), and **"I give them eternal life, and they shall never perish; no one will snatch them out of my hand. My Father, who has given them to me, is greater than all; no one can snatch them out of my Father's hand"** (John 10:28-29). As long as we are in Christ, as long as we believe and trust in Him, our salvation is assured. Just as His creation is complete, so is His redemption. The salvation we have received should be worked out with fear and trembling (Phil. 2:12) through the active use of the means of grace. We know that when Paul says, **"Work out your salvation,"** he is not referring to earning salvation but urging the Philippians to live lives worthy of the gospel of Christ. This is not about accomplishing salvation but making the salvation that Jesus has accomplished our own. It means to activate salvation in every area of life. Therefore, this does not apply to those who have not repented. God will keep His people until the very end. He will be with us until the end of the world.

❷ A true Christian cannot lose their salvation. The perseverance of the saints teaches that those truly born again by the Spirit will not fall away from grace. They may face difficulties, fall into sin, or experience seasons of doubt, but they will never completely fall from grace. A true believer is preserved by God's grace through faith. "**For I am convinced that neither death nor life, neither angels nor demons, neither the present nor the future, nor any powers, neither height nor depth, nor anything else in all creation, will be able to separate us from the love of God that is in Christ Jesus our Lord**" (Rom. 8:38-39). The Almighty God will "**keep you from stumbling and to present you before his glorious presence without fault and with great joy**" (Jude 24). God's work of salvation never stops at choosing, calling, regenerating, or justifying; He will bring believers into glory and will ensure they will dwell with Him forever. His absolute sovereignty and grace never fail in the work He has determined. How amazing and great is the grace that God is our God! Therefore, even if we face suffering or even the threat of death, we will not be ashamed. On the contrary, we have boldness because we know who is the author and finisher of our faith, and that He will complete our race of faith. He is the one who can keep all those who come to Him (2 Tim. 1:12).

The perseverance of the saints should not be misunderstood as if it means there is no need for proof of salvation. It is not a safety net that requires no evidence. Faith and good works must go hand in hand.

Those who live without repentance or who turn away from the faith (1 John 2:19) have no evidence of salvation. One must bear the fruit of the Spirit (Gal. 5:22) or the fruit of light (Eph. 5:8-9). The branch that remains in Christ will naturally bear fruit because it is nourished by Him. A lack of this fruit is evidence that the person is not truly united with Christ. The perseverance of the saints accelerates the bearing of the fruit of salvation.

Lastly, let us briefly consider the eternal state of humanity. Humans were created innocent, but due to sin, they fell. The fallen human is redeemed by the blood of Christ. The redeemed will ultimately reach their final state, the heavenly rest, where they will dwell forever in the presence of God.[33] The **"glorious state"** refers to the ultimate destiny where those justified will experience eternal happiness, communion with God, and freedom from sin and suffering in the presence of God. Here, what was partial will be made complete in perfect knowledge. There will no longer be a longing soul seeking the Lord, as in Psalm 42, because we will be in constant communion with Him face to face. All effects of sin and fallenness will be completely eradicated, and we will be transformed into the likeness of Christ (2 Cor. 3:18). At the resurrection, when spirit and body are united, we will receive glorious bodies, without the limitations of the flesh. In this place, there will be no sorrow, tears, separation, or sickness, but eternal joy and satisfaction (Rev. 21:4). Until this glorious day, the redeemed saints must follow the path of the Lord wholeheartedly.

The virtues that follow here are the things of following Jesus and

---

[33] If you want to learn more about *the Fourfold State of Man*, I recommend reading the book written by Thomas Boston. It has been translated and published by *Revival and Reformation Press*.

resembling Jesus. We must not deviate to the left or right but follow only our Lord, Jesus Christ, who is the goal of our lives. Whether He leads us to the valley of Achor, to a wilderness, to a palace, to the hill of Golgotha, or to the garden of Gethsemane, where His sweat became like drops of blood, we must deny ourselves, take up our cross, and follow Him. There is no turning away, no betrayal—only faithfulness. Faith and faithfulness cannot be separated. Anyone who serves in the church must not display their personal ambitions, philosophical ideologies, or political views. Rather, they must be faithful servants who clearly make known God's Word. We find the greatest glory in seeing God's will accomplished in our lives. To resemble Jesus is to become like Him in His perfection. Moving toward perfection involves allowing the truth of God's Word to lead us, being fully submitted to the guidance of the Holy Spirit, and working in cooperation with the pastor who feeds and cares for us with the truth that makes us holy, as described in 2 Tim. 3:16-17. Let us think deeply about Jesus, the author and finisher of our faith. May we be blessed saints who eagerly long for Jesus alone.

Review of Learning Content

01. What is the difference between the old person and the new creation? (2 Corinthians 5:17, Ephesians 2:2-3)
    Why is the new creation unable to grow?

02. What is the path of learning about Jesus?
    * Direct path: The Bible, Bible commentaries, and doctrinal interpretations. Public means of grace.
    * Indirect path: Theology is life. The path of refinement is walked in the field of life. Using discernment.

03. The content of learning is broadly divided into two categories:
    (1) Who is God?
        ① Explain the Almighty God.
        ② Explain the relationship between the Father and the Son.
        ③ What are the four main works of the Spirit of Truth, the Holy Spirit?

    (2) What does the fourfold state of humanity refer to?
        ① Explain total corruption and fall.
        ② What are the three doctrines learned from the redemptive work of Jesus Christ?
        ③ Explain the nature of sin and the nature of atonement.
        ④ Explain the final end and judgment.
        ⑤ The perseverance of the saints and their eternal state.

    (3) Why reject the theory of evolution?

Chapter 3

Following Jesus

"After he has laid down all his own sheep, he goes ahead of them, and because the sheep know his voice, they follow him. But they will never follow a stranger, for they do not recognize a stranger's voice and will run away from him."
(John 10:4-5)

"But you do not believe because you are not my sheep. My sheep listen to my voice; I know them, and they follow me."
(John 10:26-27)

"Whoever wants to be my disciple must deny themselves and take up their cross and follow me. For whoever wants to save their life will lose it, but whoever loses their life for me and the gospel will save it."
(Mark 8:34-35)

• Chapter 3 •

Following Jesus

To follow someone involves a mixture of fondness and curiosity. It is a desire to not be satisfied by rumors about the person but to meet them personally, see them with one's own eyes, listen to them with one's own ears, and experience them directly. This curiosity leads to a desire to know more and continues to stimulate the urge to follow the person. This desire may grow into a deep understanding of their character, their way of life, and even a longing to be like them. Of course, from the human perspective, as we know more, we might experience disappointment and frustration as we come to see the flaws in the person. But following the Lord never results in disappointment. It only becomes pure knowledge that never leads to regret. Those who follow the Lord sincerely always speak with one voice about the admiration, deep emotion, joy, satisfaction, thanksgiving, praise, and amazement they experience. I hope that the readers of this book will taste this joy in their lives.

What Does It Mean to Follow Jesus?

In truth, following Jesus is not an optional subject. It is not a mandatory course required to graduate or earn credits. Following Jesus is an instinctive spiritual desire of a born-again believer. This is because, at the moment of faith, they are united with Jesus Christ. They are firmly grafted into Him with a bond that no one can break. The believer is in Christ, and Christ is in the believer. How could anyone who believes not follow Jesus? Many people desire to follow Jesus. They first hear rumors about Him. Just as the saying goes, **"A word without feet travels a thousand miles,"** rumors about Jesus draw people to Him. A representative starting point is the story of Andrew telling his brother Simon Peter that he had met the Messiah and introducing him to Jesus, leading Peter to receive a new name (John 1:40-42). Another example is Philip telling Nathanael that he had met the Messiah predicted by Moses and the prophets, leading him to Jesus (John 1:45-48). Similarly, Nicodemus came to Jesus at night (John 3). Moreover, the Samaritan woman, who had five husbands and was living with another man, met Jesus at a well. Afterward, she went to her town and told the people about Jesus, leading many of them to come and meet Him (John 4:27-30). Not only that, but there was the woman who had suffered for twelve years with a hemorrhage and had spent all her money on doctors, but when she heard of Jesus, she came to Him and was immediately healed (Matthew 5:25-34). In Luke 7, a centurion heard of Jesus and came to Him, seeking healing for his sick servant. Jesus praised his faith, saying, **"I have not found such great faith even in Israel"** (Luke 7:1-9). Even those who came to follow Jesus with the intention of being with Him wherever He went were met with Jesus' response that He had no place to lay His head (Matthew 8:20). Indeed, many followed Jesus after hearing rumors about Him, but not all had pure intentions. Some even sought to kill Him, as seen in Mark 3, where Jesus' family, hearing rumors, tried to take Him away, thinking He was out of His mind. Even some, following Him for personal gain, would abandon Him when their needs weren't met, as seen with the crowds who followed Him for bread (John 6:26). These people did not come to learn from Jesus or to know Him; they were merely seeking to fill their bellies with earthly food. However, the type of following that I mean is following Jesus as a true Savior, regardless of one's background. Jesus' answer to such followers is as follows:

"Whoever wants to be my disciple must deny themselves and take up their cross daily and follow me." (Luke 9:23, Matthew 16:24). **"Anyone who loves their father or mother more than me is not worthy of me; anyone who loves their son or daughter more than me is not worthy of me. And whoever does not take up their cross and follow me is not worthy of me."** (Matthew 10:37-38). **"Peter replied, 'We have left everything to follow you!' 'Truly I tell you,' Jesus replied, 'no one who has left home or brothers or sisters or mother or father or children or fields for me and the gospel will fail to receive a hundred times as much in this present age—homes, brothers, sisters, mothers, children and fields—along with persecutions—and in the age to come eternal life. But many who are first will be last, and the last first.'"** (Mark 10:28-31).

These words demonstrate that following Jesus is not possible for those who do not have a deep relationship with Him. For those who are on the path of belief and learning, following Jesus will involve profound lessons. It is not only about self-denial and taking up one's cross, but also about giving up everything—home, family, and possessions—for the sake of Jesus and His gospel. It is not an easy path, as it requires giving up the strongest human bonds and desires. Just as a builder must count the cost before starting, one must remember that following Jesus comes with a price. Without considering the cost, one might be criticized and ridiculed for acting in a hypocritical, irresponsible, or cruel way. What does it truly mean to follow Jesus?

Following Jesus means recognizing that it is not about appearance, wealth, or status. Regardless of one's background, anyone can follow Jesus, but they must do so on the condition of self-denial, taking up their cross, and prioritizing love and obedience to Him. Just because someone calls out "**Lord, Lord**" does not mean they will enter the Kingdom of Heaven. As Jesus declared, only those who do the will of His Father in Heaven will enter (Matthew 7:21), following Jesus is not just about walking behind Him; it requires the correct motives and understanding. Many followed Him in His time, but not all were genuine disciples—some shouted for His crucifixion, and others, like Judas Iscariot, betrayed Him. Those who followed Him for personal gain often left when they did not get what they wanted. The path of following Jesus involves risks, including the possibility of losing one's life. It requires discernment to navigate the trials, obstacles, and temptations along the way. If we do not remain vigilant, we may find ourselves drifting away from Jesus, as seen with the five foolish virgins who were waiting for the bridegroom but missed Him. In order to follow Jesus properly, we must mature spiritually and develop discernment. Only through spiritual training, by consuming solid food and using our minds, can we navigate the path of following Jesus. This is the way forward.

Entering Through the Narrow Gate

Following Jesus is, above all, entering through the narrow gate. Those who follow Jesus do not avoid the narrow road. The ones who enter through this gate are those who have made a firm resolution not to give up, even though harsh realities may await them. They are those who are determined to willingly endure even the hardest training. Patience and refinement are part of this journey, and they do not avoid them. Jesus' disciples were trained for three years. If it took three years to be trained under a master like Jesus, we cannot help but wonder how much more time it would take to be trained under a weak human master, lacking strength and ability. In fact, the process of patience and refinement is something that cannot cease until the Lord comes. There are many twists and turns along the way, and temptations that seek to cause those who wish to follow the Lord to stumble. Even the temptation to betray Jesus, their Master, came. On the night Jesus was arrested, all the disciples ran away. Although it is heartbreaking, we do not need to condemn their fleeing. If we had been in the same reality, we cannot deny that we too would have walked the path of betrayal. However, their failure did not lead to success because of their will or faith, but because of Jesus Christ, who rose from the dead on the third day. Through His grace, the weak and powerless were transformed into people who could bear fruit. Therefore, we do not avoid the narrow road.

In this way, those who follow Jesus with a faith without falsehood must first exert every effort to learn the gospel of Jesus with their whole being. It is not a smooth path. The path of flowers cannot be expected. Most of it is an unpaved road. However, those who enter this path will experience that, even if they fall seven times, they can stand up again with the Lord's help, who forgives seventy-seven times, and walk and run with the power to do so. They cannot look back after putting their hand to the plow. With true faith, which is the substance of things hoped for and the evidence of things not seen, they confess that the present suffering is nothing compared to the glory that is to come. Even if they fall, they rise again. They only look to the Lord, who is the goal, and rejoice in the glory of God, enjoying the joy of spiritual life. But this path is one that will lead to suffering in this world. This suffering brings patience, patience brings refinement, and refinement strengthens hope (Romans 5:2-4). Every step in this process is like a training of self-discipline. Even though it may seem unbearable, the Lord, who opens a way of escape, makes it possible to endure with Him. This training is not just physical training, but a different dimension altogether. The training leading to godliness has a clear promise both in this life and the life to come, so it cannot stop or be abandoned (1 Timothy 4:8). This is the way of abandoning the temptation to take the easiest path and choosing the most secure path, even though it may seem dangerous. Without suffering, there is no glory. So, what kinds of training, refinement, or exercises leading to godliness must we undergo to reach the glory that is to come?

The training of self-denial, the training of carrying one's cross, and the decision to live for the Lord even if we die, are all part of the daily path. Following and obedience are twins. Neither following without obedience, nor obedience without following, is valid. However, following and obeying cannot be done by one's own strength. At the very least, the strong work of the Holy Spirit and the cooperation of fellow workers are required. Just as Jesus chose twelve disciples to train, we too need fellow workers. Church leadership is not entrusted to a single pastor but is a collaborative leadership, working together with ruling elders. It is important to have fellow workers who can speak the same words, think the same thoughts, and be united with the same purpose. Salvation is individual, but the way of faith is not walked alone. The fellowship of believers is an essential part of the church, and it is through working together that we are trained in virtues. Just as a child raised among siblings grows with a unique character, so too does spiritual growth happen within a community. In the world, the term **"single-person household"** is used, but in Christianity, we do not refer to a believer as a **"solo church."** Through the fellowship of saints, virtues are cultivated, such as: considering others better than oneself, doing everything with humility and gentleness, serving rather than ruling, being without complaints or disputes, loving and respecting one another, seeking the benefit of others, and speaking the truth in love. These are the highest forms of service that must be realized even in this time.

Peter teaches the believers, who have escaped the corruption of the world and have partaken in the divine nature, to add to their faith the following: **"For this very reason, make every effort to add to your faith goodness; and to goodness, knowledge; and to knowledge, self-control; and to self-control, perseverance; and to perseverance, godliness; and to godliness, mutual affection; and to mutual affection, love. For if you possess these qualities in increasing measure, they will keep you from being ineffective and unproductive in your knowledge of our Lord Jesus Christ. But whoever does not have them is nearsighted and blind, forgetting that they have been cleansed from their past sins. Therefore, my brothers and sisters, make every effort to confirm your calling and election. For if you do these things, you will never stumble, and you will receive a rich welcome into the**

eternal kingdom of our Lord and Savior Jesus Christ" (2 Peter 1:5-11). Peter's recommendations are for those who enter through the narrow gate and walk the narrow road. Through this process, we strengthen our calling and election. Ultimately, following Jesus deepens our learning of Him, and that learning must bear fruit. As a result, our calling and election become more certain, and we are guaranteed to enter the eternal kingdom.

Those who have strong curiosity about learning will also have a strong desire to follow. As they follow, change will occur. Without this, a life of faith is completely fake. The early Christians were called Christians by the people of the world because they followed Jesus (Acts 11:26). This happened when the first Gentile church was established in Antioch, under the leadership of Paul and Barnabas, who were filled with the Holy Spirit and wisdom. The faith, learning, and following of Jesus grew simultaneously. They would have been far removed from the criticism of the Gentiles that resulted from Jews boasting about possessing the law of God, which caused God's name to be blasphemed among the Gentiles. In the early Jerusalem church, it was clear that those who heard the gospel, repented, and returned showed by their actions what it meant to follow, learn, and follow Jesus. "**And they praised God and enjoyed the favor of all the people. And the Lord added to their number daily those who were being saved**" (Acts 2:47). This was also seen in the early history of Christianity in Korea, where the faithful "**Jesus people**" created an environment for rapid growth. Unfortunately, the foundation was broken when the example of following Jesus was lost, preferring the broad road instead of the narrow one. This happened when they focused on the prosperity gospel, seeking things that perish. The lack of spiritual training, avoidance of hardship, absence of leaders filled with the Holy Spirit and wisdom, the loss of spiritual discernment due to lack of doctrinal education, the focus on religious rituals, and the shift from theocentrism to anthropocentrism all led to this situation. If this continues, destruction is inevitable. Even those who do not attend the church, the so-called "**Canaan**" believers, are not safe if they avoid fellowship with other believers in truth.

How many Christians today cause non-believers to be curious and want to believe in Jesus? Of course, there are people who are morally pure, honest, kind, and friendly. But aren't these virtues also found among conservative non-believers? Christians who think that moral goodness is all there is will not make the world attracted to following Jesus. Indeed, ethical and moral excellence, along with cultured manners and life attitudes, should be part of the package. But without a deep, personal communion with the holy, good, righteous, and merciful God, such virtues cannot exhibit the taste of heaven. Only those who enjoy spiritual intimacy with the Lord can walk the narrow road, deny themselves, and willingly carry their cross, making following Him possible. The spiritual richness that comes from following the Lord and the deep love that binds us together will help us overcome trials and live a life that testifies to the Lord's living power.

In fact, the quickest way for a person in the world to recognize the invisible divine presence is through the lives of those who follow that divine presence. Their language, actions, and character will serve as stepping stones, leading others to thoroughly follow our Lord Jesus Christ. True Christians praise: "**There is nothing more precious than Jesus, nothing can compare to the wealth of this world. The amazing love of the One who died for me, I can never forget. I have given up all worldly pleasures and pride. There is nothing more precious than Jesus. There is no one but Jesus**" (Hymn 94, verse 1). Everything visible pales in comparison to Jesus, and everything heard must be His voice. Whether we live or die, we follow Christ alone. His sheep do not doubt that He will always lead them to green pastures and still waters. Seeing others walk the same path strengthens our confidence that the path we are on is not in vain.

Let it not be misunderstood that this following is pure and voluntary, with no coercion. National defense duties must be followed out of obligation. But the Lord's soldiers follow willingly, not as conscripts but as volunteers. They are not mercenaries paid to serve, but volunteers who would even pay to serve. Today, some forces in the military operate like mercenaries, and strangely, the church follows this pattern. The primary factor in recruiting church workers nowadays includes welfare benefits, a departure from the past. However, self-denial required in following the Lord is different from all that. It involves complete turning away from the path of those who are children of wrath. It is closely tied to the death of sin. It is a spiritual battle. This battle is one against the self, against the world, and against the devil. The self, which was dead in trespasses and sins, has no room for divine will. Even though fallen humans still retain God's image and can discern good and evil, public and private matters, they cannot think about a relationship with the divine nor understand the spiritual world. The path of mortifying sin is, as the Heidelberg Catechism teaches, the path of sanctification, the pursuit of holiness. It is a journey of dying to sin and living to righteousness. The human heart is **"deceitful above all things and beyond cure"** (Jeremiah 17:9). Even those who are given new life through God's grace need strong external help to suppress the continuing activity of their sinful nature. This power comes from God. As Paul writes in his first letter to the Corinthians: **"No temptation has overtaken you except what is common to mankind. And God is faithful; He will not let you be tempted beyond what you can bear. But when** you are tempted, He will also provide a way out so that you can endure it" (1 Corinthians 10:13, The cursive writing is the author's emphasis.).

Above All, Guard Your Heart

"Above all else, guard your heart, for everything you do flows from it." (Proverbs 4:23)

Those who walk the narrow path must always guard their hearts firmly. If left unattended, our hearts will turn into factories of idols. Calvin described the corrupted and fallen human heart as 'a perpetual forge of idols.'[34] The attempt to shape the image of the Spirit of God is something that has not disappeared throughout the history of fallen humanity. The fact that the redeemed people of Israel made a golden calf is evidence of this. Just as Jesus was tempted, we too are always close to temptations. Good things come from the good stored in our hearts, and evil things emerge from the evil we store there. As stated in Romans, the spiritual desires that cannot subdue the fleshly desires of the heart are false. Christians are those who live according to the spirit of Jesus. Therefore, those who follow the flesh only seek the works of the flesh, while those who follow the spirit seek the things of the spirit. The thoughts of the flesh lead to death, but the thoughts of the spirit bring life and peace (Romans 8:5-6). However, the god of this world and the devil stimulate our desires to prevent us from experiencing the work of the Holy Spirit. They often boldly lead us to paths that are

---

34 John Calvin, *Institutes of the Christian Religion*, 127.

enemies of God. But those who have Christ within them and are led by His Spirit eagerly fight against sin and rejoice in walking the holy path prepared by God for the redeemed. Those in Christ are the beneficiaries of the blessings achieved by Jesus Christ. Therefore, following Him means that, just as He obeyed everything commanded by God the Father without adding or subtracting, we too move forward into places where spiritual benefits are prioritized, even if there may be physical loss. The Spirit of Christ constantly proves that we are children of God (Romans 8:15-16) and trains us to be heirs who will inherit the kingdom of God with Christ, leading us into the position of sharing His glory. This is why suffering is beneficial. Through suffering, we learn God's decrees, participate in His holiness, and are protected from falling into the emptiness of sin as believers.

Thus, self-denial is the way of dying to sin, which leads to freedom from bread, freedom from wealth and glory, and freedom from the kiss of compromise and ease. [35] It is the path that governs the various emotions stirred in our hearts, such as 'envy,' 'insult,' 'disappointment,' 'hatred,' 'vengeance,' 'anger and fury,' 'distress,' 'shame,' 'indifference,' 'helplessness,' 'regret,' 'worry,' 'lust,' and others. Jesus said, 'It is not what goes into a person's mouth that defiles them, but what comes out of their mouth, this defiles them' (Matthew 15:11). Peter, who did not fully understand this teaching, asked Jesus to explain the parable. Jesus' explanation was as follows: 'Do you not see that whatever enters the mouth goes into the stomach and is expelled? But what comes out of the mouth comes from

---

35 John Owen, *The Mortification of Sin*, translated by Kang *Seomun*, SFC, 2009; Thomas Brooks, *Precious Remedies Against Satan's Devices*, translated by *Shu* Changwon, Elmen, 2007. Please refer to these.

the heart, and these things defile a person. For out of the heart come evil thoughts, murder, adultery, sexual immorality, theft, false witness, slander. These are what defile a person. But to eat with unwashed hands does not defile anyone' (Matthew 15:17-20).

The way to kill these sinful thoughts and fulfill the Lord's will is through prayer. Prayer is also the optimal tool for self-emptying. I open my heart, hoping that the Lord's will will be fulfilled in me. Just as we know a tree by its fruit, 'A good person out of the good stored up in their heart brings forth good, and an evil person out of the evil stored up in their heart brings forth evil. For the mouth speaks what the heart is full of' (Luke 6:45). The evil things that come from the human heart are things the Lord hates, so we need to train ourselves to store up good things in our hearts.[36] To follow Jesus is to fix our often distracted hearts on the Lord and to be filled with Him. We believe that the Holy Spirit, who dwells in us, enables us to put aside the thoughts of the flesh and be filled with the thoughts of the Spirit, bringing life and peace (Romans 8:5-9).

In the meanwhile, carrying one's cross leads to becoming a stronger believer through suffering, becoming a giant of faith who the world cannot overcome. There is no resurrection without the cross, and no glory without suffering. Life itself is filled with toil and sorrow, but through the winding paths, the roots of faith are firmly planted. Despite occasional shakings, the misfortune of being uprooted never comes.

---

36 *"There are six things that the Lord hates, seven that are detestable to him: haughty eyes, a lying tongue, hands that shed innocent blood, a heart that devises wicked schemes, feet that are quick to rush into evil, a false witness who pours out lies, and a person who stirs up conflict in the community."* (Proverbs 6:16-19)

Instead, we move forward with hope, looking to God, who gives us the strength to overcome all tribulations. Even if everything around us seems full of misery, ruin, and destruction, we can quietly reflect and, like Jeremiah in the midst of affliction and disaster, confess with hope: "**I remember my affliction and my wandering, the bitterness and the gall. I well remember them, and my soul is downcast within me. Yet this I call to mind and therefore I have hope: Because of the Lord's great love we are not consumed, for His compassions never fail. They are new every morning; great is Your faithfulness. I say to myself, 'The Lord is my portion; therefore I will wait for Him.'"** (Lamentations 3:19-24).

Jeremiah had sufficient reason to leave God and could have justified his complaints. However, he did not succumb to that justification but obeyed God's purpose. This is the grace that is obtained through continually looking to God, the Lord of hosts, in the battlefield of self-denial. Doubt, anxiety, and dissatisfaction are elements of the devil's work that are subdued through the training of self-denial. The most effective self-denial is to kill sin while firmly trusting in the authority of prayer and the Word. In fact, prayer is the means to break my will and establish God's will within me. It is an opportunity to be filled abundantly by the Lord. Prayer is the power that makes us experience the living and active Word of the Lord within us. Thus, we walk the path of continuous prayer and meditation on the Lord's Word day and night.

Furthermore, self-denial is like emptying oneself. Letting go of the self is a good example of following Jesus. Jesus emptied Himself for the salvation of sinners. Though He was in the very nature God, He made Himself nothing, taking the nature of a servant, being made in human likeness, and humbled Himself by becoming obedient to death, even death on a cross (Philippians 2:6-8). Jesus' self-emptying (Kenosis theory) involved taking on what He emptied Himself of. He was the Lord of the universe, yet He emptied Himself to become a servant under the law (Galatians 4:4). People did not see Him as a pretended servant; He was actually a servant, the suffering servant of the Lord, who washed His disciples' feet. Despite being sinless, He took on the cursed death of the cross. He humbled Himself to nothing. He emptied Himself so that through Him, we might receive the abundant grace of salvation. **"For you know the grace of our Lord Jesus Christ, that though He was rich, yet for your sakes He became poor, so that you through His poverty might become rich."** (2 Corinthians 8:9). This is very important. Though self-denial may seem like great loss, it is in fact the way to become rich in Christ Jesus. In other words, self-emptying leads to self-filling. Therefore, following Jesus means laying down the fleshly and carnal instincts that work among the disobedient sons, abandoning one's own physical advantages for Christ's sake. And to those who empty themselves, to those who deny themselves, the Lord fills them with great things. That is, He fills them with the Spirit of truth, the Holy Spirit.

Be Filled with the Holy Spirit

In fact, following Jesus can be described as being filled with the Holy Spirit. When the disciples and about 120 believers prayed together in the upper room on the Day of Pentecost, they were all filled with the Holy Spirit (Acts 2:4). It wasn't just the eleven disciples who were filled, but everyone who gathered and prayed, and the Holy Spirit came upon each of them. They naturally began to speak in tongues as the

Spirit enabled them. So, what does it really mean to be filled with the Holy Spirit?[37]

We must first clarify some terminology. We need to understand the difference between being filled with the Spirit and being baptized in the Spirit. Some argue that receiving the Holy Spirit and being filled with the Spirit are different. In the Bible, there are phrases like "**being filled with the Spirit**," "**being baptized in the Spirit**," and "**receiving the Holy Spirit**" or being marked by the Holy Spirit. Can we distinguish these? Can we define them as distinct experiences? Professor McCloud argues that it's impossible and that they actually refer to the same experience. In other words, "**being baptized in the Holy Spirit means being filled with the Holy Spirit, and receiving the Holy Spirit means possessing the Holy Spirit, which is the same as being marked by the Holy Spirit.**" He says this because the events of Pentecost described exactly these things. In Acts 1:5, Jesus predicted, "**You will be baptized with the Holy Spirit.**" However, even though this was to happen on Pentecost, the people didn't say they were baptized in the Spirit. Instead, as mentioned earlier, it is described that each person "**was filled with the Holy Spirit**" (Acts 2:5). In Acts 10:47, Peter, recalling what happened in Cornelius' house, said, "**These people have received the Holy Spirit just as we have.**" In other words, he referred to the Pentecostal experience as receiving the Holy Spirit. Therefore, receiving the Holy Spirit is equivalent to being baptized in the Holy Spirit, and being baptized in the Holy Spirit is equivalent to being filled with the Holy Spirit. Professor McCloud states, "**A person who has not been baptized cannot receive the Holy Spirit, and a person who has not been**

---

[37] This content is an excerpt from Chapter 13 of Donald McCloud's book, *A Faith to Live By*.

baptized cannot be filled with the Holy Spirit."[38]

Therefore, we must never forget that receiving the fullness of the Holy Spirit is always a gift from God the Father or God the Son. This is important because the one who fills us with the Holy Spirit is either God the Father or God the Son. In other words, we are not baptized by the Holy Spirit or filled by the Holy Spirit on our own. The Holy Spirit is the mediator who allows us to be baptized, and He is the means by which we are filled. The Holy Spirit is the spirit of the Father and the Son, through whom they pour out their fullness upon us until we are completely soaked. Baptism is always an experience of being filled with or extremely full of the Holy Spirit. To clarify, when we are baptized, we do not receive just a part of the Holy Spirit's personhood. We are filled with the Holy Spirit and baptized by the Holy Spirit. "**We receive the fullness of the Holy Spirit's divine personhood and the fullness of all His activities. The Holy Spirit does not only work partially or perform some functions in the Christian life. The Holy Spirit works with all that He is and does all that He can.**"

Of course, this raises some questions. How can the immense Holy Spirit enter into our humble lives? And if God fills us with the Holy Spirit, why do we not always feel it in our daily lives? God, in His personal glory, comes into our humble lives, and as a result, we become the temple of the Holy Spirit (1 Corinthians 6:19) and experience all the work of the Spirit. However, is this experience shared by all Christians, or is it a privilege for just a few? The Pentecostal denomination claims that the baptism of the Holy Spirit and being filled with the Holy Spirit are not for all believers, and that they are not given at baptism but are a second blessing that some experience after conversion, once

---

38 Donald Macleod, ibid, 164.

they have become God's children. In other words, it's possible to be a believer but still remain without being filled with the Holy Spirit. A born-again Christian can be saved and united with Christ but might remain a Christian who has not yet experienced the baptism of the Holy Spirit. However, this is a biblically erroneous claim. The truth is that anyone who has not been baptized with the Holy Spirit is not truly a Christian. Of course, some Christians are like spiritual infants (1 Corinthians 3:1). However, the fleshly person (carnal) cannot receive or understand the work of God's Spirit (1 Corinthians 2:14). Being baptized with the Holy Spirit or being filled with the Holy Spirit is the experience of every true Christian. Why? Because ❶ Acts 2:4 says so. All those who were praying in the upper room received the fullness of the Holy Spirit. Everyone was baptized with the Holy Spirit. The prophecy of Joel was fulfilled (Acts 2:17). ❷ The follow-up events of Pentecost also confirm this. After hearing Peter's sermon, 3,000 people repented. Peter promised that they would all receive the Holy Spirit as a gift (Acts 2:38). Peter did not say, "**Repent, and then wait for another experience,**" but instead said, "**Repent and be baptized, and you will receive the Holy Spirit.**" All 3,000 repented, were baptized, and received the Holy Spirit. Moreover, 1 Corinthians 12:13 says, "**We were all baptized by one Spirit into one body.**" This declares that the promise of Acts 1:5 is a universal phenomenon, as stated in 1 Corinthians 12:13. The phrase, "**We were all made to drink of one Spirit,**" means, in the original language, that we were all "**immersed in one Spirit.**" In other words, like plants planted in God's garden, we all grow as we are watered by the Holy Spirit. It is unimaginable that God, the Gardener, would water only some plants and neglect others. If a plant does not receive water, it will wither and die. But God did not plant it to let it die, did He?

Our bodies are made up of complex irrigation systems as organisms. Just as each part of the body is nourished through this system to function properly, if it gets blocked (such as in cases of dehydration), it causes severe damage. Similarly, the body of Christ is spiritually organized in an irrigation system, where the head, Christ, is the center. **"The whole body, joined and held together by every supporting ligament, grows and builds itself up in love, as each part does its work"** (Ephesians 4:16). To ensure the smooth functioning of this process, each part is soaked through by the same Holy Spirit. Branches that are not connected to Christ die (John 15:5), so every converted Christian is baptized by the Holy Spirit and filled with the Holy Spirit. Therefore, to speak of the baptism of the Holy Spirit as something reserved only for a select few undermines the foundational elements of Christian soteriology. Reformed theology teaches that those who are saved by faith possess all the blessings of salvation. The doctrine of the baptism of the Holy Spirit experienced by certain individuals, as claimed by the Pentecostal movement, contradicts the Bible's teaching that all believers are united with Christ. If the Spirit of Christ is not poured out on all those united with Christ, then all the spiritual blessings we enjoy in Christ would be false. As believers are united with Christ, we testify to the blessings we receive in Christ, such as our adoption and predestination in Ephesians 1:5, the grace of redemption and forgiveness of sins in verse 7, and the enjoyment of all spiritual blessings in the heavenly realms (1:3). If we say that we are in Christ but exclude baptism in the Holy Spirit, the sealing of the Holy Spirit, and the fullness of the Holy Spirit, how can we claim to have all the spiritual blessings in Christ? Therefore, the concept of a limited Holy Spirit baptism cuts off the very core of Christian faith in redemption.

The grace of Jesus Christ's redemption means enjoying all of God's promises in Christ, which naturally includes the grace of the fullness of the Holy Spirit (the promise of the Spirit) (Galatians 3:14). Can we say that someone who has received the grace of redemption does not have the Holy Spirit? No. A believer receives the promise of the Holy Spirit by faith and, by faith, possesses the Holy Spirit in Christ. Therefore, we cannot speak of the baptism of the Holy Spirit or the fullness of the Holy Spirit as a second blessing. The Pentecostal claim that speaking in tongues is a proof of having received the Holy Spirit is also incorrect. Many Christians who spoke in tongues did not experience the Pentecostal baptism, and many who were baptized with the Holy Spirit did not speak in tongues. Every Christian who has received the grace of Christ's cross is already filled in Christ (Colossians 2:10). In fact, the meaning of the original text is that we are complete in Christ. So, what is lacking that would require a second blessing? In Christ, we receive all spiritual blessings, and we are filled with all the fullness of God (Ephesians 3:19).

There is a counter-argument based on Acts 8, where the Samaritans, who believed after Philip's preaching, did not receive the Holy Spirit until Peter and John came and prayed for them. This event is used to support the need for a second blessing. However, this should be understood as a special case with intentional divine intent. The Samaritans, according to Jewish thought, were considered people with whom one could not associate. However, after they believed in Jesus Christ through Philip's preaching, Peter and John went to verify this. They saw that the Samaritans had not yet received the fullness of the Holy Spirit, so they prayed for them, and the same Holy Spirit that had been received by the apostles and the 120 believers in Jerusalem came upon them. This event confirms that the Samaritans were baptized by the same Spirit and shared the same citizenship as the believers in Jerusalem. The same applies to the event in Cornelius' house. It shows that the gospel of Jesus Christ, which began in Judea, must also be proclaimed in Samaria and to the ends of the earth, demonstrating the universality of the gospel and confirming that the believers are one in Christ. The fullness of the Holy Spirit and the gifts of the Spirit can only be experienced in union with the body of Christ and in communion with the apostles. This means experiencing the renewing grace of the Holy Spirit in the church where the Word is faithfully preached. The experience of the Ephesians believers in Acts 19, who knew only John's baptism, can also be understood in this context. Such occurrences should be seen as special situations that do not happen elsewhere in the New Testament.

Then, why was the command to be filled with the Holy Spirit given to the believers in the Ephesians church, who had already believed? If baptism with the Holy Spirit and being filled with the Holy Spirit are the same as receiving the Holy Spirit at the time of salvation, then why give the command to be filled with the Holy Spirit again? This raises a question. The answer is that the fullness of the Holy Spirit is not a one-time, eternal blessing but something that is needed continuously throughout the believer's life. In fact, the literal meaning of Ephesians 5:18 is to **"be constantly being filled with the Holy Spirit."** This is emphasized because, in a believer's life, there is the possibility of grieving the Holy Spirit (Ephesians 4:30) or falling into sin that undermines the unity of the Spirit (Ephesians 4:3). The fullness of the Holy Spirit is not a one-time event; it must be a continuous process. We need to seek to be filled and, by faith, receive the fullness of the Holy Spirit. Much of the weakness, defeat, and powerlessness we experience in our spiritual lives stems from not continually being filled with the Holy Spirit. Therefore, a **"constantly being filled"** lifestyle is necessary. The grammar of ancient Greek also indicates two important things here. First, the verb is in the passive voice, meaning it is not an experience we create ourselves. Second, it is imperative, meaning it is essential and not a selective experience of certain Christians, as some Pentecostal movements claim. As mentioned before, being filled with the Holy Spirit means being filled with Jesus. It is about abiding in Jesus, communing with Him, and being filled with the joy of knowing Him more. This is the continuous faith life of living by the Spirit and walking by the Spirit (Galatians 5:25).

To walk in the Spirit is to keep in step with the Spirit. This is different from the term "**walk by the Spirit**" used in verse 16 of the same chapter. The latter uses the word "**peripateo**" (περιπατεω), which means to walk in a general sense, describing one's life journey. It refers to being open to and sensitively responding to the influence of the Holy Spirit within us, allowing that influence to shape our character according to the Spirit's guidance. As emphasized before, the Holy Spirit leads us to live a Christ-centered life (John 14:16-17, 14:26, 15:26, 16:13-15). The word used in verse 25, "**stoicheo**" (στοιχέω), means «**to walk in step with**" or "**to walk alongside.**" Paul uses this word here to refer to walking in step with the Holy Spirit. In other words, we are to follow the guidance of the Holy Spirit. As the Holy Spirit is the source of our life, living according to His guidance is what it means to live a life filled with the Holy Spirit. The verb "**stoicheo**" is used in the present imperative, meaning that walking in step with the Holy Spirit should be the habitual practice of believers.

However, because we are easily tempted to follow the desires of the flesh rather than the desires of the Spirit, we must actively use the means of grace that God has given us in the church to walk a holy life in step with the Spirit. To be filled with the Holy Spirit means to receive from the One who gives. As mentioned earlier, the Holy Spirit is sent by the Father and the Son, and we are filled with the Spirit, the Spirit of truth, who leads us into all truth. To live a life filled with the Holy Spirit is to follow Jesus, deny oneself, and be filled with Jesus. This is the opposite of drunkenness. The command, **"Do not get drunk on wine, which leads to debauchery. Instead, be filled with the Spirit,"** is often misunderstood as a call to be **"drunk"** with the Spirit or to become ecstatic, but this is not the case. The Bible does not portray Jesus as someone who was drunk or out of control. Drunkenness causes a loss of self-control, as described in Proverbs 23:33-35, and this is the opposite of the life that being filled with the Holy Spirit brings. Being filled with the Holy Spirit is not about wild behavior, but about a life of self-control and self-denial, becoming a person of dignity and grace. It is a life where one is controlled by the Spirit, and our desires, emotions, and impulses are all shaped by the Spirit. Nowhere in the Gospels is Jesus described as being in a drunken state. We cannot use the term **"drunk in the Spirit"** to describe Jesus because He was perfectly filled with the Holy Spirit (John 3:35). To be filled with the Holy Spirit is to live a life that is characterized by passion, devotion, emotion, love, agility, and even sorrow—all within the control of the Holy Spirit, resulting in a life of high-quality, rational judgment and dignity.

A life filled with the Holy Spirit also leads to a moral and ethical distinction. The Holy Spirit works in every area of our lives to make us better, more complete believers. In relationships, such as marriage, parent-child, employer-employee, the believer faithfully fulfills their role and honors the rights of others. They do not fall into traps of unrighteousness, deceit, hypocrisy, envy, and malice. This does not mean they are without mistakes or failures, but they strive to be vigilant in prayer and earnestly seek the guidance of the Holy Spirit. This is why the command to be filled with the Holy Spirit is given. A believer who is filled with the Holy Spirit focuses on fulfilling their duties in relationships rather than asserting their rights. Whether as a husband, wife, child, parent, employer, or employee, they fulfill their roles faithfully while respecting the rights of others. This is the fruit of self-denial in following Jesus.

Take Up Your Cross

What does it mean to take up your cross? While there may be many discussions on this, it essentially means prioritizing God's work over human concerns. The avoidance of the burden of the cross is to be a helper in accomplishing the work of the devil. In fact, when Jesus spoke these words to His disciples, it was after He had foretold His own suffering, rejection, and death on the cross. In the midst of their grief, Jesus told them that whoever wishes to follow Him must deny themselves and take up their cross. This meant following the same path Jesus walked. Jesus did not come to be served, but to serve. His purpose was not to elevate His divine authority on the backs of others' sacrifices but to offer His life as a ransom to save many. Through one man's disobedience, all humans became sinners and fell into a situation where they could not escape the wrath of God. But through the obedience of the second Adam, Jesus Christ, many are granted life. This is the meaning of following Jesus. Taking up your cross means that, while the one who bears the cross walks a path of life, they also lead others to eternal life in Christ.

When I first came to faith in Jesus, I faced harsh persecution from my beloved parents. I willingly endured it as grace, and through that suffering, the living testimony of God's presence was made known, and as a result, my entire family came to faith in Christ. In Jesus' time, the cross was a brutal tool of execution, without any mercy. It was a means of execution with no other purpose. It was not a decoration hanging in Christian homes or cars, nor was it a piece of jewelry. The cross was a tool of severe punishment, filled with blood and pain, with cries of agony echoing around it. Yet, today we cleanse and decorate the cross, using it as an ornament. For us, Jesus says, **"If you want to follow me, take up your cross every day and follow me."** This is where the Apostle Paul's confession of dying daily comes from. A Christian is one who dies to sin every day and lives for righteousness.

Taking up the cross is not a tourist attraction or a round-trip ticket to heaven. It is a singular path, filled with annoying situations, uncomfortable detours, and even the threat of life, which we must pass through as pilgrims on a journey. This is not about temporarily participating in ascetic practices like medieval monks carrying wooden crosses or joining Easter processions in the Philippines, where people physically carry a cross and have nails hammered into their bodies. The cross-bearing journey is a lifelong commitment. It is a spiritual life that must continue until we are embraced by the Lord. Taking up the cross is not about showing how religious we are. Those who bear the cross know that the cross itself cannot save them. Bearing the cross is a lesson in humility, and it means embracing the heart of Christ. It is not a temporary form of self-discipline, but a constant surrender to Christ, longing for God's will to be done, not our own.

Along the way, something mysterious happens. The wounds and pains we encounter on our pilgrim journey transform into **"well-ripened wounds,"** and the traces of knowing Jesus are gloriously etched upon us.[39] These wounds begin to exude the fragrance of Christ, a fragrance that leads to life. Life is naturally a path where we get hurt and try to avoid pain. But an existence filled only with labor and sorrow cannot escape trials, poverty, persecution, or hardship. Therefore, we must embrace these struggles with joy, for the path of the cross becomes a way that leads to victory, even in the face of unavoidable trials. It transforms into a "**well-ripened wound**" that bears fruit, radiating the fragrance of life. The Lord will provide us with the strength to endure and grace in times of need, filling us with hope of receiving rewards from Him. Thus, when the Lord asks us to take up our cross, He is not calling us to a life of meaningless sacrifices but to a life of eternal glory. Interestingly, the word "**bless**" in English, meaning to bless, shares the same root as the French word "**blessure**," meaning "**wound**." Just as pearls are produced from well-ripened wounds, the suffering we endure for Christ and His gospel is not just something to overcome but a stepping stone toward glory. The wounds Jesus endured—being torn, trampled, beaten, and pierced—led to His resurrection and eternal glory, where He is forever worshiped by the hosts of heaven. Those who faithfully follow Him will also dwell forever in His presence. The suffering is transformed into joy, pain into a crown, and trials into glory. We praise God who turns sorrow into joy, and pain into glory.

Taking up the cross also means seeking not our own gain but the benefit of others. Those who seek glory and comfort without walking

---

39 *Regarding the Poem 'Scar' by Bok Hyo-geun"*
The burn my sister received long ago / Somehow resembles a flower. / All the pain and sorrow I carried in my youth / Has now gathered,/ And from my sister's eyes, / The scent of flowers rises... (excerpt) / In the heart of a person from whom a fragrance emanates, / There is a large wound. From a well-ripened wound, / The scent of flowers rises

the path of the cross are not true Christians, and they are not following the Lord. By nature, humans resist self-denial and endlessly pursue self-satisfaction. Therefore, the daily training of self-denial is necessary. Dying daily is unnatural to our nature and something we may despise. However, if the life of Christ is within us, we become a new creation. We no longer judge people according to the flesh or elevate human excellence to a divine position. Instead, as new creations, we live for the One who died and rose again for us (Galatians 2:20, 2 Corinthians 5:15-17). The only hope of the reborn person is found in the power of the resurrected Lord. So, like the Apostle Paul, a Christian, empowered by the truth of God's word and the resurrection power, can confidently say: **"As unknown, and yet well known; as dying, and, behold, we live; as chastened, and not killed; as sorrowful, yet always rejoicing; as poor, yet making many rich; as having nothing, and yet possessing all things"** (2 Corinthians 6:9-10). Therefore, bearing the cross is a form of giving up in order to be filled, a sacrifice to gain life, and a death that leads to life. A life without this commitment and dedication is like an empty shell, devoid of life, and such a life will not be respected or feared by others. It is because of such Christians that the term **"cult Christianity"** is used to mock the faith, and the sentiment of **"Jesus is good, but the church is bad"** is growing. True Christians, however, are the light of the world, and their lives must produce good fruit that dispels the darkness around them, bringing blessings to the world and glory to God.

Take Up the Whole Armor of God[40]

On the night when Jesus was about to be arrested, Peter drew his sword and struck at the soldiers. One of the servant's ears, except for the high priest's servant, was cut off. In a situation where a battle could have erupted at any moment, Jesus said: **"Jesus said to him, 'Put your sword back in its place, for all who draw the sword will die by the sword. Do you think I cannot call on my Father, and he will at once put at my disposal more than twelve legions of angels? But how then would the Scriptures be fulfilled that say it must happen in this way?'"** (Matthew 26:52-54).[41] While Peter could have argued that his actions were legitimate self-defense, Jesus stopped him and quietly complied with the fulfillment of Scripture. Jesus demonstrated that God's will was more important than His own safety. The fulfillment of God's will is more precious than personal honor or gain. To follow Jesus is to emulate what He did. Though this aspect will be discussed further at the end of this book, I want to briefly mention here that Jesus came to destroy the works of the devil. In other words, Christians face the devil's attacks regularly while following Jesus. How do we resist these attacks and walk in the same path that the Lord walked? This is the concern of those who walk with the Lord. To participate in the Lord's mission of destroying the works of the devil, we must guard ourselves

---

40 Excellent books on the Armor of God include William Gurnal's The Christian's Complete Armor, Christian Digest, 2019, and Lloyd-Jones' *Ephesians 6:10-20, The Christian Soldier*. The full armor of God is mentioned as consisting of six pieces, but this is not the entirety of the armor of God.

41 The 'legion' used here refers to a Roman legion, which consists of 6,000 infantry soldiers and 700 cavalry horses

from lies, divisions, conflicts, impurity, greed, idolatry, and sin.

Thankfully, the Lord not only told us not to worry and to trust and follow Him, but He also confirmed this through the mighty work of the Holy Spirit dwelling within believers. Moreover, in the Holy Spirit, the Lord has provided us with enough spiritual weapons to withstand the attacks of the evil one. This is what we will examine here: the full armor of God. The words Apostle Paul wrote to the church in Ephesus are as follows: "**Finally, be strong in the Lord and in his mighty power. Put on the full armor of God, so that you can take your stand against the devil's schemes. For our struggle is not against flesh and blood, but against the rulers, against the authorities, against the powers of this dark world and against the spiritual forces of evil in the heavenly realms. Therefore, put on the full armor of God, so that when the day of evil comes, you may be able to stand your ground, and after you have done everything, to stand. Stand firm then, with the belt of truth buckled around your waist, with the breastplate of righteousness in place, and with your feet fitted with the readiness that comes from the gospel of peace. In addition to all this, take up the shield of faith, with which you can extinguish all the flaming arrows of the evil one. Take the helmet of salvation and the sword of the Spirit, which is the word of God.**" (Ephesians 6:10-17). In short, the full armor of God is the most useful tool for overcoming and destroying the works of the devil.

God gives all the necessary equipment to those who believe in the Savior, Jesus, and empowers them to engage in spiritual warfare with all that is needed. The ancient Greek word for 'armor' is used only once in the New Testament. In Luke 11:21-22, Jesus spoke of a strong man who is fully armed, but when one stronger comes and overpowers him, all his armor (equipment) is taken away. We know that Jesus disarmed all principalities and powers through His cross (Colossians 2:15). Moreover, the armor He gives to the saints is from God and belongs to God. In the Old Testament, it was the Lord who wore this armor (Isaiah 59:17). Now, He shares this armor with the believers who follow Him. Having equipped us with God's armor, it is natural for us to be more than conquerors (Romans 8:37)[42]. In fact, winning abundantly is not a boast, but a guarantee of truth. This is because our commander, Jesus Christ, ensures victory for those who follow Him every day. In the above passage, Paul uses the word 'able' (or 'strong') three times. This war, in fact, belongs to the Lord, and victory or defeat does not depend on the number of people or weapons. Therefore, true Christians live a life of 'thanks to God, who gives us the victory through our Lord Jesus Christ' (1 Corinthians 15:57). Now, let's briefly reflect on the content of the full armor.

❶ Stand Therefore! In reality, soldiers going to war can be overwhelmed by the enemy's weapons or numbers and become fearful. However, the spiritual battle of the saints is one of high morale. There is no room for fear, despair, discouragement, retreat, or surrender. Our God is the Lord of hosts, mighty in battle. Therefore, we stand firm and resist the enemy, the devil. The Bible urges us: **"Resist the devil, and he will flee from you"** (James 4:7). Those who stand on the side of God, who gives **"greater grace"** (James 4:6) to His people, are brave and fearless soldiers of the cross who, empowered by His grace, boldly stand against the enemy. The only reason a believer may be defeated is one: pride, when they attempt to become a hero without relying on God.

---

42 In our Korean Bible, it is translated as 'We are more than conquerors.'

God resists the proud, so we must humble ourselves before Him. Stand firm against the enemy, but humble ourselves before God. The one who humbles themselves before God and submits completely to Him will rise to the position of victory. Humility means submitting fully to God. He created us, and through the blood of His Son, He redeemed us to be His possession. Not submitting to God is a path to disaster. Without obeying Him, we cannot even begin to resist the devil. However, as the hymn goes: "**If we follow Jesus and obey the gospel, our way will be clear. Those who trust and obey will have the Lord with them always. The way of trust and obedience is joyful and blessed in Jesus.**" When we humbly submit to God, we resist the devil and step into a guaranteed victory.

To resist the devil means to boldly stand against all of his deceit and threatening efforts. Have we not seen the promise of the Lord that if we resist the devil, he will flee from us? Faith is to stand firm on the Lord's promises and act on them. In fact, what James is saying is not that someone else will cast out the devil on our behalf, but that each Christian is called to treat Satan as a defeated enemy. Satan is someone we can and must personally resist. The word "**resist**" in English comes from two Greek words: "**stand**" and "**against,**" meaning to stand firm and oppose. Therefore, if we humbly rely on the name of our leader, Jesus Christ, and stand firm, we can surely defeat the devil, who roams like a roaring lion, seeking someone to devour. Just as the young David, when tending sheep, boldly faced lions, bears, and wolves to protect the flock, those who trust in the Lord and follow Him can always taste victory, empowered by His help.

In mentioning the full armor of God, the phrase "**stand firm!**" is said. This is not about boldness relying on each of our individual dispositions, like a young puppy that does not know the fear of a tiger. Rather, it is about being strong and courageous through the power of the Lord, "**in the strength of His might**" (Ephesians 6:10). Standing firm and confronting is the basic action to "**stand against**" the schemes of the devil with strength. It's not about narrowly winning. It's about winning abundantly. There is no need to breathe a sigh of relief. It's not about trembling or sweating in fear. The word 'able' is used three times (in verses 11, 13, and 16) to emphasize that victory is assured. To stand firmly in the evil day, one must put on the full armor of God. This is the bold walk of faith where there is no fear, no timidity, and no hesitation. This armor is essential for every Christian. The trials, pains, temptations, and persecutions we face threaten us, make us afraid, and confuse us. But God's wisdom and power, who works all things together for good, bring ultimate victory to His people who love Him. Therefore, we are to stand boldly and not succumb to circumstances but obey God. Even if victory seems hard-won, it guarantees a valuable victory. In truth, being saved from a life-threatening crisis is the best opportunity to experience the power of Almighty God. Victory is with the Lord. Believers are not refugees or helpless wounded soldiers but strong and courageous soldiers of the living God.

The fact that we are in the army of Christ doesn't mean we won't face attacks or threats of injury. We may be surrounded, oppressed, persecuted, or even knocked down. But we will not be discouraged, forsaken, or destroyed (2 Corinthians 4:8-9). Paul speaks in 2 Corinthians 6 of some of the harsh realities of his life: "**in everything commending ourselves as servants of God... by endurance, by afflictions, by hardships, by beatings, by imprisonments, by tumults, by labors, by sleeplessness, by hunger...**" (verses 4-5). But he continues with a confession: "**in purity, in knowledge, in patience, in kindness, in the Holy

Spirit, in genuine love, in the word of truth, in the power of God, by the weapons of righteousness for the right hand and the left..." (verses 6-7). So, when we are told to 'stand firm,' it's a command not to give up, not to be discouraged, but to be bold. Paul faced difficulties and challenges too. He encountered setbacks. He faced unexpected intrusions. But he tells us not to panic, to be bold. There is no need to show weakness.

Satan's strategy is cunning, and he targets our vulnerabilities. As a result, we may feel far from God's promise of victory. We may begin to feel like failures or outcasts. Were the recipients of Ephesians the kind of people who had never experienced failure? No. They were people just like us, who wrestled with all the challenges of life. To these people, the Apostle Paul says, **"Stand firm."** The Apostle Peter, writing to the scattered believers throughout Asia due to the gospel, knew this well and advised them: **"Beloved, do not think it strange concerning the fiery trial which is to try you, as though some strange thing happened to you; but rejoice to the extent that you partake of Christ's sufferings, that when His glory is revealed, you may also be glad with exceeding joy..."** (1 Peter 4:12-13). The giants who stood boldly in faith, the soldiers of the cross who endured the world's opposition, can be seen clearly in Hebrews 10 and 11. The sufferings and trials they faced were unavoidable, given that Satan exists and sin surrounds us. However, these did not lead them to despair or betrayal; instead, they rejoiced in sharing in Christ's sufferings and eventually received the crown of victory. They never doubted the certainty of victory in the battle. In his commentary on Ephesians, Lloyd-Jones says: **"If Christianity is a task, if worshiping God in His house is something we have to force ourselves to do, we are already defeated. We are not stand-**

ing; we are stumbling and standing crookedly. **We need to be supported by others or pushed by something other than our own strength."**[43] Following the Lord is not something we are reluctantly driven into, but it is a voluntary dedication. Following the Lord means being sober, alert, and diligently pursuing Him as brave soldiers of the cross, standing firm against the devil. We must stand in grace (Romans 5:2), stand in the gospel (1 Corinthians 15:1), stand in courage and strength (1 Corinthians 16:13), and stand in faith (2 Corinthians 1:24). We must stand in the freedom of a Christian (Galatians 5:1), stand in the unity of Christians (Philippians 1:27), stand in the Lord (Philippians 4:1), and stand in God's will, complete and perfect (Colossians 4:12). Take up the full armor of God.

❷ The Belt of Truth: The belt is not something someone else can put on for you; it is something you must wear yourself. It is not merely ornamental, nor is it a necessary accessory for decoration. It is the belt of truth. It is an absolutely essential weapon in the armor. If we look at the function of the belt, we see that in Paul's time, most common attire was long and loose. If we compare it to the clothing worn in the Middle East today, we can understand that in times of war, the utility of the belt becomes crucial. You must tightly fasten it around your waist to move swiftly. The belt helps you go into battle without any hindrances. By fastening the belt firmly, the soldier is now ready for action. With one hand holding the shield and the other holding the sword, he can engage in battle without any obstruction. There is no need to worry about tripping over clothes or getting caught in any part of them. The belt allows the soldier to confidently advance toward

---

[43] D M Martin Lloyd Jones, The Christian Soldier, The Banner of Truth, 1977, 160. The translation is author's own.

the enemy. This is why Jesus also said, "**Let your waist be girded and your lamps burning**" (Luke 12:35). In other words, He is telling us to fasten the belt of truth and raise the torch of truth. We must be ready to act immediately. Soldiers train continuously in preparation for battle, fortifying national defense and security. The attacks of the evil devil, who is constantly watching and waiting, could come at any time, from anywhere, in any form. Therefore, Christians must be firmly prepared to face the devil. The belt that will tightly bind us to immediately engage in battle is the belt of truth.

What does this truth refer to here? Some people interpret this passage, because later in the text there is a reference to the sword of the Spirit, which is the word of God, as meaning that the truth of the belt is not the objective truth of God's Word but rather a kind of subjective reality—traits like "**sincerity, fairness, honesty, and generosity**" of the person wearing it.[44] This interpretation is very dangerous because in spiritual warfare, victory does not depend on the subjective qualities of individual soldiers; it must be a unified response, entirely dependent on the Lord's truth. We are not perfect enough to trust in ourselves. If we acknowledge that our being is entirely by the grace of the Lord, then we must firmly trust in all the objective truths of God in Christ Jesus, and we must unite with those truths. We must fasten our minds and hearts firmly to that truth. It is that truth that will allow us to enjoy freedom from the schemes of the devil. We must wear the belt of truth, which leaves no room for doubt or uncertainty, and diligently follow the true Lord who is the truth. Moreover, because Satan is the father of lies, he will try to distort and misinterpret the truth to make us fall. That is why we must firmly hold on to the universal truth

---

44 Lloyd Jones, Ibid, 186.

of the Lord's word.

The distortion and confusion of truth is a strategy that Satan has planted in the church. Therefore, we must strive to be those who rightly divide the Word of God, as those who are approved, workmen who do not need to be ashamed, but who present themselves to the Lord (2 Timothy 2:15). In particular, we must be soldiers of the cross, firmly bound with all the truth necessary for salvation. In the context of God's full armor, we must deeply understand Paul's gospel proclamation spirit: **"For the weapons of our warfare are not carnal, but mighty in God for pulling down strongholds, casting down arguments and every high thing that exalts itself against the knowledge of God, bringing every thought into captivity to the obedience of Christ"** (2 Corinthians 10:4-5). Therefore, to stand firm, we must tightly fasten the belt of truth to be victorious.

❸ Put on the breastplate of righteousness. The breastplate is the piece of equipment that protects the most important organs of our body. A soldier can fight somewhat effectively without a shield. However, a soldier of the cross cannot fight against spiritual enemies at all without the breastplate of righteousness. This is not our own righteousness or a feeling of righteousness. It is the righteousness of the Lord received through faith in Jesus. Some may try to understand the breastplate of righteousness as one derived from the hardened experience of a battle-hardened warrior, but Paul said, **"Put on the breastplate of righteousness."** We are often tempted to rely on precious experiences of spiritual warfare against the devil. While faith without experience is false, our faith does not depend on experience but entirely on the truth of God's Word. Our experiences confirm the objective truth of the Lord. However, experiences and emotions are always fluid and can change dramatically depending on circumstances. But the clothing of Christ's righteousness is unchanging, unwavering, and no one can take it away. Do not forget that it is the full armor of God, prepared by Him. In Philippians 3, Paul expressed that, although he had excelled in the things people boast about, after knowing Christ, he considered those things as garbage. He confessed that all his new desires were found in knowing Jesus Christ, saying: **"I want to be found in Him, not having a righteousness of my own that comes from the law, but that which is through faith in Christ—the righteousness that comes from God on the basis of faith"** (Phil 3:9). The Jews, who did not know this truth, committed the sin of rejecting God's righteousness because of their zeal and attempts to display their own righteousness (Rom 10:2-3). This was the same sin Paul committed before he believed in Jesus.

This phenomenon can easily be seen in the church today. Many people boast about their own achievements or merits. They tend to trust their devoted accomplishments for the Lord more than the righteousness of Jesus Christ. However, as stated before, we must not forget that our being is entirely by God's grace. We must clothe ourselves with the righteousness of God, which is Jesus Christ, received through faith. **"Let us behave decently, as in the daytime, not in carousing and drunkenness, not in sexual immorality and debauchery, not in dissension and jealousy. Rather, clothe yourselves with the Lord Jesus Christ, and do not think about how to gratify the desires of the flesh"** (Rom 13:13-14). This righteousness is the righteousness that is imputed to those who believe in and follow Jesus Christ (imputed righteousness). It is also imparted righteousness.[45] Modern Christians may not fully

---

45 Martin Lloyd-Jones, in his exposition of Ephesians, distinguishes between imputed righteousness and imparted righteousness, explaining as follows: "The

understand what this means, so preachers must make it clear and certain, as reformers and Puritans did. The doctrine of justification by faith means that the righteousness of Christ has been imputed to those who believe in Jesus Christ as their Savior through faith.[46] This is what it means to clothe ourselves with Christ. When it comes to the righteousness of the law, even Paul, who boasted of being blameless according to the law, had no choice but to confess that he was a sinner before the brighter light of Christ. Even people who can live morally and ethically without the law must confess that they are stained with sin from head to toe before the holy and righteous God. The closer we get

---

difference between imputed righteousness and imparted righteousness is that if we stop at imputed righteousness, I remain where I was before. I am clothed and covered with the righteousness of the Lord Jesus Christ, but there is no righteousness in me at all. That is just the beginning. It is what makes me a Christian. It is the foundation. But God does not stop there; He now begins to work the righteousness of His Son within me. He grants it to me, makes it a part of me, and places it inside me. This necessarily happens as a result of being born again, regenerated, and living a new life. A new seed of life has been planted within me." (ibid. 230). However, he believes there is no need to separate the two concepts. Imputed righteousness itself includes imparted righteousness. The author believes that Lloyd-Jones never stopped at the historical work of salvation represented by imputed righteousness and that being justified by faith in Christ is not only the beginning of regeneration but also includes being able to stand before God as a holy and righteous people.

46   For readers who want to understand the key arguments and the main dispute concerning the imputation of Christ's righteousness, refer to Sin Ho-seob's *Reformed Doctrine of Imputation* (Seoul: Jipyeongseowon, 2015). In fact, the doctrine of imputation is generally divided into three main parts. First, the sin of Adam and Eve was imputed to their descendants. Second, the sins of sinners were imputed to Christ. Third, the righteousness of Christ is imputed to those who believe in Him. Therefore, it is not enough to merely say that our sins have been removed; what we need is the righteousness that is recognized by God, a holy, just, and supremely good God. There is no other way than for the essential righteousness of Christ to be imputed to us.

to God, the more our sin appears magnified. The more we strive to live a better life, even attempting to follow Jesus' Sermon on the Mount, the more our sin clings to us, and we will despair in front of our hopeless condition. By the standards of God (Matt 22:37-39), we are nothing but sinners, less than dust or worms. **"Wretched man that I am! Who will rescue me from this body of death?"** In the face of such lamentation, Paul instills confidence, saying: **"Therefore, there is now no condemnation for those who are in Christ Jesus"** (Rom 8:1). It is because of the righteousness of Christ.

There is nothing we can do to obtain God's righteousness. The harder we try, the more our sins increase. We must hold on to Christ, who saved us from such sin. There is no solution other than His grace. In Him alone, there is no condemnation, and we are counted as righteous. Those who trust in God's promise to believe in Jesus Christ, His Son, who is without blemish or sin, are those who have put on the breastplate of righteousness through faith. **"God made Him who had no sin to be sin for us, so that in Him we might become the righteousness of God"** (2 Cor 5:21). There is no other way except to receive what God has done. Only in Jesus Christ can we stand before God as holy, without fault, and blameless. It is not because we kept God's law perfectly (for we could not), but because Christ perfectly kept it for us. **"A person is not justified by the works of the law, but by faith in Jesus Christ. So we, too, have put our faith in Christ Jesus, that we may be justified by faith and not by the works of the law, because no one will be justified by the works of the law"** (Gal 2:16). The Heidelberg Catechism, created in 1563, teaches in question 3 that we come to know our sin and misery through God's law. Because we cannot fully keep this law, we are justified through Jesus Christ, who satisfied the law's demands. This is mentioned in questions 60 and 61: **"How are** you righteous before God? Only through true faith in Jesus Christ. Even though I have greatly violated all of God's commandments and have not kept even one, and my conscience accuses me of still having a sinful nature, God grants me the righteousness, holiness, and complete satisfaction of Christ as a gift. God considers me as though I had never sinned and as though I had obeyed perfectly, because of Christ's perfect obedience. I receive this gift through faith alone." "Why is it said that only by faith are we justified? It is not because of any worthiness of my faith that God accepts me, but only because of Christ's satisfaction, righteousness, and holiness, which become my righteousness before God. I can only receive this righteousness by faith and make it my own."[47] The Christian who is clothed in the perfect righteousness of Christ is untouched and uncondemned by the law. Therefore, with confidence in victory, they can boldly engage in spiritual warfare. As long as we are in Christ, there is no reason to doubt the assurance of our salvation. All saints who love the Lord, remembering that the grace given by the Lord to those who follow Him is greater than all the power of their enemies, are strong and courageous soldiers of the cross.

❹ Prepare your feet with the gospel of peace! The **"shoes"** mentioned here are not ordinary shoes that regular people wear. They are military boots worn by soldiers going into battle. These were shoes designed to help soldiers move quickly and protect their feet during combat. While they were not as advanced as modern military boots, they were essential for soldiers in ancient times. At that time, they were

---

47 *Heidelberg Catechism*, published by Seongyak Publishing House, 2004, pages 94-95.

more like sandals, but for a soldier, they were a crucial piece of equipment. If a soldier's feet were injured, moving would become difficult, and attacking would become even harder. Therefore, it was important to protect the feet to maintain mobility on the battlefield. The Bible defines these shoes as the "**shoes of the gospel of peace.**"

It does not simply say to wear shoes, but to wear shoes that are "**prepared**" or "**made ready.**" What does this mean? The gospel of peace is something that Christians can easily understand. It refers to the gospel of the cross of Christ, which reconciles us to God and removes the dividing wall of hostility. Wherever this gospel is preached, the barriers are broken, and people are brought near through the cross, becoming fellow citizens and members of God's household. But why is the word "**prepared**" (or "**readied**") used here? There are two general interpretations for this term. One interpretation is that it refers to the firmness given to us by the gospel of peace. There is no doubt that the gospel proclamation brings peace to sinners, and this is certain. The second interpretation is that it refers to a state of readiness for battle. This is a description of soldiers who are prepared to go to war, similar to the use of "**prepared**" in Titus 3:1, which talks about being prepared for good works. In other words, it refers to a state where everything is ready for battle, and one is prepared to act at any moment when commanded. What kind of training do we need in times of peace to be prepared for battle?

Generally, military training includes both offensive and defensive strategies. The same applies to spiritual warfare. Defensive tactics involve holding fast to orthodox theology and doctrinal systems to defend against heresies. Offensive tactics involve actively proclaiming the gospel of Christ's cross, whether the time is favorable or not. In fact, the effectiveness of these tactics is greater in real-life situations than in theoretical training. Therefore, one must demonstrate the ability to engage in spiritual warfare by applying sound doctrine learned through study. Doctrinal education should not be a one-time thing. Just as military tactics require constant repetition, so must doctrinal education be reinforced through repeated study to effectively combat the subtle challenges of heresies. A person who is familiar with the Westminster Confession of Faith and the Westminster Shorter and Larger Catechisms should be ready to engage in spiritual warfare. At the same time, Christians must actively engage in the Great Commission that our Lord has given us: **"Go therefore and make disciples of all nations, baptizing them in the name of the Father and of the Son and of the Holy Spirit, teaching them to observe all that I have commanded you"** (Matthew 28:19-20). Those who are well-trained in the commands of Christ will be able to fight as seasoned warriors in any situation. However, those who are not properly trained will easily fall prey to the enemy. The apostle Peter gives this encouragement in relation to gospel proclamation: **"But in your hearts honor Christ the Lord as holy, always being prepared to make a defense to anyone who asks you for a reason for the hope that is in you; yet do it with gentleness and respect"** (1 Peter 3:15-16).

Of course, as Lloyd-Jones points out, Paul does not specifically mention the propagation of the gospel in this passage. He is talking about spiritual warfare against the wicked one, so there may not be a direct emphasis on preparing for effective gospel preaching. However, being prepared to firmly present and affirm the truths we believe will undoubtedly increase the chances of successfully overcoming the wiles of the devil. In this sense, the final piece of armor mentioned, the **"sword of the Spirit, which is the word of God,"** is highly significant. This is the only offensive weapon in the armor of God. It implies that we should not neglect doctrinal learning but rather embrace and boldly proclaim the truths we have learned as an effective strategy to defend sound doctrine and defeat the forces of darkness. Isaiah 52:7 also speaks of this: **"How beautiful upon the mountains are the feet of him who brings good news, who publishes peace, who brings good news of happiness, who publishes salvation, who says to Zion, 'Your God reigns.'"** Therefore, putting on the **"prepared"** shoes refers to a decisive determination and readiness to carry out this command. It symbolizes a stance filled with confidence and resolve.

One of the reasons why contemporary Christianity is lukewarm is the lack of pure gospel proclamation that strengthens our resolve. There are fewer and fewer committed believers who stand firm in the gospel, and many are slipping into compromise with the world. This situation is connected to the failure to boldly sound the trumpet of the gospel of peace. The enemy, Satan, laughs at the church. There is too much room for him to infiltrate within the church. Therefore, each believer and the church as a whole must continually remember and proclaim the truths of our faith. Many are ready to compromise, and they quietly prepare to retreat. The spiritual war we face is not about finding a middle ground between faith and the world; it is about standing firm in the truth. We cannot serve two masters. God's truth must be properly discerned, for truth often brings division—between believers and unbelievers, between the people of heaven and the children of hell. There is nothing that can go against the truth; it must be upheld at all costs (2 Corinthians 13:8). Once we compromise, not only doctrinally but also in our practical lives, the foundation starts to crumble. The standard set by God becomes flexible. We begin to speak with double tongues, and our outward and inward lives are no longer aligned. However, the truth of the gospel is clear. It is not vague or ambiguous. It is a visible and understandable path, a clear standard for life. Truth defines how we live in the church, in our families, and in society. If it doesn't, it is not truth.[48] Just as we cannot serve two masters, we cannot live with one foot in the world and one in the church. There is only one path—the path God has set before us. We must always be alert and vigilant, for we do not know when or where the enemy will strike. The watchman's vigilance allows the people of God to be at peace and stay faithful to their mission. Therefore, church leaders and Christians, who are the light of the world, must continue to stand firm in faith, remaining strong and courageous (1 Corinthians 16:13). Satan, who attacks us, never tires or sleeps. He constantly commands the principalities and powers, leading evil spirits to shoot fiery darts at God's chosen people. He is wiser and more cunning than the saints, and that is why, without unwavering resolve to follow Christ, we are bound to fall prey to him. Anyone who tries to gain personal glory is an easy target for Satan. Can we afford to go into battle without proper training, lazily and complacently? Absolutely not. We must move swiftly and decisively, like soldiers of the cross, boldly confronting the enemy. Only then can we resist the attacks of Satan, who prowls around like a roaring lion, seeking to devour.

❺ Take the Shield of Faith. The phrase, **"Take up the shield of faith above all,"**[49] suggests that in addition to all the essential gear that a soldier of the cross must have when entering battle, there is something else that must be equipped. That is the shield of faith. What is signifi-

---

48   The author strongly recommends reading *Theology is Life* (Christian Renaissance, 2023) for further insight on this matter.

49   Our Korean Bible uses the word 'have,' but (in the KRV and the NKRV versions) this is a mistranslation.

cant here is not just the command to 'have' the shield of faith, but to 'take' it. This verb emphasizes that it is something we actively use. As the text explains, the purpose of this shield is to "**extinguish all the fiery darts of the wicked one**" (verse 16). Lloyd-Jones divides the six pieces of armor into two sets[50]: the first three pieces of armor are those that are attached to the body by special fastenings. The belt, the breastplate of righteousness, and the shoes must be firmly fixed to our body. In contrast, the last three do not attach to our body. These are the shield of faith, the helmet of salvation, and the sword of the Spirit. These are items we take up when going into battle. We take them up and use them, but they are not always firmly attached to our body. They can be separated from our body as needed. This is why the apostle used the term "**take**" instead of "**have.**" The first three must always be with us, but the last three are items we can take as needed, depending on the situation. The last three are used in actual combat, while the first three must be worn not only during battle but also when resting. The first three must be worn during tactical training, and the last three are to be taken up when we are actually engaged in combat.

The shield we think of might be small and light, something we can hold and move easily, but the shield used by Roman soldiers was quite large—about 120 cm in length and 75 cm in width. It was like a door, large enough to shield the entire body behind it. Interestingly, while the shield was made of wood, its surface was lined with fireproof metal, so when enemy fiery arrows were shot at the soldier, raising the shield would cause the arrows to land on the fireproof lining. Therefore, this shield, in combination with the previously mentioned three pieces of armor, effectively provided protection. This is also why the text mentions

---

[50] in Lloyd Jones, Ibid, 297.

that the shield of faith can extinguish all the fiery darts of the wicked one. Satan shoots fiery arrows from all directions to create confusion among both allies and enemies. When a path opens, it is one of the tactics for an army to advance. Right now, Satan is shooting these fiery arrows at the children of God, causing great confusion in our ranks. The unity is collapsing. The reason why the church is fragmented into hundreds of different branches today, because of theological differences, is that it has fallen lower than even the centralized Roman Catholic Church. Armed with philosophies, theories, reason, and science, the devil and his collective attack have caused the church, which once stood united in truth, to scatter in all directions. Of course, the world rejects God, but it also refuses to believe in the existence of the devil. There is a growing tendency to deny the existence of evil spirits. However, the Bible still speaks about **"principalities, powers, rulers of the darkness of this world, and spiritual wickedness in high places."** Therefore, God's full armor is not an outdated concept. It is still highly useful in spiritual warfare today. These are weapons that come from the eternal and unchanging God, so how could we regard them as expired relics? The evil devil uses all those who are aligned against God. Therefore, the enemy we face mobilizes a formidable army and weapons. It is not an abstract entity, but very specific and real. If we fail to recognize this, following Jesus would remain at the level of a leisurely walk or a tourist's journey. However, a true Christian does not see the reality of things, but goes into battle looking to Christ, who gives daily victory. We train ourselves to be familiar with the weapons He has given and use them to extinguish all the fiery darts of the wicked one. The necessity of God's full armor is only truly realized in the midst of warfare. We must be soldiers of the cross who, through our Captain Jesus Christ, wear the crown of victory in the fight against sin, the world, and the devil.

Now, let's address what the fiery darts that Satan shoots at us are. In short, they are the various distractions and unnecessary things that prevent us from focusing on God. They include anything that hinders our worship of God, prevents us from concentrating on prayer, or leads our hearts and lips away from true confession. Even fleeting thoughts or distractions that pass through our minds are enough to create confusion and prevent us from following the Lord. A momentary lapse in focus can cause devastating damage, just like athletes who experience a loss of concentration in a game. Similarly, a brief moment of distraction in spiritual warfare can become the trigger for the destruction of the entire camp. There is a campaign to prevent drowsy driving with slogans like, "**The destination of drowsy driving is not this world**" and "**A brief nap could lead straight to death!**" Isn't that chilling? In spiritual warfare, even a brief moment of drowsiness or distraction can lead to disastrous consequences. We must always stay awake. Just as we cannot guarantee safety tomorrow just because we are safe today, we cannot be assured of victory in tomorrow's spiritual battle just because we've blocked Satan's fiery darts today. The vows made during a pastor's ordination or a church officer's installation are serious and real confessions, but ignoring those vows and giving in to pragmatism or convenience is another way the fiery darts of Satan cause harm. Acts that undermine the authority of the Bible, such as misusing the name of Christ in the name of academic freedom or twisting God's infallible word, are also part of the wicked one's schemes. In such an era of tolerant and uncritical attitudes, the practical remedy is to hold firmly to our faith. We must be diligent in repeating, meditating on, and proclaiming the truth. As Paul said in 2 Corinthians 2:17, "**We do not peddle the word of God for profit, but speak with sincerity, as from God, before God, in Christ.**" Even when fiery trials approach, do not let go of the shield of faith. Hold onto the promise of the Lord, who is with us to the end of the age, and praise Him for the victory He gives. What else can comfort us besides the voice of the Lord, and what else can make us stand as victors besides His word?

❻ The Helmet of Salvation: The phrase used here also evokes the image of a Roman soldier. Just as soldiers wore helmets, Roman soldiers also wore helmets as part of their armor. Just like the full armor that protects the body, the helmet of salvation can be seen as a protective or defensive tool. The helmets of that time were said to resemble hats made of leather, which gradually became reinforced with metal plates or spikes for added protection. So, when soldiers went to battle, they would wear their armor, carry shields, wear helmets, and take swords with them. When thinking about the purpose of a helmet, we cannot help but think about how to apply this to Christians in spiritual warfare. Since the helmet is worn on the head, it functions as a protective device for the head. But what is it protecting us from? Since this helmet is called the helmet of salvation, it is associated with salvation. It is related to defending against thoughts that might make us doubt the certainty of our salvation and allowing those thoughts to dominate our hearts and minds. It is directly connected to our intellect and the way we think and understand. When Satan, the father of lies, tempted our first parents and led them to fall, it was a matter of their thoughts and minds. If Adam and Eve, created without sin, easily fell, how much more likely are we, with our inherent tendency to sin, to fall? Just as the shield of faith was related to tactics and strategies, the helmet of salvation is not so much about fundamental doctrines like salvation by faith (justification by faith), but rather something more general. Lloyd-Jones connects it to feelings of weakness, exhaustion, and giving up that

Christians often experience.[51] Christians face difficult situations where there seems to be no hope of life, or they are surrounded by enemies. There are times when they feel as though they have fallen into a barren desert with no water. Though they do not completely abandon their salvation, they become passive in their training, lukewarm in the battle, and may even sit down or retreat. With this in mind, the Bible tells us to wear the helmet of salvation to protect ourselves from thoughts and emotions that are unhelpful.

In our spiritual journey, we sometimes feel that our efforts are in vain. We may pray, but there is no answer, and after working hard, we experience no reward or benefit. In such cases, it is natural for believers to fall back. For this reason, the Bible offers words of comfort and encouragement to those who have had such experiences: **"Let us not become weary in doing good, for at the proper time we will reap a harvest if we do not give up"** (Galatians 6:9). The phrase **"if we do not become weary"** can be understood as **"if we do not weaken."** In other words, if we do not give up or become discouraged, we will surely reap what we have sown. Jesus also gave us a similar message. In Luke 18, He taught the parable of the unjust judge, who, despite his indifference to God and people, was moved to avenge the widow's complaint. Jesus said that how much more will God, who is full of mercy and grace, respond to the cries of His chosen ones who cry out to Him day and night. Therefore, we should not give up on praying, whether we see immediate responses or God seems silent for a time. The writer of Hebrews challenges Christians who have undergone severe persecution and trials, saying: **"But we do not belong to those who shrink back and are destroyed, but to those who have faith and are saved"** (Hebrews

---

51 Martin Lloyd Jones, Ibid, 310.

10:39). In other words, despite suffering and persecution, we are those who have faith, and we should have strong assurance that we are not on the path of apostasy or destruction. In this sense, we wear the helmet of salvation and go into the battle.

At times, due to heavy burdens, the indifference of people, or their lack of recognition, we can fall into discouragement and be caught in a web of negative emotions. As the saying goes, **"In a prolonged illness, even a devoted child is of no use,"** when the war drags on or when material or mental damage seems irreversible, we might feel like throwing up our hands and giving up. At that moment, we might blame God, doubt our salvation, and withdraw from fellowship within the community, almost falling into a state of stumbling. These experiences are not just someone else's issues; they are existential realities that can come to each of us. The situation the church faces today feels incredibly grim. The church is caught in a chaotic state where it can offer no hope. Satan approaches such a church and pours fuel on the fire. With issues like homosexuality, human rights, gender equality, women's ordination, and disputes over church authority, the church finds itself in a confusing situation, with powerless churches and Christians growing in number. The approval of the people is at an all-time low, and many sociologists predict that soon churches will be empty due to young people turning their backs on the church. What we are seeing in the Western churches is now happening in our own country. The enemy, Satan, seems stronger, and the people of the Lord appear weak and frail. The number of those who have turned away from the church has greatly increased. According to some, the number of **"Canaan believers"** who do not attend church exceeds 2 million (though the exact number is unknown). Why has the church come to such a state? The favorable conditions for Christianity have almost disappeared. The portrayal of Christianity in films and dramas often mocks and ridicules it in exaggerated ways, creating negative images. We live in an era where genuine hope is hard to find.

Look at how the Apostle Paul, who was in a state where even his hope for life had been cut off, encourages others: "**For we do not want you to be uninformed, brothers, of the affliction we experienced in Asia. For we were so utterly burdened beyond our strength that we despaired of life itself. Indeed, we felt that we had received the sentence of death. But that was to make us rely not on ourselves but on God who raises the dead. He delivered us from such a deadly peril, and he will deliver us. On him we have set our hope that he will deliver us again**" (2 Corinthians 1:8-10). The smell of blood and death may follow us to the grave, but think of the confession of Shadrach, Meshach, and Abednego, who were delivered from the fiery furnace: "**King Nebuchadnezzar, we do not need to defend ourselves before you in this matter. If we are thrown into the blazing furnace, the God we serve is able to deliver us from it, and he will deliver us from your majesty's hand. But even if he does not, we want you to know, your majesty, that we will not serve your gods or worship the image of gold you have set up**" (Daniel 3:16-18).

Such confessions are not just those of Paul or Daniel's friends. They are found throughout the history of Christianity, especially in the history of martyrs. They did not discard the helmet of salvation in the face of their circumstances. Though God's promises may seem delayed, in His time and in His way, He will fulfill them. Let us not forget to take up the helmet of salvation, which is unwavering. Listen to the confession of Luther, a great warrior of spiritual warfare: "**A mighty fortress is our God, a bulwark never failing; our helper he, amid the flood of mortal ills prevailing. For still our ancient foe doth seek to** work us woe; his craft and power are great, and, armed with cruel hate, on earth is not his equal. Did we in our own strength confide, our striving would be losing; we're not the right man on our side, the man of God's own choosing. Dost ask who that may be? Christ Jesus, it is he; Lord Sabaoth, his name, from age to age the same, and he must win the battle. And though this world, with devils filled, should threaten to undo us, we will not fear, for God hath willed his truth to triumph through us. The prince of darkness grim, we tremble not for him; his rage we can endure, for lo, his doom is sure; one little word shall fell him. That word above all earthly powers, no thanks to them, abideth; the spirit and the gifts are ours, through him who with us sideth. Let goods and kindred go, this mortal life also; the body they may kill, God's truth abideth still, his kingdom is forever."** Amen! Even when it's easy to fall into discouragement and the temptation to give up, the true Christian remembers: The Lord is strong. He gives strength to those who fear Him. Yes, we may stumble, but we will not be utterly cast down, for the Lord upholds us with His mighty hand (Psalm 37:24). We are forever protected. **"The young lions lack and suffer hunger, but those who seek the Lord shall not lack any good thing"** (Psalm 34:10). However, the wicked may seem to prosper for a while, but they will eventually be destroyed, like smoke fading away. Though the righteous may face many troubles, believe that God will deliver them from all adversity, mockery, persecution, and reproach. Therefore, the helmet of salvation is necessary. **"For God gave us a spirit not of fear but of power and love and self-control"** (2 Timothy 1:7).

Before we address the final part of the full armor of God, let us briefly consider what salvation means in the context of the "**helmet of**

salvation." Lloyd-Jones, while acknowledging that salvation is the deep realization of being saved that a believer experiences, disagrees with Charles Hodge's interpretation. Based on 1 Thessalonians 5:8, he interprets the helmet of salvation as the "**hope of salvation**."[52] The phrase "**hope of salvation**" does not imply that we are not yet saved, but rather that we are looking forward to the complete fulfillment of our salvation in the future (Romans 13:11). This hope of salvation is similar to how believers live with the hope of eternal rest, even though they have already found peace in Christ. As we live in this world, we long for the day when our salvation is fully realized. Until that day, we are working out our salvation with fear and trembling. If one expects that the process of following Jesus will lead to a utopia, that would be a great mistake. Of course, we do experience true peace that the world cannot give. Even though we may be treated as obscure, poor, or as though we have nothing, we live as those who are rich and possess everything in Christ Jesus, because the crown of righteousness awaits us—the glory we will receive from our Lord Jesus Christ. This is a spiritual benefit far beyond the expectations and values of the world.

Because we have this hope, even in the midst of a long and exhausting battle, when we find ourselves weak and in distress, we continue to pursue the fullness of hope. This is so that we may "**imitate those who through faith and patience inherit the promises**" (Hebrews 6:12). Jesus walked this path, and His disciples followed Him in the same way. The salvation of the Lord encompasses the past, present, and future. Believers have been saved by faith. They have been justified by faith. Therefore, they are under grace, not the law. However, our salvation on this earth is not yet complete. We are running toward the

---

[52] Martin Lloyd Jones, Ibid, 315.

completion of our salvation. Until the glorious day arrives, we do not live as abandoned or forsaken individuals; rather, we live under the guidance of the Spirit of the Lord, who is always with us. And we will advance toward the perfection of our salvation. We must be fully protected from all external whispers that would cause us to doubt or deny this truth. This is why the full armor of God is necessary. Lloyd-Jones divides this hope of salvation into three temporal stages: the past (justification), the present (sanctification), and the future (glorification).[53] A perfect, final, absolute, flawless, and irreproachable salvation will unfold before us.

The helmet of salvation is a helmet of hope, and it guarantees a certain, clear, and eternal salvation. Jesus said, "**I give them eternal life, and they shall never perish; no one will snatch them out of my hand. My Father, who has given them to me, is greater than all; no one can snatch them out of my Father's hand**" (John 10:28-29). In this sense, God's calling is irrevocable. The helmet of salvation protects us from discouragement, from the desire to give up, and not only helps us know that we are saved but also assures us that we will be saved. It gives us the confidence that God will be victorious.

❼ Take the sword of the Spirit, which is the Word of God. This verse shows that the Holy Spirit provides a sword for believers, and that sword is the Word of God. Using this sword effectively is not about treating the Bible like a magical spell book or an amulet related to fortune-telling. The most effective use of the sword of the Spirit is to firmly trust that it is the Word of God. This Word comes from the Holy Spirit, who is the Holy Spirit, the Spirit of Truth, the Spirit of

---

53 Ibid, 319.

the Son, and the Spirit of God. We should have no doubt about this. As the sword of the Spirit, it brings the dead to life, makes the ignorant wise, strengthens the weak, encourages the discouraged, fills the sorrowful with joy, and gives hope to the hopeless. Because it is the Word of the Holy Spirit, it transforms the dry bones in the valley of Ezekiel into a great army. The Holy Spirit has not only given us the Bible, but He has also made it alive to us (or we have made it alive in the Bible), and He has prepared us to wield the sword at the right time. Think of a soldier or a gladiator training, practicing their thrusts, movements, and posture. Whether a gladiator or a soldier, they continually train. Only by practicing beforehand will they be able to perform effectively in battle. If someone is an excellent warrior with strong instincts, they will immediately remember which thrust or posture is most suitable for the precise moment in battle. However, without prior preparation, they would not be able to defend themselves, let alone use offensive instincts during battle.

Especially, church workers should be people who are skilled in the Word. A master at using the sword does not let the sword move separately from their body. The sword moves as swiftly and sharply as part of the body. Ministers of the Word must have a clear grasp of the truth to avoid going beyond the written Word of God. All of Satan's attacks seek to leave us either ignorant, negative, or distorted about God's Word. Misunderstandings, misinterpretations, and misguided preaching lead us further away from fully following the Lord. Consider Satan's reckless attack: he tempted Jesus, who is the Truth, and who holds all treasures of knowledge and wisdom, with the Word of God. How easily, then, would we, who are ignorant, be tempted and fall? One must be familiar with God's Word in order to perform a proper operation to heal the sick, as well as to instantly crush all schemes of the evil one. Look at what the book of Hebrews says about the characteristics of the sword of the Spirit: **"For the word of God is alive and active. Sharper than any double-edged sword, it penetrates even to dividing soul and spirit, joints and marrow; it judges the thoughts and attitudes of the heart. Nothing in all creation is hidden from God's sight. Everything is uncovered and laid bare before the eyes of him to whom we must give account"** (Hebrews 4:12-13).

The Word of God is not a dead letter. It is a living, active Word. The words of men scatter in the air as soon as they leave their mouths, and if not written down, they can never be found again. However, God is not known solely by the written words of the Bible. God revealed Himself through His creation, imbuing His divinity and power within His creation. In other words, even general revelation proves that God is a speaking God, because what He said has been fulfilled. Although special revelation, the Bible, is necessary for salvation, general revelation is also the result of God's power. However, we cannot know God fully through general revelation alone, which is why Jesus Christ, the invisible image of God, came to earth in the flesh. The Word became flesh and dwelt among sinners. The Holy Spirit, who helps us understand, remember, and apply all the truths that Jesus taught and preached, uses this truth Himself.

The power of the Word of God is sharper than any sword that humans can create. A sword of the flesh may be able to cut through a person's body, but it cannot pierce the soul, spirit, joints, or marrow of a person, nor can it reveal the thoughts and intentions of the heart. However, the Word of Truth can do all of this. While the weapons of the flesh may kill the body, the sword of the Spirit is a weapon that can heal both the body and the heart. At the same time, this sword not only attacks the enemy but also plays a defensive role by blocking attacks. Unlike other armor that protects only parts of the body, this sword protects the whole body. A doctor's scalpel is a vital tool in removing harmful tissue and healing wounds, but a sword in the hands of a child could become a dangerous weapon, causing great harm or even death. Similarly, those who are skilled in using the Word of God can bring the dead to life, heal the sick, strengthen the weak, and bring wisdom to the ignorant. Those who have experienced this will long for the Word more than gold and find it sweeter than honey, confessing and praising it. As we read in 2 Timothy 3:16-17: "**All Scripture is God-breathed and is useful for teaching, rebuking, correcting and training in righteousness, so that the servant of God may be thoroughly equipped for every good work.**"

The Bible is the greatest textbook, guidebook, and the only standard. It details what to believe and teaches how to live.

Believers recognize, as Jesus said, "**Man shall not live by bread alone, but by every word that comes from the mouth of God**" (Matthew 4:4). However, in the physical world, one might say they believe in the Lord after eating bread and being satisfied or by becoming a member of the church, but in the spiritual world, that is not enough. The path for believers is not to follow the trends or customs of this world but to follow the statutes and laws given by God (Leviticus 18:1-5). Ignoring the Lord's Word is like not loving Him. The difficulties and darkness people experience in this world are all the result of rejecting God's Word (Psalm 107:11-12). Therefore, the only thing that can save humanity is the Word of God.

The powerlessness of the church and the weakness of individual believers are linked to the sword of the Spirit. The lack of one of the essential pillars in the church, which is the pillar of truth, or the lack of sufficient spiritual nourishment, leads to these symptoms. Darkness only operates in places where light does not penetrate. But when light comes, darkness is immediately defeated and disappears. If there are places in the church where light does not shine, darkness will take over and create evil works. The power to oppose the devil comes from the Lord's Word, the true light. The Word of truth is what drives away the king of darkness, Satan. It is the only thing that can instantly tear down the devil's fortress, which is surrounded by error and lies. The allure of human wisdom and philosophy may seem attractive, with their sophistication, beauty, freshness, logic, and appeal, but these things are not equipped with the dual aspects of defense and offense, preservation and attack, that the Word of God provides. Even if these human ideas seem appealing, they cannot transform the corrupted and fallen human soul. Modern science, with all its excellence, cannot challenge the absolute authority of the Bible. The ideas and theories that undermine the Bible will eventually kneel before the perfect truth. Those who may appear uninformed, inflexible, or lacking in tolerance for wanting to preserve and teach the Bible as it is, will be vindicated by the truth itself. The ideas of man opposing the Bible are fleeting, but the Bible is unchanging. The Lord said that heaven and earth will pass away, but His words will never pass away (Matthew 24:35). Although it may seem natural for a changing world to reject the unchanging truth of the Lord, Christians who have been reborn by the truth must hold on to the Word as more precious than life itself, for without it, existence is impossible. **"But you who held fast to the Lord your God are alive today, every one of you"** (Deuteronomy 4:4). This truth still stands today, displaying its power. Believers are to lift the banner of truth that was given to those who fear the Lord (Psalm 60:4). The only way to save those in lawlessness, ignorance, and powerlessness is under the banner of truth.

The Holy Spirit, the source of the Word, uses the power of that Word to save souls, giving spiritual strength to those saved to become veteran soldiers fighting for the Lord in a corrupt and evil world. The more we know and understand the Word that the Holy Spirit has given us, the more effective soldiers we become in carrying out God's will and learning more effective tactics to confront the enemies of our souls. Becoming familiar with the sword of the Spirit that drives Satan to flight is the blessing of following Jesus. While reading D. Martyn Lloyd-Jones' commentary on Ephesians, I was shocked by something he revealed. I had been curious about why the Roman Catholic Church changed its policy to allow the laity to read the Bible in their own language, but I hadn't investigated it. However, what Lloyd-Jones revealed in his book was astonishing. He stated that the reason people no longer fear the Bible is that **"Protestants no longer believe in the Bible. Those who destructively criticize the Bible have damaged people's trust in it. Therefore, we are the only ones who can defend the Bible."**[54] Those who follow Jesus must remember that they are to live by every word that proceeds from the mouth of God, which includes the entire Bible. We should not be lazy or negligent in taking up the sword of the Spirit, the Word of God. Whether or not we know science or philosophy, we must believe that God's Word is sharper than any sword and can bring every human theory and thought to submission. However, our knowledge or ability regarding the Bible is not what enables us to resist the attacks of the evil one; it is the Holy Spirit who works through us. That's why the apostles constantly urged us **"to pray in the Spirit and to be vigilant, always praying for those who preach the gospel"**(Ephesians 6:18-19).

---

54 Martin Lloyd Jones, Ibid, 353.

Jesus is calling me. Jesus is calling me. Wherever I go, I will follow the Lord. I will go with Him. Following His guidance, Following His guidance, Wherever I go, I will follow the Lord, I will go with Him.
(Korean Hymn 324)

Review of Learning Content

01. What are the essential conditions for following the Lord?

02. Is there a way to overcome the realistic reasons for hesitating to enter through the narrow gate?
    (1) Find the lessons in 2 Peter 1:5-11.

    (2) What is our answer to Jesus' question in John 21:15?

03. What blessings are gained from guarding the heart? (Proverbs 4:23, Philippians 2:5-11)

04. What does being filled with the Holy Spirit mean? (Acts 2:4, 17)
    Post-Pentecost follow-up actions: Samaria, Cornelius (Ephesians 4:16, John 15:5, Ephesians 1:5, 5:18)

05. What do you think is the most urgent thing to do in order to align with the Holy Spirit?

06. What does taking up your cross mean?
    (1) What does it mean to become a "well-ripened wound"?

(2) Is the benefit of others first, or my own benefit first?

(3) What does 2 Corinthians 6:9-10 mean to me?

07. What is the importance of the full armor of God? (Ephesians 6:10-17)
(1) Stand firm then

(2) The belt of truth

(3) The breastplate of righteousness

(4) The readiness that comes from the gospel of peace

(5) The shield of faith

(6) The helmet of salvation

(7) The sword of the Spirit

• Special Meditation 1 •

The Battles the Believer Fights

War with the World

"For whatever is born of God overcomes the world. And this is the victory that has overcome the world—our faith."
(1 John 5:4)

Governments often declare wars against their citizens. Wars on drugs, crime, prostitution, terrorism, and inflation are examples. But that's not all. In this world, wars are endless. There are wars between individuals, conflicts between groups, and fights between nations, including economic wars, diplomatic wars, water wars, resource wars, and ideological wars. Countless people die in these wars. Those who lose in war suffer severe pain and hardship. How many people disappear from the stage of history due to wars? Generally, people prefer peace over war, not only because of the horrors of war but also because they know that it leads to mutual destruction. Having experienced not only invasions from foreign powers but also the pain of civil wars, we long for the day when such tragedies will never occur on this land again. Whether it's a war for unification or an invasion war, war must be avoided, and the best way to preserve the most valuable heritage of humanity is for people to come together peacefully. It is also about loving precious life.

However, the believer faces a war that cannot be avoided. It's not temporary but a war that must be fought every day as long as we breathe on this earth. It is a battle against the one who caused all human tragedy. This is the fight with Satan or the devil, and in short, it is called the **"spiritual war."** The reformer Martin Luther described this spiritual war as a triple battle. That is, Christians must fight three wars: the war against the world, the war against the flesh, and the war against the devil. These wars come at the believers with terrifying weapons. The battle with them is never a fair fight. Sometimes they attack in groups, and at other times, they lure you into traps with clever tactics. Satan is an expert in surprise attacks. The flesh is an internal enemy that is a hindrance to the Holy Spirit, causing great damage to the believer.

The more we try to please the good and righteous God, the more inevitable it becomes to fight these enemies, and as long as we exist in this world, it is a battle we must face. It would be nice if we could avoid it, but the world will never leave us in peace. As a believer who constantly faces such battles, I cannot help but meditate on the verse from 1 Corinthians 15:57: **"But thanks be to God, who gives us the victory through our Lord Jesus Christ."** In short, the victory in this battle is obtained from our Lord Jesus Christ. He is the cause of our victory. The passage from 1 John 5:4 tells us that the secret to overcoming the world in this battle is faith. But that faith is the faith in our Lord Jesus Christ, and this faith is a gift from God, not something that comes from within ourselves. Therefore, the believer's battle can be called a war that has already been won. But why do we often fail? As the saying goes, **"Know yourself and your enemy, and you will be victorious in every battle,"** to win in this war, we must understand the enemy well. Victory in this war is a difficult task, so we must be well-informed and appropriately respond to the world, the flesh, and the devil, who are our enemies. What kind of world do we live in? Years ago, the drama *"The Rose of Sharon"* reached the highest ratings, but most people are deceived by the sweet temptations of the world. The mentality of the world, that is, the value system of the fallen created world, cannot be separated as we distinguish the flesh and the devil. The flesh is a part of the fallen world, and the devil is the prince of this world. In a world ruled by this devil, the prince of darkness, there is no place that is safe.

There is no Demilitarized Zone

Saints are a part of this world. Citizenship may be in heaven, but we live in this world. We are influenced directly or indirectly by the cultures and trends of this world. We are soldiers of the cross, deployed into the battlefield of the spiritual war. This battlefield is not limited to the Korean Peninsula, Ukraine and Russia, or Israel and Hamas. While Christians are born of God, our homeland is also this world, and this country is part of the world. However, we are born and die on this battlefield. Every place in the world is a site of spiritual warfare. There is no demilitarized zone in this battlefield. There has never been a time, across all places and eras, when there was no war. The entire planet Earth is a corrupted world, and all of creation groans, waiting for redemption. Even countless planets in the heavens, untouched by human footsteps, become horrific battlefields the moment humanity steps foot on them. Isn't nature the same? Even ancient forests, once untouched, begin to be ruined and polluted as soon as humans start to tread upon them. Wherever sinners exist, there is a fierce battlefield.

We live in a world ruled by the law of survival of the fittest. Therefore, we long for a new heaven and a new earth, where the wolf will dwell with the lamb, and the child can play with the cobra without harm. But right now, shepherds never tell wolves to live with the sheep. Terrible beasts are not limited to wolves; countless creatures, including the snakes that crawl on the ground, can bring harm to the spiritual battle of saints. Especially, the world seems to exist to make the saints miserable, producing cruel outcomes. The world is a tempter. It strives to extract our attention and devotion. The world is very close to us, easily visible to our eyes, and appears irresistibly alluring. It excels in obscuring our vision of heaven. It steals our hearts and minds with its visible grandeur. It succeeds in blocking us from seeing the better city that God has created and rules. Those intoxicated by what the world offers sadly fail to see the hook hidden behind the bait.

Christians live in such a spiritual battlefield where such humans abound. There are no occasions where pleasing the world aligns with pleasing God. Pleasing people is also not always the same as pleasing God. However, pleasing God leads to pleasing both people and creation, because the all-powerful and wise God has made His people so. Saints should not conform to this world. The phrase **"overcoming the world"** in the text itself does not describe the world as a friend or an object of worship. It describes it as an enemy that must be fought and defeated. This is the teaching of the Bible, but the world, in contrast, whispers to us that we should be friends and partners with it. The world lures us with its most dazzling and sweet things. The temptation is so intense that most people's eyes and ears are drawn to it.

Nowadays, it feels as if the church is desperately trying to please the world. It seems to be struggling to gain the approval of the world. Instead of conquering the enemy, it throws flirtatious gestures toward them, as if it must gain their approval, while seeking the praise and popularity of people. Even though the saints know these things are like bubbles, they eagerly strive to achieve at least one more success in the pride of this life. They are falling for Satan's crafty tactics. It is similar to how South Korean officials, obsessed with getting along with North Korea, have led to a society where communists have gained power in a country that was once armed against them. Just as the enemy has shifted, causing extreme confusion, the church is no longer trying to conquer and rule the world, but instead acts as if it is eager to walk alongside it. Some have already become prey to the enemy. Even those who have learned not to rely on the world's applause often stumble because they haven't learned to ignore it.

For the sake of becoming **"popular,"** it is happening all too often that people forsake what pleases God. They tremble, afraid that the world might hate them. They waste energy and money trying to avoid conflict and trying to conform. By following the world's patterns or structure to gain popularity, they easily fall for the world's smooth words. Even while feeling internal conflict, they just resign, saying, **"That's how the world is, what can you do?"** and fail to stand up. As Christians, they neglect what should be done and get distracted by what shouldn't be done. **"You have to do it for social life! There's no other way!"** they console themselves, rationalizing it. They don't dare to fight and seem to be constantly strategizing on how to get along with the world.

Every era and every culture has its dominant and prevailing spirit. The Germans captured this concept with the term 'Zeitgeist,' which is a combination of the word 'Zeit,' meaning time, and 'Geist,' meaning spirit. This is how the term 'spirit of the time' came into being. What is the spirit of the age in which we live? It is 'secularism.' The emphasis of secularism is on this world, on this time. It pays little attention to things beyond this world. We only briefly think about eternal matters at funerals, no more and no less. Our concerns are always those we face in the place we live. It is the reality of the present moment. Living for the here and now, living for the pleasures of the present, is the spirit of this world.

The generation born in the 70s and who attended university in the 90s is called Generation X. A report by the Dong-A Newspaper interestingly captured their current situation as parents raising children. These mothers, while raising children, never give up their own personal pursuits. When they were growing up, the characteristics of the time were described as an era where people only knew 'me' rather than 'us.' Now that they have grown and become mothers, the articles describe how they believe that they must be happy first for their children to be happy. This mindset contrasts completely with the past when parents sacrificed everything for the happiness of their children. These individuals argue that 'We shop, therefore we exist,' and they seek a life of happiness and self-satisfaction centered around themselves. Of course, this is not a phenomenon of only yesterday or today, but it is certain that people's attention is directed toward earthly matters. This phenomenon has only intensified.

The spirit of the time, which is absorbed in how to live happily in this world and how to enjoy the pleasures of life, existed even during the time of Jesus. The Lord instructed us to set our eyes on the eternal world. He told us to store our treasures in heaven. He said, 'What good will it be for someone to gain the whole world, yet forfeit their soul?' (Matthew 16:26), but these words are of no consequence. Even church pastors reflect this spirit of the time by focusing on how to enjoy life to the fullest in the world. The happiness of this world is often presented as though it is the entirety of a believer's life. Such books become popular and bring in significant profits. The work of turning our eyes from the world to heaven is truly unpopular. Those who attempt it are always hungry, often tired from the difficult struggles, and many give up and collapse because they cannot endure it. They easily become accustomed to a life of contentment in reality, claiming that what is good is good. The virtues of suffering, persecution, self-discipline, and sacrifice for the Lord's righteousness and truth now occupy the wide space of antique shops.

Are we citizens of the heavenly kingdom, or are we people of this world? Do we desire to possess the things of this world, or do we seek to gain our souls? Do we wish to please the world, or do we seek to please God? These are the things we must examine as Christians living in this world. If we are to conform to this world, we must be prepared to lose our souls. The world assigns no value to the soul. According to today's spirit of the age, the visible body is considered more valuable than the invisible soul. The spirit of the world says, 'Enjoy today, pay for it tomorrow.' Of course, the emphasis is on today. This is the popular lifestyle. No one knows what tomorrow will bring. Therefore, if a Christian is to reject the temptations of the world, they must be ready to swim against the current of the times. To please God, they must be prepared to not please people. Listen to the teaching of the Apostle John: 'Do not love the world or anything in the world. If anyone loves the world, love for the Father is not in them. For everything in the world—the lust of the flesh, the lust of the eyes, and the pride of life—comes not from the Father but from the world' (1 John 2:15-16)."

Loving the world means giving in to the lust of the flesh, the lust of the eyes, and the pride of life. It means being drawn to what is visible and following where the body leads. It is like chasing after something that is ultimately insubstantial, yet investing oneself for the sake of popularity. The result is a heap of sin. Therefore, the love of the Father cannot dwell in such a person. Loving the world makes one an enemy of God. It overflows with things God hates. Jesus teaches: 'Blessed are you when people insult you, persecute you and falsely say all kinds of evil against you because of me. Rejoice and be glad, because great is your reward in heaven, for in the same way they persecuted the prophets who were before you' (Matthew 5:11-12). The Lord clearly demands that we seek the reward of heaven over the reward of the world. The key phrase here is 'because of me.' The greatest reason not to conform to the world is 'for the Lord.' Anyone can become a nonconformist and attract attention. Standing alone with a protest sign at a candlelight vigil can certainly draw attention. In a society where personal will is respected, it's not necessarily bad to be on the opposite side. However, in the spiritual realm, the standard for distinguishing between cheap and true nonconformity is 'for the Lord.' It is not about acting out for no reason but rather acting for the Lord. This is how believers fight against the world. It must be selective and have a clear purpose. The Lord does not want opposition for opposition's sake.

The World, the Stage of God's Redemption

The Apostle John pointed out that the world is the enemy we must fight and conquer, and he said that the way to victory in this battle is through faith. Christians are not those who love the world like people of the world. They are saints who have been transformed and become new people. In Christ Jesus, they are created in righteousness and truth, a new creation. To become a new person does not mean to turn away from the world. If we had to turn away from the world, there would be no reason for the Lord to leave us in this world. After all, if the world is a battlefield opposing God, why would God place His redeemed people—whom He saved through precious blood—into a fierce battlefield? A monastery is not needed. The reason He placed us in this world is to fight and overcome through faith, transforming the world. The best weapon in this mission is a firm faith in the Lord, a mind that fully follows Him. This is a powerful weapon that shows those who are satisfied with secularism that living beyond the confines of this world is the greatest happiness.

Saints should neither succumb to the world nor avoid it. They must show the spirit of the heavenly kingdom that the Lord revealed. They must penetrate the barriers of this world. While living in the world, they should not align with it. In other words, Christians should not become worldly people who conform to the mentalities, trends, and customs of this age. For this reason, Christians face suffering and persecution. Still, Christians must love the world. They must love with the heart of Christ, not with greedy nature. This is because it is the Lord's will to save those who are in this evil world. If we flee or turn away from the world, how will the work of salvation be carried out?

The stage for God's redemption of sinners is this world. How can God's saving power be revealed if we leave this world? Jesus, who is God, came to this world in the form of a human. Christ, who broke the power of sin and death and destroyed the works of the devil, did not want His disciples to lock themselves in a room and hide, afraid of death and persecution. He did not desire them to build a retreat on Mount Transfiguration. Instead, He commanded them to go and be His witnesses in Jerusalem, Judea, Samaria, and to the ends of the earth. Jerusalem is in this world, and so is Judea, and so is Samaria. Even the ends of the earth are in this world. Therefore, it is not the Christian attitude to despise this world and seek to escape to the mountains or hide. It is a grave mistake to think that by turning away or fleeing, one can please the Lord. **"This is the victory that has overcome the world, even your faith."** Living for the Lord, the author and perfecter of our faith, is the only way to transform and rule the world.

As God's People, We Must Learn How to Live in the World Alongside the World. Martin Luther spoke of the mature Christian's growth. He mentioned that when someone becomes a Christian, they go through a period of turning away from and forsaking the world. A true convert is someone who has **"seen the world and is done with it."** They must let go of all the attitudes they once had when they were conforming to and compromising with the world. A period of retreat is necessary. During this period, saints immerse themselves in the things of God. Before being sent as an apostle to the Gentiles, Paul first went into the wilderness of Arabia. Before being sent to Pharaoh's court, Moses had to spend time alone in the wilderness of Midian with God. Just as this retreat to spend time with God is a normal and healthy part of growth, it is not the end of the journey. Luther stated that only when one reaches the second stage can they reach the fullness of spiritual maturity. In other words, just as God loved the world and gave His only Son, Christians must return to the world and embrace it.

God the Father does not despise the world right away. He loves the world to the extent that He makes it the stage for His redemptive work, sending His Son into it. He does not abandon or forsake the world. Saints must learn to model this heart of God. They must not embrace the world in the same way they did before believing in Jesus, but they must regard the world as the stage for redemption and carry it in their hearts. The world is not only a battlefield but also our workplace. It is the stage where God created and where Christ, having taken on human flesh, completed the work of salvation. Therefore, without trust in the incarnate Lord, we cannot embrace the world. As God's people, we must learn how to claim ownership over the world on God's behalf.

Now, we must not conform to the world or yield to its temptations, but rather we must testify of Christ in the world and change it, thereby showing that the world belongs to the Lord. God desires for us to live holy lives and to shine brightly like stars in this fallen world. If our hearts are transformed and we begin to live by faith, we can actively participate in God's good work, making this world, though it has become useless, the stage for God's redemption. This is what pleases the Creator God and is living for our Savior, Jesus Christ.

There is no demilitarized zone in this world. There is no safe refuge. It is only a battlefield. We must not live in harmony with the world but instead, we must recognize the world as the field of spiritual warfare. The world is the enemy we must fight and overcome, not a place where we should live in captivity like prisoners. We must not conform to the power of the world and the allure of secularism but must become those who, by faith in the Lord Jesus Christ, overcome the world. This happens when we do not rise by carrying the world on our backs but when we love the world with the heart of Christ.

Being acknowledged by the world does not make one a true church or a true saint. It is normal to be hated by the world, because we belong to the Lord. But with the Lord's heart, who loved the world and brought about the salvation of sinners, we must become the lead actors in God's redemptive stage, joyfully walking in the midst of it.

• Special Meditation 2 •

The Battles That Believers Must Fight

The Battle with the Flesh

"I say then: Walk in the Spirit, and you shall not fulfill the lust of the flesh. For the flesh lusts against the Spirit, and the Spirit against the flesh; and these are contrary to one another, so that you do not do the things that you wish. But if you are led by the Spirit, you are not under the law. Now the works of the flesh are evident, which are: adultery, fornication, uncleanness, lewdness, idolatry, sorcery, hatred, contentions, jealousies, outbursts of wrath, selfish ambitions, dissensions, heresies, envy, murders, drunkenness, revelries, and the like; of which I tell you beforehand, just as I also told you in time past, that those who practice such things will not inherit the kingdom of God." (Galatians 5:16-21)

Let us now look at the second of the three battles that Martin Luther described for believers to fight: the battle with the flesh. Just because we've won the battle with the world once doesn't mean we are free from it. As long as we are breathing on this earth, the battle with the world is an ongoing, present war. Because there is no demilitarized zone in this fight, if we do not stay alert, secularism can gradually infiltrate us and begin to dominate our lives without us even noticing. Therefore, we must always be vigilant. Even in times of peace, a watchman must always stand guard at the tower. Since the enemy's attack could come at any time, the watchman watches for the enemy's movements and blows the warning trumpet, preparing for both attack and defense.

Just because I believe in Jesus today doesn't mean I am no longer a person of the flesh and only filled with the Spirit. The continuous temptation of sin still torments our hearts and bodies. Those who face this battle often confess the truth found in Matthew 26:41, where Jesus says, **"The spirit is willing, but the flesh is weak."** This verse expresses the deep inner conflict that every child of God experiences. The Apostle Paul makes a similar confession in Romans 7, where he says, **"For the good that I will to do, I do not do; but the evil I will not to do, that I practice"** (Romans 7:19).

Unbelievers might describe this struggle as a matter of the heart, a conflict between conscience and the desires of the flesh. However, since the conscience of unbelievers is corrupted by sin, it is impossible for their conscience to overcome all the desires of the flesh. Believers, too, have fallen consciences, but they also have something that unbelievers do not: the Holy Spirit of God. This Spirit rules over us, and thus, the thoughts of the flesh and the thoughts of the Spirit are completely opposed. This internal conflict is what is referred to as **"the battle with the flesh."** The Holy Spirit, who dwells within us, leads us and His thoughts stand in direct opposition to the instincts of our corrupt nature.

If the thoughts of the flesh dominate this battle, sinful words and actions will follow. However, if the thoughts of the Spirit prevail, the holy, righteous, and truthful spiritual strength of godliness will manifest in the life of the believer. But who among the believers does not desire to live a holy life? Everyone's heart is willing, but the weakness of the flesh causes frequent failure. All believers who long to become better Christians should reflect on the nature of the battle with the flesh and look to the way they can overcome it.

The Battle with the Flesh is the Battle with the Fallen Human Nature

The nature of the battle with the flesh is primarily the battle with the fallen human nature. To understand this part well, we need to understand what the term **"flesh"** means in the context we are using. Does **"flesh"** refer to our body? Or does it refer to the fall? In the Bible, there are two Greek words that are used for the word **"flesh."** One is **"soma"** (σῶμα), which is most commonly used, and the other is **"sarx"** (σάρξ). Generally, «**soma**,» which refers to our body, does not carry the meaning of sin or fall. However, «**sarx**» refers to the body but also contains the notion of human›s fallen nature. In John 1:14, where it says, **"The Word became flesh and dwelt among us,"** the meaning of **"flesh"** is not that the Word (Logos) became corrupted, but simply that Jesus, the Logos, took on a human body. The word is also used when referring to kinship or close family ties.

However, **"sarx"** is also used to represent the fallen nature. In this case, it does not only refer to our physical body but to the entire person. In other words, human's total fall, where sin has infected all of human existence, and as a result, humans have become beings who cannot do anything good. In other words, it indicates that our hearts, minds, and bodies are all fallen. Therefore, it says that **"there is no one righteous, not even one,"** and that **"every inclination of the thoughts of the human heart is only evil all the time."**

The specific actions that this fallen human nature, or flesh, commits are clearly described in the passage from Galatians: **"The acts of the flesh are obvious: sexual immorality, impurity and debauchery; idolatry and witchcraft; hatred, discord, jealousy, fits of rage, selfish ambition, dissensions, factions and envy; drunkenness, orgies, and the like. I warn you, as I did before, that those who live like this will not inherit the kingdom of God"** (Galatians 5:19-21).

Here, there is a strict contrast between the flesh and the works of God's Spirit. This is not a conflict between the body and the mind or between the conscience, but rather a war between the old man, who is under the rule of the fallen nature, and the new man, in whom the Spirit of God dwells. The Spirit of God and the flesh are clearly opposing concepts. There is no compromise between them, and there is not even the slightest possibility of reconciliation. It's either one must die or the other must die, but they cannot walk together. This is the biggest reason why people hesitate to come to the Lord. The flesh, with its fallen nature, cannot tolerate the rule of the Holy Spirit, for the flesh resists and tries to overcome the Holy Spirit with all its might.

At the Same Time, the Holy Spirit is an Enemy to the Flesh. The Holy Spirit is an enemy to the flesh. What the flesh loves the most, the Holy Spirit hates the most. What the flesh hates the most, the Holy Spirit loves the most. So how can these two coexist? They can only be separated. Paul begins by comparing the works of the Spirit and the works of the flesh in the text: **"I say to you, walk by the Spirit, and you will not gratify the desires of the flesh. For the desires of the flesh are against the Spirit, and the desires of the Spirit are against** the flesh; for these are opposed to each other, to keep you from doing the things you want to do" (Galatians 5:16-17). "**But the fruit of the Spirit is love, joy, peace, forbearance, kindness, goodness, faithfulness, gentleness, and self-control. Against such things, there is no law**" (Galatians 5:22-23). These two are so diametrically opposed that they can never coexist or reconcile.

The Apostle Paul also teaches the distinction between the works of the flesh and the works of the Spirit in Romans 8: "**Those who live according to the flesh have their minds set on the flesh, but those who live according to the Spirit have their minds set on the Spirit. The mind governed by the flesh is death, but the mind governed by the Spirit is life and peace. The mind governed by the flesh is hostile to God; it does not submit to God's law, nor can it do so. Those who are in the realm of the flesh cannot please God. You, however, are not in the realm of the flesh but are in the realm of the Spirit, if indeed the Spirit of God lives in you. And if anyone does not have the Spirit of Christ, they do not belong to Christ**" (Romans 8:5-9).

As such, the pursuit of the flesh, or the body, and the pursuit of the Spirit represent two extremes that can never find common ground. A person who belongs to the flesh cannot think about the things of the Spirit. A person who belongs to the Spirit can think about the things of the flesh, but the person belonging to the flesh can never understand spiritual things. This is because spiritual things can only be discerned by the Spirit. The difference between a Christian and a non-Christian is the difference between being ruled by the grace of the Holy Spirit and being ruled by sin, and because of this, they can never be one. This is why when these two meet, they will inevitably be at odds and fight.

When we examine the works of the flesh in more detail, one aspect surprises us. In this list, there are not only sins related to the flesh but also sins that have a non-physical character. For example, sexual immorality and drunkenness are sins related to the desires of the flesh and bodily functions. However, the same list includes sins such as rivalry, envy, heresy, and idolatry. Of course, rivalry and envy are related to our body, because, in reality, we do nothing without our body. But rivalry is not a physical act; it is related to our mental attitude and belongs to our mind and thought processes. Idolatry can also involve our bodies, but the essence of idolatry is not in the outward gestures; it is in the inner attitude of the heart.

Therefore, the conclusion is this: when the New Testament speaks directly about the flesh (sarx) in contrast to the Holy Spirit, it usually refers not to the body but to the fallen nature of humanity as a whole. It is the conflict between two ways of life—the life dominated by the desires of sin and the flesh, and the life led by the Holy Spirit, which guides us to live as citizens of the Kingdom of God in righteousness, joy, and peace. This conflict is inevitable.

As believers, our bodies should be used to glorify God. This is because our bodies were bought with the precious blood of Christ. However, at the same time, since believers are still under the influence of their fallen human nature, they must fight the desire of the flesh throughout their lives on this earth. What is the way to do this? Before considering this answer, let's think about a question that every believer often wrestles with. In 1 John 3:9, it says, **"No one born of God will continue to sin,"** so why do believers often live in sin? Those who believe in Jesus have put off the old self and become a new creation, so why do we still suffer and weep because of our sins? Is it impossible to experience perfect freedom from sin?

A renowned pastor explains this issue through an interesting illustration, referencing the **"dominion of sin and grace."** He states that the **"dominion of grace in the believer's life does not refer to a state where the believer lives without sin. Even though sin still resides within the believer, grace continues to have actual dominion over their heart and soul. This means the believer lives under the influence of God's grace…"** To help you understand, he offers an illustration: Imagine that in a city, occasionally, armed terrorists appear on the streets. But even so, if the police quickly arrive and eliminate them, the lawful government still maintains control over the city. Sometimes only a few terrorists appear, and other times a dozen or more, but as soon as they emerge, they are swiftly subdued by the legitimate authorities.

Although terrorists or criminals may show up, they are easily dealt with. This is similar to how a believer, even though they may commit small sins, is still under the dominion of grace. However, if those terrorists begin to organize, take control of the city center, control civilian movement, roam the streets with powerful weaponry, set up a military headquarters, collect taxes from the residents, and recruit young people for military training, then it is no longer a few terrorists appearing—it is the beginning of the rule of an illegal government. If sin operates in this way within the believer, it indicates that the believer is under the dominion of sin."

This is the reason we must fight a spiritual war: the **"terrorists"** that often emerge within us. The way to overcome them and become someone who lives under the grace of the Holy Spirit, not under the dominion of sin, is the path to take.

John Owen explains that while sin wields tyrannical power, God's grace, through Jesus Christ, is the sovereign power that governs the believer's life. Grace not only frees the believer from the penalty of sin but also breaks the power of sin, allowing the believer to live in obedience to God's law.⁵⁵ Because the war between the flesh and the desires of the Spirit continues in the believer's life, the believer must deeply rely on the grace of the Holy Spirit who dwells in their heart.

Walk According to the Spirit

In verse 16, it says, **"I say, walk by the Spirit, and you will not gratify the desires of the flesh."** This is the most effective way to reduce the influence of sin and to manifest the ruling power of grace. The use of the present tense here implies that walking by the Spirit, or walking with the Spirit, should become a continuous habit in the life of a believer. This doesn't only refer to outward actions. If being led by the Spirit is limited to external things, there's a risk that we may fall into Phariseeism. We might hide jealousy in our hearts with a kind smile, or conceal a spirit full of envy with a polite demeanor. However, the guidance of the Holy Spirit aims to purify both our external and internal lives, helping us to live honestly before God, who sees the heart. Therefore, the change in the believer's heart leads to a transformation in behavior.

Of course, some people think that what's inside is important, and that the external doesn't matter. They argue that motivation and mindset are what really matter, and that outward actions aren't significant. They don't pay much attention to things like dress or speech. This is self-deception. Many people with this mindset justify various sins. Today, among young people, some justify adultery by claiming that they are in

---

55 "Refer to John Owen's *Death of Death in the Death of Christ*."

love. While the **"flesh"** doesn't only refer to physical sins or tendencies, it does include them. Our lives are stained by our fallen nature, and there are powerful physical forces in us influenced by this nature. Physical desires are often difficult to control. It's easy to resolve to lose weight after a meal, but when hunger strikes before dinner, it attacks our will.

Living by the Spirit of Christ within us, diligently and faithfully using all the means of grace, overcoming the temptations of sin, and submitting ourselves to the active rule of grace is more necessary than ever before. Look at the times we live in. There are so many things to eat that we fail to use the gift of self-control. And there are immoral trends everywhere. In cyberspace, it's gotten out of hand. TV dramas, videos, books, and more leave us confused about where to focus our attention. In this age, we need the gift of self-control even more. The Holy Spirit commands us to restrain the desires of our flesh and put a bridle on them. Appetite itself is not a sin; it is a normal function and instinct of our body. However, if we fail to control our appetite, we will overeat, leading to obesity, which causes various diseases and ultimately leads to death.

Sexual impulses are also natural instincts of the body. That's why God instituted the lawful institution of marriage. Spouses have both sexual rights and duties towards one another. Premarital sex, adultery, and other such acts are forbidden by God. Our bodies are complex sensory organs that respond very sensitively to physical stimuli. God could have created humanity with the ability to procreate without any physical pleasure. Similarly, God could have created us with the ability to eat without the enjoyment of taste. However, God chose a better way. He gave sex as a gift, with all the accompanying physical pleasure. But using this gift comes with regulations that God has set. Sin is misusing this gift, using it in a way God has not allowed.

There are unconscious bodily impulses. You cannot make your heart beat with ethical thoughts. But not all bodily actions are unconscious. God commands us to control sexual behavior. **"And keep back Your servant from presumptuous sins; let them not have dominion over me. Then I shall be blameless, and I shall be innocent of great transgression."** (Psalm 19:13). The **"presumptuous sins"** here refer to intentional, planned sins. In other words, these are the sins we commit with deliberate intent, what we would call **"actual sins"** today. These kinds of sins can have a destructive influence on our souls, because we can voluntarily submit to the desires of sin and emotionally fall into the pleasure it provides.

Although we may not be able to control our recognition of sexual attraction, we can suppress the urge to act on it. Martin Luther explained the issue of lust in this way: **"It is impossible to prevent birds from flying over our heads, but it is another thing entirely to let them build a nest in our hair."** When we allow thoughts about the sexual to grow in our minds, simple awareness turns into lust and leads to actual sin. That is why, when listing the deeds of the flesh, the Apostle Paul declares that those who commit such sins will not inherit the Kingdom of God. In Ephesians, it says, **"But sexual immorality and all impurity or covetousness must not even be named among you, as is proper among saints"** (Ephesians 5:3). Psychologists might tell young people that sexual immorality is natural and normal. Indeed, sexual immorality may be natural to fallen humanity. But imagine justifying such actions. What would happen to society? God clearly forbids such actions.

We live in an era where maintaining chastity is extremely difficult. As sexual taboos disappear and our senses are bombarded daily with hedonistic stimuli in the secular culture, we are exposed to situations that lead us into sin through our thoughts, actions, and words. However, God's law is clear. God clearly says, "**No!**" Even though we live in a fallen culture, as His chosen people and citizens of His holy nation, He requires us to live holy lives, just as He is holy. Consider the dilemma faced by those who struggle with same-sex attraction. These individuals are in a serious quandary. God established marriage between a man and a woman, not between two men or two women. Just as God prohibits adultery for those who do not have a homosexual inclination, He demands chastity from those with homosexual tendencies as well. Nowhere in the Bible does it teach that homosexuality is lawful. Chastity pleases God. It is true that sexual purity is difficult to maintain because of the weakness of our flesh. However, it is possible to keep it. God commands us to live in chastity, and failure is sin. We must be patient with those who have fallen into sin, but it is not right to change God's standard to accommodate our weak actions. Changing God's law and calling good evil and evil good is disrespectful to God. The flesh is aligned with the world. Setting the standards of the flesh based on the world's criteria is not the proper stance of a believer.

A believer is one who lives according to the guidance of the Holy Spirit. They must live by the truth of God's Word. This is the way to live a life that pleases God. It is the path where we overcome sin and become more like the holy God. Regardless of the social customs and education that do not treat sin as sin, believers live by God's law. God wants us to live with life and peace. This is what the Holy Spirit within us desires. No one is without mistakes. However, we must not justify our mistakes but repent and turn back, living according to the guidance of the Holy Spirit, as new creations made in righteousness and truth. "**Flee from sexual immorality. Every other sin a person commits** is outside the body, but the sexually immoral person sins against his own body. Or do you not know that your body is a temple of the Holy Spirit within you, whom you have from God? You are not your own, for you were bought with a price. So glorify God in your body" (1 Corinthians 6:18-20).

We must be believers who win the battle against the flesh and live in the Spirit, bearing the fruit of the Spirit: "**But the fruit of the Spirit is love, joy, peace, forbearance, kindness, goodness, faithfulness, gentleness and self-control. Against such things there is no law. Those who belong to Christ Jesus have crucified the flesh with its passions and desires**" (Galatians 5:22-24). I dream of the history where more and more blessed saints live godly lives as people who are daily crucified to the world, declaring, "**I die daily.**" Let us thank God, who gives us victory in this war with the flesh.

• Special Meditation 3 •

The Battles Fought by the Saints:

The War with the Devil

"Finally, be strong in the Lord and in the strength of His might. Put on the full armor of God, so that you will be able to stand firm against the schemes of the devil. For our struggle is not against flesh and blood, but against the rulers, against the powers, against the world forces of this darkness, against the spiritual forces of wickedness in the heavenly places. Therefore, take up the full armor of God, so that you will be able to resist in the evil day, and having done everything, to stand firm" (Ephesians 6:10-13).

What is the hardest battle that saints, who must fight the threefold battle against the world, the flesh, and the devil every day, face? Without a doubt, it is the battle with the devil. The fight with the evil spirits, also called Satan or the devil, is the most terrifying war. Satan is not just an enemy; he is a sworn enemy. The Bible introduces many names for him: the ruler of darkness, the father of lies, the accuser of the brethren, and the cunning serpent. The battle with the devil is beyond human imagination. In verse 12, it introduces the powerful enemy that the saints face in this battle: "**For our struggle is not against**

flesh and blood, but against the rulers, against the powers, against the world forces of this darkness, against the spiritual forces of wickedness in the heavenly places."

Saints must fight not only the difficult battles against the world and the desires of the flesh but also the fierce battle against the terrifying evil spirits. Because of this, some people are so frightened by the thought of this battle that they even give up on their Christian faith entirely. Living in this world, which is full of suffering, is hard enough, and the thought of fighting a battle every day is enough to make them give up. However, dear brothers and sisters, it is too early to give up. Verse 11 encourages us to put on the full armor of God to be able to triumph in this battle. Although this battle is indeed the most terrifying and difficult one, it also assures us that it is a battle we can win. Otherwise, there would be no need to tell us to put on the full armor of God. First, let us understand who our sworn enemy, Satan, is.

The Devil is Not a Mythical Figure

Many people doubt or refuse to believe in the existence of the devil, thinking of him as merely a fictional character created by religious people. However, the devil is a real, existential being. Modern individuals, in particular, tend to view the devil merely as a type of ghost or spirit, and they make efforts to deny his existence. In Korea, due to legends and popular TV dramas like Three Thousand Miles of Legends that often feature ghost stories, the existence of ghosts is widely acknowledged. However, the devil or Satan and ghosts are clearly different. Non-believers often say that when a person dies, they become a ghost that wanders in the afterlife, and they perform rituals to appease these spirits. But the Bible never teaches that people become ghosts after death. Ghosts are evil spirits under the control of Satan. In the Gospels, the term used for demons is "**daimonion**" (δαιμονιον) in Greek, often in the plural form. These demons are always hostile spiritual beings in relation to God and humans. Since Baal-Zebul (Mark 3:22) is their king, demons are regarded as his servants. They mocked Jesus, accusing Him of being demon-possessed and performing miracles by the power of Baal-Zebul, the prince of demons.

When analyzing those possessed by demons, we see that demons are evil spirits that prevent people from being fully human, such as spirits that make people mute (Luke 11:14), cause epilepsy (Mark 9:17-18), make people wander between tombs (Luke 8:27), or cause other afflictions. Jesus proved that God's power is greater than the authority of demons by healing the possessed. He also gave His disciples the power to cast out demons and heal diseases (Luke 9:1). When He sent out 70 disciples, He allowed them to experience demons submitting to His name. Some people claim that all human diseases are related to demonic possession. However, the Bible does not teach that disease and demon possession are the same. The cases mentioned above may seem related to diseases, but they are clearly distinct. For example, in Matthew 4:24, as news of Jesus spread, people brought all the sick to Him, including those suffering from various diseases and afflictions, as well as demon-possessed individuals. The Bible distinguishes between diseases and demon possession. While simple diseases were healed through laying on of hands or anointing with oil, demons were cast out by commanding them to leave in the name of Jesus.

Demon possession, as frequently mentioned in the Gospels, is shown to be a special strategy of Satan to rally his forces against Christ and

His disciples. Therefore, even today, demons are part of the forces of evil actively opposing the Gospel. In this sense, the apostle Paul refers to the spiritual battle against evil spirits in today's passage.

If demons exist, then the existence of the devil is even clearer. If anyone doubts the existence of the devil or demons, I would ask: "**Do you believe in the existence of God? Do you believe that God is a spiritual being who has the power to influence people to do good? If you believe in spiritual beings that influence people to do good, why would you doubt the existence of spiritual beings that can influence people for evil?**" No matter how advanced science becomes or how civilization frees people from ignorance and superstition, the existence of evil spirits will remain as long as humanity exists. The image of the devil that people have is often of a ridiculous figure in red clothes holding a pitchfork. However, the Bible does not describe the devil in this childish, satirical manner. He is a far scarier, real, and dynamic being.

The Devil is a Master of Disguise

The image of the devil presented in the Bible is that of a being who excels in disguising himself as an angel of light. In 2 Corinthians 11:14, it says, "**For Satan himself masquerades as an angel of light.**" He is exceptionally skilled at presenting himself as a highly good and virtuous being, which makes it easy for most people to be deceived. For this reason, the Bible calls him "**cunning.**" This cunning refers to his exceptional craftiness in deceiving people. Satan's deception first appeared in the Garden of Eden, when he deceived Adam and Eve through the serpent, which the Bible describes as **"cunning"** (Genesis 3:1). Satan is not a foolish clown or a simple trickster. He is a deceitful fraud, a master of persuasion. His appearance is remarkably beautiful. The ruler of darkness dresses in the clothes of light. Many people fall for his elaborate rhetoric and transformation into an angel. Jesus refers to him as **"the father of lies"** (John 8:44), and we must take this teaching to heart. Satan is a master of deception, able to impersonate Christ's apostles, and he is skilled at convincing people that he is the true embodiment of truth.

How did Satan tempt Eve? He distorted the truth, making his words appear as if they were the truth. Similarly, today, if we are not spiritually alert, we too will fall under the influence of Satan's agents and stray from the truth, engaging in wicked deeds. In this way, we may forsake God's will and be led by the lusts of the flesh, indulging in the pleasures of the world, living as though these are God's true blessings. Satan will make us believe that this way of life is aligned with God's will, and will prevent us from thinking that suffering and reproach for the sake of the Gospel are necessary. Those who live in the world's comforts will see these as true happiness, dismissing the sacrifices of the faithful as foolish extremes. This is the masterful deception of Satan, who is adept at making people mistake falsehoods for the truth. As long as we fail to know the truth deeply and firmly, we will be misled into believing what is not true, and we will continue to follow after it. Therefore, we must be rooted deeply in the truth of God's word and stand firm on it. We must adhere to apostolic teaching and live by it.

Satan's disguises deceive in two ways. One way is that he makes us underestimate our own strength, and the other way is that he makes us overestimate it. In both cases, Satan's goal is to deceive us and bring us down. Peter, for example, underestimated Satan's power. When Jesus told Peter that he would deny Him and fall, Peter boldly declared that this could never happen. He said, **"Lord, I am ready to go with You to prison and to death"** (Luke 22:33). Peter had overestimated his own abilities and underestimated the relentless power of Satan. He publicly dismissed the power of Satan as described by Jesus. As a result, just as Jesus had predicted, Peter denied Him three times before the rooster crowed that night.

From this incident, believers must remember that Satan is not to be taken lightly. However, does this mean we are powerless against his deceptions? No. Satan's power is limited. While he is stronger than us, we are more than capable of defeating him, and we have an Advocate who will actually fight for us. The Bible clearly says, **"He who is in you is greater than he who is in the world"** (1 John 4:4). The apostle James also says, **"Submit yourselves, then,to God. Resist the devil, and he will flee from you"** (James 4:7). If we live by the power of the Holy Spirit, who dwells within us, we will be able to resist and defeat Satan's crafty schemes.

Satan is like a roaring lion

He has the form of a lion that roams around, roaring, seeking someone to devour (1 Peter 5:8). Recall that he was previously described as a master of disguise. The lion, which is used as a symbol of Christ, is mimicked by Satan, the archetype of the Antichrist. However, the actions of these two lions are completely opposite. Satan's work, like that of a roaring lion, is to devour, but the lion of Judah represents the Lord who redeems sinners.

The strength of a lion is that of the king of the jungle. No one dares to oppose its majesty. However, this destructive power cannot compare to Christ's strength. One of the reasons Christ came to this earth was to destroy the works of the devil (1 John 3:8). Therefore, from the moment Jesus took on human form and came to this world, Satan made every effort to kill Him.

In fact, when Jesus began His public ministry, Satan tempted Him to oppose His mission to redeem sinners. He even used Jesus' most beloved disciples to do so. Satan is like a roaring lion, tirelessly searching for someone to devour. He works ceaselessly, boasting endless energy. He never misses an opportunity and knows exactly who his prey is. Just as the ruler of the world's air, he shows the world's fleeting wealth and power, tempting Jesus after His 40-day fast, hoping He would be overcome by hunger, testing Him with bread, and questioning God's power. But we vividly remember that the Son of God, Jesus Christ, resisted all of Satan's cunning.

What believers should remember is that although Satan is weaker than Christ's power and wisdom, he is much stronger than ours. He is not as strong as Christ, but he is stronger than us. Therefore, to destroy the works of the devil, we must hold fast to the Lord Jesus Christ, who came to this world in human form. We must walk in Him, so we can gain even one prize of victory. Without this, no one can defeat Satan's power. However, the power of the Holy Spirit can easily subdue Satan's strength. Though Satan shook Peter like wheat, that was only temporary.

If we underestimate Satan, pride—the forerunner of destruction—will enter us. However, if we overestimate him, we give him undue honor and respect. We must avoid both.

Satan is only a created being. He is finite, and his power is limited. He operates only under God's permissive will. In the Old Testament, when Satan tried to test Job, he clearly operated within God's sovereign will. Satan is stronger than humans; he has the power to destroy all of Job's wealth and children in one blow.

However, he cannot compare to God. He can only operate effectively when he aligns with the side of the strong. If he sides with the weak, he might get a temporary meal, but in the end, he will be destroyed. Stand on the side of the stronger Lord. Joshua's confession, **"As for me and my house, we will serve the Lord,"** must always be our confession.

Satan's knowledge and wisdom are greater than ours, but he is not omniscient. His power is remarkable, but it is not almighty. His influence is broader than ours, but he is not omnipresent. Satan cannot occupy more than one place at a time. Like all angels, whether good or evil, Satan is bound by time and space. Statistically, you will probably never face Satan directly in your lifetime. One of Satan's lower-ranking spirits, or an evil spirit, may confront you, but Satan will use his time and space to face greater targets than us. Even when Satan directly attacked Jesus, he **"left Him for a while"** (Luke 4:13).

Therefore, in this passage, the Apostle Paul makes it clear that our struggle is not against flesh and blood but **"against the rulers, against the authorities, against the powers of this dark world and against the spiritual forces of evil in the heavenly realms."**

One thing we must address here is that, as the world becomes more chaotic, Satanism and films or dramas that feature ghosts are spreading incorrect perceptions to people. In the past, movies like The Exorcist and The Omen dominated, and now, movies about ghosts, starting with Whispering Corridors and The Coffin, continue to be made. There are countless types of ghosts, such as the Mongdal ghost, the virgin ghost, the fairy lady, the tomb ghost, the egg ghost, the tree ghost, the water ghost, and so on. Among the cults, there are those who emphasize the doctrine of ghosts. They claim that certain ghosts cause certain sins. For example, there are ghosts of alcohol, depression, and cigarettes, and many pastors emphasize the ability to cast out these ghosts. One pastor, for instance, said that expelling the cigarette ghost is indicated by a sigh, as the ghost of cigarettes has left. The cigarette ghost enters when you inhale but leaves when you exhale. Vomiting is considered evidence that the alcohol ghost has departed. They claim that all sins we can identify are associated with ghosts, and therefore we must cast them out and take necessary measures to ensure they cannot return.

However, these teachings are not mentioned anywhere in the Bible, yet people listen to them. Sadly, excessive focus on Satan and ghosts causes us to pay less attention to Christ, and rather than pleasing God, it leads people into worshipping Satan, which is part of Satan's plan. I was once shocked after hearing the story of Pastor Joel Beeke, who met a Satan worshipper on an airplane. He was on his way to a meeting in a certain area when, as the in-flight meal was being served, the passenger sitting next to him began praying fervently. Pastor Beeke, happy to see a fellow Christian, greeted him and asked if he was a Christian as well. The passenger replied that he was not a Christian. When Beeke asked whom he had been praying to, the man said he had prayed to Satan. When asked what he prayed for, he said, "**I pray that 200 churches in the U.S. close every day.**" Beeke, having witnessed firsthand a Satan worshipper and hearing their prayer, shared the experience and how he diligently preached the gospel. We must seriously consider why the church is collapsing globally. As long as we carry the gospel, we can never retreat in our battle with the devil.

Can a believer be possessed by a ghost? No. A Christian cannot be possessed because the Holy Spirit resides within them. Where the

Holy Spirit is present, there is freedom. To be controlled by an evil spirit while simultaneously being indwelled by the Holy Spirit would make the redemptive work of Christ meaningless. Therefore, true born-again believers do not fear ghosts or the power of the devil. Evil spirits work through those who are possessed by false spirits. If one is not bound by the truth, they will be captured by all kinds of powers, false signs, and wonders (2 Thessalonians 2:9-10). Focusing too much on the devil can lead to a denial of the very reality of sin. While Satan may encourage us to sin, we cannot shift the blame for our actions onto him. He is, of course, the tempter. But one does not need to be possessed by the devil to become drunk.

There is a deeply ingrained sinful tendency within us that can lead to drunkenness. We cannot excuse our behavior by saying the devil made us do it. While we may say we were tempted by Satan, we cannot claim that we were under his control or that we sinned because we were coerced. We are responsible for our own sins.

Those who claim that sin occurs because of ghostly control are wrong in two ways. First, they avoid personal responsibility for their sins. Saying **"the devil made me do it"** is simply an excuse for one's sinful actions. Second, they propagate the mistaken belief that we can only be freed from sin by casting out demons, which contradicts the concept of sanctification taught throughout the Bible. We are made holy by God's truth alone. Our holy lives are not a result of casting out demons but are a manifestation of the power of the Holy Spirit within us. Therefore, we must escape from any new cult-like, pseudo-Christian practices, such as relying on exorcism rituals and the belief that everything evil is caused by evil spirits, which is not much different from traditional shamanistic rituals. To preserve your spiritual life, you must distance yourself from such wrong teachings. You must leave them.

What Satan Can Do to Humans

When Satan attacks believers, he uses two main methods: temptation and accusation. Let's first look at the issue of temptation. The greatest temptations of Satan in the Bible can be found in the book of Genesis and the Gospel of Matthew. These two places highlight Satan's temptations at the beginning of humanity and at the start of Jesus Christ's public ministry. Let's look at what Satan's work as a tempter involves.

Before we think about Satan's temptations, there is an essential piece of knowledge we must understand: his cunning. Satan's craftiness is one of the most extensive tools he uses in tempting believers. The cunning temptations of Satan are most clearly revealed in Genesis, where Satan tempts the first humans, Adam and Eve, and in the Gospel of Matthew, where Satan tempts God's Son, Jesus Christ. In these two incidents, we can observe several things about Satan's cunning temptations. First, he tempts us by causing us to doubt the truth. In Genesis 3:1, we see this: **"Did God really say, 'You shall not eat from any tree in the garden?'"** Satan knew very well what God's command was to Adam and Eve. This is one of the reasons why we often fall into Satan's temptations so easily. As mentioned earlier, Satan, who disguises himself as an angel of light, is highly skilled in distorting God's truth. When he tempted Jesus, he also used God's word to do so. Therefore, we should never take the truth lightly or hastily. We must learn it clearly and know it firmly. We should strive to hold on to what we have learned and be certain in it.

Satan brought doubt into Eve's mind, making her question whether God's rules and commandments were harsh. He made her feel that a loving God would not prohibit them from eating the delicious fruit.

He sowed seeds of doubt by asking, **"Did God really say, 'You shall not eat from any tree in the garden?'"** To this, Eve responded, **"We may eat the fruit of the trees in the garden, but of the fruit of the tree which is in the middle of the garden, God has said, 'You shall not eat it, nor shall you touch it, lest you die.'"**

God had given Adam and Eve everything in the Garden of Eden. There was only one exception. In the center of the garden, there were two trees: the Tree of Life and the Tree of the Knowledge of Good and Evil. They were allowed to eat from the Tree of Life, but they were commanded not to eat the fruit from the Tree of the Knowledge of Good and Evil, known as the **"forbidden fruit."** As long as they obeyed this one rule, they had the freedom to enjoy everything else in the garden. How incredible is this grace! However, Satan caused them to doubt whether their freedom was truly real. Satan made them question, **"Did God really tell you not to eat from any tree in the garden?"** This question revealed Satan's cunning. His aim was to make them believe that God, who placed a restriction on one tree, was limiting their freedom. Satan wanted them to think, **"If God is so loving, why would He forbid us to eat from this tree?"** Satan's question was enough to make them doubt God's goodness, justice, and mercy.

God had freely given Adam and Eve everything in the garden—nothing in it was created by them. Not a single plant, rock, or creature existed because of their actions. Every beautiful thing in the garden, from the sky, the lush pastures, the birds in the air, the wild animals on the earth, and even the microscopic organisms, were created by God. Everything was designed for the perfect and unblemished life of humanity. In comparison, there was only one exception: the prohibition to eat from the Tree of the Knowledge of Good and Evil. God permitted them to eat from the Tree of Life because His will was for them to have eternal life, but this life could only be obtained if they obeyed His command not to eat the forbidden fruit. If they had obeyed, they would have enjoyed the blessings of eternal life in the Garden of Eden.

God's law was established based on His justice. By placing even a small restriction on them, He made them aware that they were created beings, and He also showed them that any freedom outside His law is not true freedom. Just as the freedom of fish that left the water is death, humans also enjoy true freedom only within the boundaries of God's law. Satan sought to reverse this truth. He led the beautiful humans to believe that living with restrictions was impossible, thus causing them to doubt God's goodness and justice.

This method of sowing doubt is still one of the most frequent tools Satan uses to tempt believers today. Issues like tithing or keeping the Sabbath are examples. God is the owner of everything. Whatever we earn through our work comes from God. Believers are those who acknowledge God's sovereignty over everything they have. However, unbelievers do not recognize God's ownership. Thus, they do not give even a single cent in offerings to God, as they are incapable of doing so. Money is their idol.

However, for believers, we must acknowledge God's ownership — in other words, we must always deeply remember that Adam and Eve, as creations in the Garden of Eden, were beings who could not live apart from God's law. By giving the tithe to the Lord, we demonstrate that we belong to God, His people. It is an act of faith, offering what belongs to God to God. Now, let's suppose that God required a tenth from us. Should we do it or not? We should still do it. Even if God asked for everything, we must give it — this is the principle. There is no room for choice. However, a merciful God did not ask for the entire tenth;

He only asked for the tithe — one-tenth. The other nine parts can be used and consumed freely. However, this does not mean that we should wastefully indulge in our desires or use the remaining nine recklessly. True Christians seriously contemplate how to use the remaining nine in a way that aligns with God's will, and they strive for righteous economic activity. The clear truth is that God is the owner of everything. The same applies to the observance of the Sabbath. God, who allowed the weekly cycle, commanded us to work for six days. But one day, the Sabbath, is the Lord's Day, and we are commanded to keep it holy.

Yet, just like with the tithe, Satan causes doubt about God's mercy and justice. He might ask, **"Did God really say you should keep the Lord's Day every week?"** or **"Did God really command that all the produce you earn should be given to Him?"** Satan's intention is to make us think that God is being harsh. Once such doubt and negativity take root in the heart, the issue becomes severe. We end up using the Sabbath according to our own will, claiming it is true freedom. He will make us give up the practice of tithing, convincing us that we have the right to use everything as we see fit. Ultimately, instead of enjoying God's mercy and goodness and causing us to rejoice in Him, Satan's cunning temptation seeks to make us view God as a tyrant or a harsh dictator, leading us away from Him.

The temptations experienced by the first ancestors of humanity are still the same temptations that believers face today. In fact, God has allowed us to enjoy many things, but He only forbids one thing, yet we claim that God is not allowing us to enjoy anything. This is how Satan tempts us. Let's observe the stages of Satan's temptation. He first caused Eve to doubt God's truth. Eve clearly answered that they could eat from every tree, but the fruit of the tree in the middle of the garden was forbidden by God's command, saying, **"You shall not eat it,** nor touch it, lest you die." Of course, Eve's response was not entirely accurate. However, her answer clearly reflected God's command: **"Do not eat, and if you do, you will die."**

Satan immediately countered, attacking God's truth head-on: **"You will not surely die. For God knows that in the day you eat of it, your eyes will be opened, and you will be like God, knowing good and evil"** (Genesis 3:4-5). Satan boldly denied God's truth. Once doubt enters the heart, the next step is no longer to verify the truth but to strongly reject it. Instead of seeking to understand God's truth, people move to oppose the one who established the law, God Himself. It begins with sarcastic remarks and escalates into direct attacks. The conversation spirals into an emotional battle rather than a rational one. In the end, believers are no exception to this. At this point, Eve is completely deceived by Satan's falsehood, which sounds so convincing: **"You will not surely die!" "That's true? God is deceiving us? How could He do that? It doesn't make sense! He's forbidding us because He doesn't want us to become like Him!"** Once doubt and denial take root in the heart, action becomes inevitable. Eve took the forbidden fruit and ate it, marking the pivotal moment when the tragedy of humanity began.

The issue at hand is whose words are true and factual. Eve did not engage in verifying whether God's word was true or Satan's word was true. Jesus clearly teaches that Satan is **"a liar and the father of lies"** (John 8:44). But Satan deceived Eve, saying, **"No, I am telling the truth, and God is lying to you."** This deception was so strong that it made Eve doubt God's truth. That doubt eventually led her to reject God. She believed it was true freedom and thought she was acting rightly, but the result was an irreversible tragedy. Satan's method of attacking believers has always been the same, and it still works today. It attacks the authenticity of God's truth. Satan tries to make God appear as a liar, making His truth seem useless. Moreover, Satan cleverly explained his reasoning, which led Eve to fall for the deception. Satan's lie was that God had forbidden them to eat the fruit because He was jealous. He said, **"If you eat the fruit, you will become like God, and God didn't want that,"** implying that God did not want them to gain the knowledge that He had.

How persuasive this reasoning was! The fruit from the tree of knowledge of good and evil, when compared to the fruit of the tree of life, was nothing. In terms of its effects, the fruit of the knowledge of good and evil only gave the ability to discern between good and evil. But the tree of life produced fruit that would grant eternal life. God permitted Adam and Eve to eat from the tree of life. Yet, Satan made Eve believe that God's command to avoid the tree of the knowledge of good and evil meant that God was unfair, dishonest, and unworthy of trust. This was clearly a sin.

In her innocence, Eve succumbed to Satan's logic and persuasion. This is something that still happens today. Satan attacks the integrity of God's truth. Consider the apostle Paul. People relentlessly attacked him, claiming that he was not truly sent by God, spreading malicious rumors that disrupted his ministry. How many times did Paul, in his letters, mention that he was **"called by the will of God to be an apostle"** (Romans 1:1)? He even spent considerable space in 1 Corinthians defending his apostolic authority. Today, many malicious words circulate, defaming church leaders. On the internet, some of these accusations are so shameful that it is embarrassing to even read them. People listen to such articles because they are using the most persuasive arguments to undermine the leaders of the church, claiming they are not worthy of the position God gave them. While it may seem that the attacks are directed at the individual church leaders, in reality, they are attacks on God, who appointed them. Whether the attack is on a pastor or a believer, the principle is the same. Some of these accusations aim to degrade the dignity and character of church leaders, causing God's truth to be taken lightly.

As a result, the authority of the preached word is undermined, and people begin to believe that their own opinions are more valid. This is happening in many parts of the church today. That is why the apostle Paul pleads: "**As workers together with Him, we urge you not to receive the grace of God in vain**" (2 Corinthians 6:1).

Satan's temptation here is to cause doubt about God's commands, suggesting that they are unfair and selfish. This is often the argument of the weak. Even if the strong act fairly, their actions can be seen as unfair by the weak. Even if the strong help and sacrifice for the weak, the weak may perceive it as unjust. This is something we experience in the church as well. A true Christian accepts God's truth as truth. We recognize and accept the leaders God has placed in the church. Through them, God reveals His truth. We cannot say that we receive God's grace while ignoring and despising His appointed leaders. We cannot confidently claim that we can receive grace without them. This is a work of Satan, trying to make people deny God's truth.

The gifts God has given to the church to "**equip the saints for the work of service, to the building up of the body of Christ**" (Ephesians 4:12) are His servants who preach the Word. In both the Old and New Testaments, God's servants are acknowledged as sinful human beings, just like all believers, and there is no distinction between high and low status. Even though Aaron and Miriam criticized Moses' leadership based on his clear faults, God did not say that they were innocent. Their argument was that God spoke only to Moses, not to them, and that Moses acted according to his own will. Numbers 12:2 states, **"And the Lord heard it."** God then called all three of them and said, **"If there is a prophet among you, I, the Lord, make Myself known to him in a vision; I speak to him in a dream. Not so with My servant Moses; He is faithful in all My house. I speak with him face to face, even plainly, and not in dark sayings; and he sees the form of the Lord"** (Numbers 12:6-8). Despite Aaron and Miriam's criticisms based on Moses' flaws, their actions provoked God's anger.

Of course, today's pastors are not Moses. Applying God's interaction with Moses to church leaders today may be an overstep, as no pastor today meets with God face to face like Moses did. While pastors may experience spiritual communion with God, so do believers. However, the principle we must extract is clear: any attempt to discredit God's appointed leaders in the church is an attack on God's Word. This is a temptation from Satan. Even when Saul, with his obvious faults, deserved to die, David refused to harm him because he was God's anointed. David completely entrusted the matter to God. Attacking church leaders brings no blessings to anyone. Therefore, King Jehoshaphat of Judah, facing the allied forces, declared to his people: **"Believe in the Lord your God, and you shall be established; believe His prophets, and you shall prosper"** (2 Chronicles 20:20).

In ancient battles, the main objective was always to defeat the enemy's leader. The soldiers would strive to protect their own leader because once the leader falls, the rest are easily conquered. Who does Satan target the most? Why did he target Adam and Eve in the Garden of Eden? Because they were representatives of humanity. Why did he target Jesus Christ, the Son of God? Because He was the second Adam, representing the saved people of God. Why does Satan continuously attack church leaders? Because they represent the church. When the representative of the church falls, everyone within it is easily taken. Satan's primary goal, which he constantly aims at and targets, is always the church leaders.

Satan, who never forgets his past experience of bringing down Adam and Eve in the Garden of Eden, still uses every possible method today to bring down church leaders. Any doubts, negative thoughts, or actions that prevent us from receiving the Word of Truth as it is must be avoided, even if we think we are right. We must not receive God's grace in vain. Look at how Satan is attacking God's integrity systematically. Did not Adam and Eve believe they had a right to the tree? Satan made God's commandment seem unjust, asserting that the regulation God set was unfair. He claimed that even if people could not please God, they still had the right to do whatever they wanted. This way of thinking causes many people to fall. The same demonic thought appears every day in our minds. Every time we sin, it is because we want to do what we desire rather than what God desires for us. As long as we harbor the rebellious thought deep inside us that God's law is unfair, we can never please God or obey His truth.

Consider the rights we have. Where do these rights come from? If we analyze the rights we assume are inherent to being human, we will find that they ultimately come from God. The right to rule over the entire Garden of Eden was given to humanity by the Creator, not something humanity earned on its own. God is the true owner of Eden. He entrusted it to humanity to manage, cultivate, and increase. Therefore, humanity's basic rights come from God, not from the individual. This means we must always submit to God's authority and live according to His laws in order to have a joyful and righteous faith life. Whatever rights we have, they are all given by God. We cannot exercise any right that God has not granted. Yet, humans act as if these rights are their own, and they boldly speak and act in ways that deny God's truth. I personally have much to repent about this. As Apostle Peter clearly advises, I feel that I have often acted as if certain things are mine, in pride. What does Apostle Peter teach? **"Be shepherds of God's flock that is under your care, watching over them—not because you must, but because you are willing, as God wants you to be; not pursuing dishonest gain, but eager to serve; not lording it over those entrusted to you, but being examples to the flock"** (1 Peter 5:2-3). The part that particularly struck me was the instruction not to **"lord it over those entrusted to you."** I honestly try to follow the rest of the teachings, and I believe the Lord, the Good Shepherd, knows my heart. However, I have struggled with being a good example to the flock, as I should. I fear that I may be guilty of acting with pride as a pastor, or exercising human authority as a professor.

We must continually pray for church leaders to be faithful to their role and not fall into Satan's temptations. Both pastors and congregations should be cautious and avoid falling into the sin of doubting or rejecting the truth of God. We must hold tightly to God's Word and resist the temptations of the enemy.

• Special Meditation 4 •

The Temptation of Jesus Christ[56]

The temptation faced by Adam and Eve and the temptation faced by Jesus Christ were not the same. Adam and Eve's temptation occurred in the middle of paradise. Adam had his wife, Eve, to comfort him. He had never experienced hunger. He could eat delicious food whenever he reached out his hand. Everything was within easy reach. However, Christ was alone. The loneliness was difficult, but the environment He was in was even worse. In the Judean desert, scorpions were abundant, thorn bushes grew thick, and several types of birds inhabited the area. In a situation where there was no one to share comfort with, Jesus went without food for forty days. It was then that the cunning Satan approached. Although the situations were completely different, the issue was the same: the truth of God's Word was being attacked.

Satan approached Jesus and said, **"If you are the Son of God, tell these stones to become bread"** (Matthew 4:3). The key point to note here is that Satan did not say, **"You are the Son of God..."** but rather, **"If**

---

56 Based on Matthew 4:1-11.

you are the Son of God..." The emphasis is on "**if.**" Why "**if**"? This was a tactic by Satan to cast doubt on and deny Jesus' self-awareness as the Son of God.

Do you remember the voice Jesus heard from heaven before He fasted for forty days? In the scene when Jesus was baptized in the Jordan River, Matthew records it in 3:16-17: "**As soon as Jesus was baptized, he went up out of the water. At that moment heaven was opened, and he saw the Spirit of God descending like a dove and alighting on him. And a voice from heaven said, 'This is my Son, whom I love; with him I am well pleased.'**" Luke 3:22 records the same event, saying, "**You are my Son, whom I love; with you I am well pleased.**" God had clearly proclaimed and confirmed that Jesus was His beloved Son. This was to affirm to Jesus, as He began His public ministry to save sinners, the path He must take as God's Son.

However, now after Jesus had fasted for forty days, in a state of extreme hunger, Satan came to Him and said, "**If you are the Son of God...**" In other words, "**Are you really sure you are the Son of God? If you are truly the Son whom God loves, what are you doing here? You shouldn't be here in this desolate place with nothing to eat. Let's see if your situation confirms you are the beloved Son of God. You must be terribly hungry, right? If you are truly God's Son, why don't you make bread out of these stones? It's not really wrong, is it?**"

Of course, after fasting for forty days, Jesus must have been extremely hungry. Anyone who has fasted knows that even a one-day fast can be difficult. Fasting for 10, 20, 30, or even 40 days is something only a few can do. The thought of food constantly circles in one's mind. Even when you close your eyes, you can picture a table full of food. After such a fast, it would be natural to seek food. Turning a few stones into bread would have been an easy task for the Lord. However, Jesus responded to Satan immediately: **"Man shall not live on bread alone, but on every word that comes from the mouth of God."** For Jesus, the hunger of the flesh was not as important as being spiritually hungry and thirsty for righteousness. His food and drink were clearly stated in John 4:32 and beyond, where He tells His disciples that there is food they do not know about. It was, **"to do the will of Him who sent me and to finish His work."**

The driving force behind Jesus' life was not physical hunger or thirst. As He traveled from Judea to Galilee, passing through Samaria, He was exhausted and hungry. While His disciples went to find food, He shared the gospel with the Samaritan woman. When the disciples returned, He told them He had no hunger for food; His focus was entirely on fulfilling the will of His Father to save sinners. This was the purpose for which He had come.

Satan tried to disrupt Jesus' self-awareness and mission. However, Jesus saw through Satan's deceitful words. In Jesus' heart, there was no **"if."** God had already declared Him to be His beloved Son. There was no doubt about it. There was no need for doubt. Jesus lived by every word that came from God's mouth. Adam and Eve, on the other hand, fell for Satan's temptation and denied the truth of God's Word. But Jesus did not step back even an inch. This is the lesson that believers must learn today. If God is for us, who can be against us? The Apostle Paul's declaration remains the only way to counter Satan's crafty strategies, which seek to bring us down. Satan attacks the identity of believers, using strategies that deny the truth of God's Word. He seeks to make us doubt that we are children of God. We will address Satan's second strategy of accusation in more detail later, but one thing is clear: **"To those who received Him, to those who believed in His name,**

He gave the right to become children of God." All believers who trust in Jesus Christ are, no matter what anyone says, children of God. There is no need for the word "**if**" for believers. We are the sons and daughters of God.

Satan attacked Jesus once more, but this time, he quoted scripture that Jesus Himself was using. Satan took Jesus to the top of the temple and said, "**If you are the Son of God, throw yourself down,**" and he cited a passage from the Bible: "**For He will command His angels concerning you, and they will lift you up in their hands, so that you will not strike your foot against a stone**" (Matthew 4:5-6). Of course, Satan did not use this Bible verse correctly. He misinterpreted it. By contrasting the Bible with itself, Satan twisted the meaning. He appealed to the Bible to justify sin.

But God didn't say that if Jesus jumped from the temple, the angels would protect Him from injury. What God said was that He would protect Jesus and uphold Him, so His feet would not strike a stone as He fulfilled His redemptive mission. The misused scripture Satan quoted implied: "**Okay, Jesus, you say you believe in the Bible. Then prove it. Test God. Jump down from here and let's see if angels will really catch you.**" But Jesus firmly rejected this temptation.

He responded to Satan's challenge with another scripture: "**Do not put the Lord your God to the test.**" Jesus was very clear: "**I know God's promises, but do not try to test Him with conditions attached. The Bible also says that you should not test God (Deuteronomy 6:16). I know that the angels will protect me, but I don't need to throw myself off the temple to prove it. God has said it, and I am sure His word is true.**"

After all the temptations were over, when Satan left Him, angels came and attended to Jesus (Matthew 4:11). We are often easily swayed by

Satan's tactics, and as a result, we end up denying God. God has never said it is okay to test Him. The only exception to this is in Malachi 3:10: **"Bring the whole tithe into the storehouse, that there may be food in my house. Test me in this,"** says the Lord Almighty, **"and see if I will not throw open the floodgates of heaven and pour out so much blessing that there will not be room enough to store it."** However, we often fall into the temptation to test God in other ways—trying to bargain with Him over material things, health, and blessings.

To test God in a way that denies His existence or power is wrong. Some years ago, a person drank the venom of a snake while proclaiming loudly on television that believers would not be harmed by venomous snakes. This was a clear case of testing God, and it ended in tragedy. Similarly, throwing a child into a lion's den and saying they will not be harmed is a foolish test of God, and the child would be harmed. While Daniel survived in the lion's den and his friends survived the fiery furnace, they did not throw themselves into those situations to **"see if God would save them."** They simply held onto the truth and the faith in the God who is truthful. They were ready to remain faithful even if God chose not to deliver them from the fire or the lions. In the end, God did deliver them.

In Acts 28, Paul was a prisoner on his way to Rome when he encountered a shipwreck. After being saved, Paul and the other survivors were treated by the locals on the island of Malta. While sitting by a fire, a venomous snake bit Paul, and everyone expected him to die. However, Paul showed no ill effects, and the locals were amazed, ultimately hearing the gospel. Again, Paul did not intentionally put himself in harm's way to test God.

No one in the Bible ever tested God in this way. However, we often try to bargain with God for material things or health. We ask questions like: "**If God doesn't make me wealthy, does that mean He doesn't exist? If God doesn't restore my health, is He not real? If God doesn't give me a good job, is He not faithful?**" We must never test God in these ways. But we must be faithful in giving our tithes, because God promises to pour out blessings when we do. This doesn't mean that if we give our full tithes, we will suddenly become rich, but it does mean that God will provide for us abundantly and allow us to share our blessings with others and further His gospel.

When we give our tithes, it is not a matter of calculating precisely or giving only on a portion of income, like just from our salary, while keeping the gains from other sources for ourselves. This is not complete obedience. We must give our full tithe and be generous in all aspects of our lives. God's law is clear: those who sow generously will reap generously, and those who sow sparingly will reap sparingly. Therefore, we should be faithful and generous, and God will bless us accordingly.

Let us now look at the final temptation of Jesus by Satan. This time, Satan changed his strategy. He showed Jesus all the kingdoms of the world and their glory. Then, he said, "**All this I will give you, if you will bow down and worship me.**" In Luke 4:6, Satan's specific words are added: "**I will give you all their authority and splendor; it has been given to me, and I can give it to anyone I want to. So, if you worship me, it will all be yours.**" Authority and glory—these are the things that every human being desires. This was a huge temptation. Who would not be tempted by the offer of all the kingdoms of the world and their glory? "**If I can gain all this wealth and power just by bowing down once, why not?**" we might think. But when such an offer is presented, would you be able to refuse it?

Consider if someone offered you 5 billion dollars in exchange for a single visit to a temple to bow down before an idol. Would you turn down the offer without hesitation? If you hesitate, listen to what Jesus answered: **"Jesus answered, 'Get behind me, Satan! For it is written: Worship the Lord your God and serve Him only.'"** (Matthew 4:10). Here again, Satan's purpose is clear: to make Jesus deny God's Word. If Jesus had accepted Satan's offer, He would have had to abandon God's Word. But Jesus fought back with Scripture. He quoted Deuteronomy 6:13: **"Worship the Lord your God and serve Him only!"** This response reaffirmed that Jesus lived by every word that proceeds from the mouth of God.

This scene reminds us to examine our own prayer lives more deeply. Jesus taught us not to worry about worldly concerns like **"What shall we eat, what shall we drink, or what shall we wear?"** (Matthew 6:31-32), for our Heavenly Father knows what we need. Yet, when we pray, we often assume that God does not know what we need, and we petition Him for our needs as though He is unaware. Though Jesus taught that **"man does not live on bread alone,"** we are often so easily tempted by the allure of the wealth and glory of the world, like Satan's offer, that we neglect God's Word. It becomes easier to deny God's Word and follow after worldly things.

Even if we physically attend church, our hearts may still be far from God, focused on worldly matters. How many of us skip worship because of concerns over survival or financial gain? How often do we neglect worship for personal gain or desire? Satan is crafty, and we must not be caught off guard by his schemes. Even now, we are in a spiritual battle. If we let our guard down, we will fall into temptation. Our primary concern should be seeking God's kingdom and righteousness. Jesus promises that when we do so, God will provide for all our needs, even the things that the world seeks after. We do need bread, but we do not live by bread alone. We must not worship money, power, or anything visible in place of God. We must worship God and serve Him alone. This is the key to keeping Satan at bay.

The test faced by both Adam and Jesus revolves around one issue: the reliability of God's Word. If even a small doubt creeps into our trust in God's Word, we open ourselves to temptation. Satan knows how to exploit that crack in our trust. True faith is believing in God as though we see Him, even though He is invisible. It does not mean creating an image of God to worship. God clearly commands in the Ten Commandments: **"You shall not make for yourselves a carved image, or any likeness of anything that is in heaven above or on the earth below or in the waters beneath the earth. You shall not bow down to them or serve them, for I the Lord your God am a jealous God..."** (Exodus 20:4-5).

God forbids the creation of idols or images to worship. Today, many churches create representations of Jesus, such as crucifixes and paintings, but this is not what God commanded. God wants us to obey His commands, not substitute them with representations. He kept the Ark of the Covenant and even the original Bible hidden to prevent people from treating them as idols to be worshiped. The true faith is believing and trusting in what God has spoken. When we fail to trust God's Word, we open ourselves up to all kinds of sin. Sin is choosing what we want over what God desires. Our desires must align with God's written Word, and if we place His Word aside, we leave ourselves vulnerable to sin.

Satan's ultimate goal is to make us doubt and disobey God's Word. When we focus only on what seems right to us, we move further away from obeying God's Word. Not trusting in God's Word is the root of all sin, and it is also the strategy Satan uses to tempt us. We must not forget that the attack of Satan always targets our trust in God's truth. In every temptation, the underlying issue is whether we will trust God's Word. Satan knows that if he can make us question or ignore God's Word, he can lead us astray. We must remain vigilant, trusting in God's promises and keeping our focus on His truth. Only by doing so can we resist the enemy's temptations and remain faithful to our Lord.

Satan constantly sets traps to devour us. It may seem illogical, but the way to avoid these traps is either not to pass by them or to avoid getting caught even if we see them. However, the one who sets the trap keeps these two things in mind while preparing it: he sets it in a way that we have no choice but to pass through it, and he presents temptations that we cannot resist. For a bird, he provides its favorite food, and for an animal, he sets food that awakens an irresistible appetite. A trap always has the property that if we're not alert, we'll inevitably fall into it. The way to resist such temptations might seem unrealistic, but it's either not to see them at all or to resist them once we see them. However, it is impossible to avoid something that has been deliberately placed in front of us. There are also traps set in ways that are invisible to us, and so we inevitably fall into traps that are specifically targeted at us. However, there is a third way to avoid or overcome these temptations. That is to look at something much better than the temptation and pass through the trap. When a person experiences great joy, even a small sorrow can be overcome. Therefore, those who love God and delight in Him can easily overcome the low-level temptations of this world. Even if there are traps we cannot see, God sees them, and by walking with Him—who is the light and the way—He opens our spiritual eyes through His Word so that we can see the traps. [57]As the

---

[57] This is an excerpt from Lee Kwangwoo's meditation on Psalm 119:110:

old saying goes, "**It's not the big mountains that trip us, but the small stones.**" A punch can be a knockout, but it's the repeated small jabs that wear us down. Therefore, we must always stay vigilant to avoid falling into traps, whether they are visible or invisible.

However, there is always a sense of regret. Do you know why believers' faith does not grow even though they hear the truth of God's Word? There is only one reason. It's because, even though they hear God's Word, they treat it lightly or do not unite it with faith (Hebrews 4:2). In other words, they do not believe that the Word being spoken to them is God's Word, so they do not engrave it in their hearts but simply let it go in one ear and out the other. The Apostle Paul explains this in 1 Thessalonians 2:13: "**For this reason, we also thank God without ceasing, because when you received the word of God which you heard from us, you welcomed it not as the word of men, but as it is in truth, the word of God, which also effectively works in you who believe.**" This is the secret. Satan's strategy is to make the sermon sound like the words of the pastor rather than God's Word. As a result, most believers ask, "**How was the pastor's sermon today?**" but they rarely discuss what God was speaking to them through the pastor. There is no preparation or intention to receive God's Word as God's Word. Naturally, they do not think about what God's Word has to say to them. But receiving it as the words of a man brings no benefit. One cannot experience God's grace or taste His goodness and righteousness. When we receive God's Word as God's Word, believing it is truly His Word, it will live and work in us. This is what transforms our lives, changes the way we speak, and enables us to bear the fruit of the Holy Spirit, making us more like God. When a pastor prepares a

---

"The wicked have laid a snare for me, but I have not strayed from Your precepts."

sermon believing it to be God's Word, yet the congregation receives it as mere human words, what kind of spark can there be in the delivering and receiving of it?

The Lord clearly stated that unbelief is sin, especially in the temptation of Satan. Not trusting God's Word is to dishonor God's righteous character. Not trusting the Lord's Word is akin to claiming that God either doesn't know what He is saying through the pastor or written Word or that what He is saying is essentially evil. In either case, it is an attack on God's honesty and righteousness. We are not asked to believe God's Word blindly. Blind faith is based on superstition and irrational prejudice. It means believing without any reason to trust. However, what God demands is not blind faith. Humans may appear truthful, but there is much falsehood within us. We often fall into self-contradictions. But God has no such flaws. Even if you tell a liar to believe someone who always lies and never keeps promises, they will not believe them. But God is not that kind of being. He has never broken a promise and cannot lie.

In the Roman Catholic Church, there is a concept called 'fides implicitum,' which means believing the church is infallible and blindly relying on it. However, if the church were truly infallible (which it isn't because it's made up of sinners), then the church could become the object of faith. But no one is without fault except God. Only God is worthy of 'fides implicitum.' That is why it is said that without faith, we cannot please God. Will you trust the lies of Satan, a liar, or will you trust the true and unchanging God? There are many around us who, deceived by Satan's lies, leave God's truth and act wickedly in the name of truth, in the name of the Church, or the General Assembly. We must hold firm to the truth of God's Word, worship the Lord, follow Him, and become like Him.

· Special Meditation 5 ·

The Accuser Satan

Satan not only excels in tempting the saints but also exerts terrifying power in accusing them. The tactics Satan uses to bring us down are all aimed at undermining the sincerity of God and distorting the truth. To achieve this, Satan employs indiscriminate attacks, regardless of time or place. Previously, we reflected on these tactics, and now, I wish to consider another strategy that complements them. This is the strategy of Satan's accusations against us, using undeniable facts to launch his relentless attacks. How do we defend ourselves from his onslaught and strengthen our position, while continually singing songs of improvement? Let us reflect on this together.

Satan often traps us in moral confusion, preventing us from escaping. At times, he may make us feel at peace when we should be grieving, bringing us to tears of repentance. Yet at other times, when we should be at peace, he can cause us to experience immense suffering. These occurrences often arise from the obvious sins that saints commit in their daily lives. In Zechariah 3, we read of the high priest Joshua being attacked by Satan. Satan dares to stand before the all-powerful God, boldly opposing God's holy servant and accusing him with a triumphant attitude. He audaciously challenges God's judgment and tries to erase the mercy God extends to the saints.

Joshua, though standing before the holy God, is not dressed in pure white but in filthy clothes. Satan, pointing out that Joshua is wearing filthy clothes, questions how such a person can stand before God. His accusation is based on undeniable facts—Joshua is indeed wearing filthy garments. He has skillfully pointed out Joshua's weakness. Ironically, Satan, the dirtiest of all, tries to conceal his own filth and instead accuses God's servant, Joshua. In response, God acknowledges Satan's accusations, asking, **"Is this not a brand plucked from the fire?"** Then, God commands the angel of the Lord to remove Joshua's filthy clothes and dress him in beautiful garments. Moreover, God declares that He has removed all of Joshua's sin. This is an amazing comfort and encouragement for saints who are struggling under Satan's schemes today.

All saints are like the scorched wood pulled out of the fire. They are like the wood pulled from the fires of hell. The key point here is that once the wood is pulled from the fire, it is no longer consumed by the flames. It may be scorched for a time, but it is not beyond revival. In due time, leaves will grow, flowers will bloom, and fruit will be borne. However, the fact remains that it is still scorched wood. Whoever touches it will get their hands soiled with soot. These saints are those who battle with the flesh. Their outward appearance may not be different from those of the world and the devil. Though they are pulled from the flames of hell by the Lord's hand, they are still covered in ash. The blackness remains. They may have been rescued from the flames, but they are still covered in soot. In other words, while they are redeemed by faith in Jesus Christ, it is still clear that they are not without sin. Therefore, Satan will never overlook the black parts of us and will continue to point them out. His accusations do not lead us to contemplate God's mercy but rather make us more conscious of our sins, trapping us in guilt and preventing us from approaching God.

We must remember that while saints are indeed scorched wood pulled from the fire, they are saved by God's grace. However, there are still those who are sinking deeper into the raging fire of hellish desires. Satan does not tempt them, as they are already obedient to his every word. Many are being pulled deeper into the fire of hell. How can people escape this fire? It cannot be done with money or by doing good deeds. A tree burning in the fire must be pulled out by someone else in order to avoid being consumed. When God asks, **"Is this not a brand plucked from the fire?"** He is implying, **"Isn't this the one I just rescued?"** Joshua was someone who had been rescued by the Lord's saving hand.

Without help, sinners cannot escape the burning pit on their own. Born into sin, they can only live a life of sin. Without being rescued, there is no way to escape the punishment of hell. The way of salvation is prepared by a loving God who desires to save sinners. That way is through faith in Jesus Christ, who suffered, died, and was resurrected for sinners. Anyone who calls on the name of the Lord will be saved. Those dead in sin and trespasses are given eternal life through faith in Jesus Christ. This is the gospel. Those who do not have this gospel are not subject to Satan's accusations because they are on the same side and have no need to accuse.

However, the saints are accused because they are children of God who have been saved. But even after salvation, they still bear traces of soot. When others touch them, they too become soiled. Satan, with his sharp eyes, will never overlook our soot. He will relentlessly accuse the saints, focusing on their weaknesses. His accusations are not false—they are true. Our sins of immorality, deceit, corruption, hypocrisy, jealousy, hatred, and bitterness, the pride and greed that ensnare us, are all visible to Satan. When he accuses us, we cannot argue because it is all true. Just like Joshua, we are silent in the face of Satan's accusations.

However, at that moment, the saints will hear God's defending voice, rebuking Satan's accusations: **"The LORD who has chosen Jerusalem rebukes you."** God steps in to shut the mouth of Satan, the accuser. This process is like a final judgment scene in a courtroom. God the Father is seated on the judge's bench. Before Him stands the sinner, Joshua. Satan, representing the prosecution, accuses and demands judgment upon him. On the other side, there is a defense team representing Joshua. The defense objects to the accusations, saying, **"I object. This man is one of the scorched trees I pulled out of the fire."** The judge, God, acknowledges this objection. Who is this defender? It is clearly the Son of God, Jesus Christ, who appears in the New Testament. He is the one who rescued Joshua from the fire with His own blood. Jesus Christ acknowledges that Joshua is a sinner, and God the Father also acknowledges this. But Jesus' defense is far more compelling than Satan's accusations. Satan focuses solely on the facts that make the sinner guilty, but Jesus, the sinless one, persuades with His own blood that He is the one who saved him. God the Father supports the defense of His Son, and in this divine courtroom, Satan, the accuser, is left speechless.

The angel of the Lord, who is Jesus Christ, takes off Joshua's filthy garments and clothes him in a beautiful robe of righteousness. A clean crown is placed on his head. What does this symbolize? It is similar to the teaching Paul gives in Romans 13: **"Let us put on the armor of light, walk decently as in the daytime, not in orgies and drunkenness, not in sexual immorality and debauchery, not in dissension and jealousy. Rather, clothe yourselves with the Lord Jesus Christ, and do not think about how to gratify the desires of the flesh"** (Romans 13:12-14). Yes, we must take off the old, corrupt ways of life and put on the new self, created to be like God in true righteousness and holiness. We put on the righteousness of Christ. This is what it means to be a saint. Furthermore, placing a clean crown on the head signifies that the saints will reign with Christ and inherit the kingdom of God as His heirs. How can those who are doomed to hell find themselves in such a glorious position? They are people who, acknowledging their sin and humbling themselves, weep and confess, **"I am a sinner."** Yet, they are able to stand with bright smiles on their faces, crowns on their heads, confidently standing before the righteous God because of the love and grace of the Lord who died on the cross for them. Our salvation is not due to our works but through faith in God's grace (Ephesians 2:8).

Is there anyone reading this who, like Joshua, is wearing filthy clothes? But how long will you wear those filthy clothes? Take them off now. Put on only the robe of righteousness that the Lord Jesus Christ gives you. Satan will no longer be able to accuse you. When Satan points out the sins we have committed, we must boldly declare, **"Yes, I am a sinner. But because of my sins, I believe in Jesus Christ, who was crucified for me. I believe that my sins have been washed away by His blood. 'I, a sinner like me, have been forgiven and made righteous before God, and this is assuredly true, for I have been redeemed by the blood of the Lamb, Jesus.'"**

The garment the Lord provides is not a temporary rental. We may borrow clothes to attend important events, but no one will enter the heavenly banquet wearing borrowed garments. The Lord will give us an everlasting, perfectly fitting wedding garment. No one can enter the feast without this garment. Even if someone were to enter without it, they would be immediately cast out from the banquet table by God's all-seeing eyes. We may be able to pretend in church, wearing fake clothes and acting like we belong. In this world, a man may dress as a woman or a woman as a man and deceive others. In the church, those who are not truly born again may act as though they are. They may receive church positions and even preach. But at God's banquet table, this will not be possible. God's eyes can detect any falseness. No one can escape from His gaze. Even Satan, the master of deceit, cannot hide his true identity from God. How much less can we?

Do not try to deceive God. The Bible urges us to reconcile our hearts with God, the Lord. In other words, before the righteous and just God, we must live truthfully and honestly. No matter how real a mask may seem, it will be exposed before God. We will only be ashamed. Put on the garment that God has provided. No matter how well the world may dress you or how excellent the clothes people provide, you cannot stand before God wearing them. Put on the garment of righteousness that God has made for you through faith. This garment is the righteousness of our Lord Jesus Christ. Whether you are tall or short, young or old, male or female, the Lord has prepared the perfect garment for each of you. Let us praise Him for it.

In today's passage, we see that the Lord removes Joshua's sin and clothes him in clean garments. God, like a kind and gentle teacher, admonishes Joshua, who is likened to a scorched piece of wood pulled from the fire: **"I have taken away your iniquity from you, and I will clothe you with rich robes."** This statement from God includes both rebuke and mercy. It is not a harsh, threatening rebuke but a gentle, compassionate voice that is meant to correct and guide.

While one might not be familiar with the atmosphere of a courtroom, it's easy to understand that the prosecutor's accusations are relentless and unforgiving. However, the voice of the defense attorney, armed with solid arguments, will sound sweet to the sinner who is in the courtroom. This reminds us of the hymn **"When my heart is full of sorrow and my tears flow endlessly,"** a song that reflects the burden of sin. But when we hear the voice of the Lord, our defender, it becomes a source of comfort and relief, as expressed in the hymn **"Who is there to comfort me, but Jesus, my Savior, who is my friend when I am in despair?"** The voice of the Lord, who defends us, is the one that brings us peace, just as we sing with grateful hearts (hymn 83).

In this passage, Joshua simultaneously hears the accusations of Satan and the admonition of God, much like what Christians experience. Every time we sin, we hear Satan accusing us, telling us that we are guilty. At the same time, the Holy Spirit gently convicts us of our sin and calls us to repentance. What is the difference? Satan's accusations, like those of a prosecutor, seek only to destroy us. He wants to cast us into the prison of hell and separate us from God. On the other hand, the Lord's voice seeks to lead us to repentance, to draw us closer to God. It is the Holy Spirit working within us. Satan uses our clear sins to condemn us, while the Holy Spirit seeks to save us from sin.

When we participate in the Lord's Supper, Satan often whispers, **"How can you, of all people, participate in this sacrament?"** He accuses us, reminding us of our unworthiness. But the Holy Spirit leads us to confess our sins and draw near to the Lord, encouraging us to live as children of the light, leaving behind the ways of sin. The Lord's Supper is a beautiful expression of the forgiveness we have through Jesus Christ's sacrifice and a reminder that we are no longer in the fire but are now united with the living God as His children. It is a sacred act of repentance and restoration.

The voice of the Holy Spirit calls us to repentance and assures us of God's grace, while Satan's voice entangles us in guilt and despair, pushing us away from God's grace and leading us deeper into sin. Satan's accusations are destructive, but the Lord's voice brings restoration and comfort. The Lord's Supper is the perfect evidence of this, containing the very essence of the gospel. Satan does not want us to repent and draw near to God. Even if sinners turn away from sin, Satan's followers will not rejoice. Satan desires us to remain in sin, trapped like pigs in a pen. Those under his influence often fall into despair, questioning, **"Why has God made me this way?"** and **"Why does He allow me to live in such misery?"** This is Satan's ultimate goal — to make us believe we are hopeless, that we are nothing but worthless. Satan wants to keep us away from God's grace, constantly accusing us, saying our clothes are filthy, and our sins are too great for a holy God to forgive.

But the voice of the Lord is one of restoration. It transforms us into new people, forgiving our sins and welcoming us into God's loving embrace. 'Yes, recognizing our sins is painful, but it pushes us toward the Father's love. Unlike Satan, who wants us to remain in sin, God's desire is for us to come back to Him, even if we have fallen. Returning to God, even after sin, is what pleases Him.'[58]

We must trust in the grace of Jesus Christ and resist the accusations of Satan. How do we resist him? Through the full armor of God, described in Ephesians 6. When we look at the armor, we see that it is all related to our Lord Jesus Christ. By faith in Him, we possess the **"belt of truth, the breastplate of righteousness, the shoes of the gospel of peace, the shield of faith, the helmet of salvation, and the sword of the Spirit."** Just like the Apostle Paul, we can boldly declare, **"There is therefore now no condemnation for those who are in Christ Jesus, for the law of the Spirit of life has set you free from the law of sin and death"** (Romans 8:1-2). **"Who shall bring any charge against**

---

[58] R. C. Sproul, *How to Please God*, Life Word Publishing, p. 95.

God's elect? It is God who justifies. Who is to condemn? Christ Jesus is the one who died — more than that, who was raised — who is at the right hand of God, who indeed is interceding for us" (Romans 8:33-34).

Let us resist Satan's accusations and declare: "**Slanderer, be gone! Accuser, be silent! Who can bring any charge against God's chosen ones? My Savior has wiped away my sins. He prays for me even now. If you don't want to hear His intercessions for me, then cover your ears. Christ is my righteousness. His merits are mine. Nothing can separate me from His love!**" Amen!

Chapter 4

Resembling Jesus

"For those whom he foreknew he also predestined to be conformed to the image of his Son, in order that he might be the firstborn among many brothers. And those whom he predestined he also called, and those whom he called he also justified, and those whom he justified he also glorified." (Romans. 8:29-30)

• Chapter 4 •

Resembling Jesus

The hymn "**I Want to Be a Christian**" contains the lyrics, "**I want to be like Jesus, truly, truly.**" Have you ever met a Christian who resembled Jesus? The author's thought on this question is that, since I am not yet a likeness myself, how could I expect anyone else to be? It is nearly impossible to think, speak, and act like Jesus, but the thought that a believer should be a little Jesus cannot be erased. A Christian is one who follows Christ and must become like Him. If there is no resemblance at all, it means Christ has not had any impact on me, and therefore, there is no reason to follow Him. However, throughout Christian history, there have been countless people who resembled Jesus Christ. They were not extraordinary individuals; they were ordinary people like us. Yet, they were spiritually extraordinary. Their hearts for the Lord were different from others. For them, only Jesus mattered. They were filled with the Lord and satisfied with Him. Even in a dry and barren land, they thirsted for the Lord (Psalm 63:1). Their pilgrimage was to praise the Lord for their whole lives. Their strength was in rejoicing in the Lord. Their wisdom was in revering the Lord. Their treasure was God Himself. Their boasting was in the Lord alone. Their sorrow was in loving the Lord less. Their sighs were for the fact that believers did not obey God's Word. It was about the godly being cut off and the foundations of the righteous being destroyed. Their hope was placed solely in God. This way of life made them resemble Jesus. They were filled with thoughts of the Lord all day, every day. They knew that the ultimate purpose of human life is to glorify God and enjoy Him forever.

They were far from merely honoring the Lord with their lips. They thoroughly preferred obeying God to listening to human words. They considered the reproach, abuse, and rejection for the sake of the Lord's name to be of greater worth than the pleasures, honors, and powers of the world. They lived looking toward the better city, built and governed by God, through faith. Therefore, they could not help but resemble the Lord. Why is this important for us? The truth is, if we do not resemble the Lord, we could be cast out in heaven as well. Romans 8 says: **"For those God foreknew, He also predestined to be conformed to the image of His Son, that He might be the firstborn among many brothers and sisters. And those He predestined, He also called; those He called, He also justified; those He justified, He also glorified"** (Romans 8:29-30). Since God predestined us to be conformed to the image of His Son before the foundation of the world, and when the time came, He allowed us to believe in Jesus Christ, the path of our faith is the path of becoming like Jesus. In fact, wanting to resemble someone is impossible without love and respect. By following Jesus, you will have experienced that the depth and extent of that love, and the measure of respect, surpasses any self-imposed limits.

Love the Lord with All Your Heart

We love the Lord because He first loved us (1 John 4:19). Though we have never seen Him with our physical eyes, we, as Christians, are those who believe, hear, know, love, revere, and serve Him by faith. To not love or honor the Lord, who gave His body to save us—those dead in trespasses and sins, rescuing us from the power of sin and death—is unthinkable for anyone who is not someone whose conscience is seared. Therefore, we live drawn by a desire to know the Lord more, to follow Him wherever He goes, to emulate whatever He does, and to become more like Him. This desire is not a fleeting impulse; it is a yearning that does not fade away until the last breath in this world. We are compelled by His love. This love keeps our focus on Him, even in the midst of severe trials. Just as the Lord's love for us is perfect, so our love for Him must be perfect.

Let's examine what the Lord required of the people of Israel after they were delivered from Egypt, as a way to understand this: "**Hear, O Israel: The Lord our God, the Lord is one. Love the Lord your God with all your heart and with all your soul and with all your strength**" (Deuteronomy 6:4-5). Jesus echoed this in His conversation with the law teacher: "**What is written in the Law? How do you read it?**" He replied, "**Love the Lord your God with all your heart and with all your soul and with all your strength and with all your mind; and love your neighbor as yourself.**" "**You have answered correctly,**" Jesus replied. "**Do this and you will live**" (Luke 10:26-28). In response to the question about how to obtain eternal life, Jesus' answer was to love God, and this love for God involves a complete reverence of Him, full support and obedience to His commandments. Without this, we cannot avoid the judgment of being false before the Lord, who sees the heart. Why does God require this whole-hearted love? The reason is that God did not give us a fraction of His love but loved us with His whole being. He gave His only Son, and His Son, Jesus Christ, willingly gave His life as a ransom for us. If we understand that nothing is more precious than life itself, then we realize that God loved us with His whole life, and therefore, He expects us to love Him with all our life in return. To not love the Lord with all our heart means that there is something we love more than the Lord, and that is idolatry. Idolatry means worshipping something that has a mouth but cannot speak, eyes but cannot see, ears but cannot hear, hands and feet but cannot move. The Lord did not pour out His life for us so that we would worship idols. We are to abandon empty idols and serve the living God, who speaks, hears, acts with power, and is with us at all times and places. Those who serve the living God and follow Jesus are the ones who resemble Him. Only such people can truly walk the path of becoming like Jesus.

The phrase **"Shema Israel"** mentioned in Deuteronomy 6 is actually a declaration of faith for the people of Israel. It is a confession of who God is and what our duties are toward Him. Here, it clearly teaches how to love and serve the God who led Israel out of slavery in Egypt and gave them the land of Canaan, flowing with milk and honey. Those who truly know who God is will know how to rightly act toward Him. This is because the guidance of the Holy Spirit dwells in the believers. Anyone who understands the love of God, who did not spare His only Son and gave Him for our salvation, will pour out a complete love in return. Since the love God gives is perfect, our love for Him must also be perfect. This is why we must love the Lord our

God with all our heart, soul, mind, and strength. This is not optional, but a necessity. No Christian is exempt from this demand for love. What God most desires from us is our wholehearted love for Him. We often think that God demands money, time, effort, will, obedience, and hundreds of other things from us, but what He truly desires is our perfect love. When we genuinely love the Lord with all our heart, soul, and mind, everything else we give to Him is done freely. If we give money, time, effort, and will to the Lord, yet our love for Him is partial or conditional, then our offerings are in vain, and He may not remember them at all. True, perfect love for the Lord leads us to love our neighbors as ourselves, because if we claim to love an invisible God but do not love visible brothers and sisters, we are lying to ourselves.

Those who have received God's perfect love will fulfill their duties and responsibilities as husbands and wives, parents and children, servants and masters, citizens to the nation, and leaders to the people. All of these duties stem from love for God. There is no area of life where the love of God does not reach. Therefore, anyone who loves God will also love creation. Efforts to protect the environment, expose human rights abuses, fight against injustice, and promote good over evil all stem from God's perfect love. Of course, there are those who do these things without knowing God, and they may even be more enthusiastic than Christians. However, such actions cannot become a means or condition for receiving God's blessings, nor do they bring glory to Him. They only showcase their own righteousness. On the other hand, the good and righteous actions of Christians, though imperfect in many ways, are the fruits of God's infinite love. Hence, we cannot boast about them. Our existence is entirely by God's grace.

Loving the Lord is shown by an exceptional expression of respect toward Him. Those who respect the Lord are also respected by Him, while those who despise Him are scorned (1 Samuel 2:30). Furthermore, those who love the Lord and honor His name will receive the blessing of being recorded in the book of remembrance before Him (Malachi 3). The Lord will protect such people, as a father protects his son, and rescue them from all the traps set by their enemies. The evidence of despising the Lord is disobedience to His commandments. Therefore, we must always read and listen to the Lord's words and act according to them. We should value His words more than fine gold and eagerly desire them. The reason why every word from the lips of someone we love is sweet like honey is because it is an expression of love. Loving the Lord means that keeping His commandments. However, we often fail in this regard. We try to obey His commandments like homework, rather than obeying with joy and without expecting anything in return. Yet, we often expect God to reward us because of our obedience and devotion. We end up treating God as if He owes us. How rude is that? In the past, laws and commandments were objects of fear and terror, but for Christians in Christ, the love and respect for the Lord is expressed in their journey as pilgrims.

Respecting the Lord means valuing what belongs to Him. We should cherish and respect other members of the body, whom He purchased with His own blood. We do not discriminate based on education, wealth, appearance, social status, or age. Instead, we consider others better than ourselves. We seek the benefit of others more than our own. If someone asks us to go one mile, we go two; if they ask for our coat, we give them our shirt as well. In this respect, there is much for us to repent of. When we think about the Beatitudes taught by the Lord, we cannot lift our heads. Yet, we cannot set aside things that are impossible to practice. Just as God the Father is perfect, we must also be perfect, and just as God is holy, we must also be holy. In fact, even in the human world, when brothers live in harmony and show strong affection for each other, it reflects their respect and honor for their parents. In the same way, when Christians turn their backs on each other, quarrel, and judge one another, it dishonors our Father God, our Savior Jesus Christ, and grieves the Holy Spirit who dwells in us. I once visited a retired pastor who had served his entire life in ministry. He now lives in a rural town, tending a vegetable garden, reading the Bible, praying, and exercising throughout his days. Despite losing one of his legs, he never complains. His wife, who has been with him for 52 years of marriage, said that she never heard him speak a sinful word. I was deeply moved by this. In contrast, I often express my anger towards politicians and others who criticize and slander the church, not just in my heart, but openly, using harsh language. Even though I am just as deserving of criticism, I mock and condemn others without realizing it. I tremble at the disrespect shown by some politicians, which is a clear sign of a generation that has lost the spirit of respect. I realize that I still have a long way to go in becoming like the Lord. To love the Lord is to respect and care for others.

Also, we should not steal what belongs to the Lord. Keeping the Sabbath holy and recognizing that everything comes from the Lord, especially the commandment to give a tithe, should not be hesitated. It is no exaggeration to say that the observance of the Sabbath has completely broken down in today's world. Recently, I was glad to visit some churches that still hold evening services instead of the Sunday afternoon services. Although it is widespread to steal the Lord's Day for one's own use and business, if we love the Lord more than anything or anyone else in this world, we must cherish the Lord's Day. This is not optional; it is a command. Misusing what the Lord has instituted is disrespecting the Lord. The prophet Isaiah speaks of the blessings of keeping the Sabbath, saying: **"If you turn your foot from the Sabbath, from doing your pleasure on My holy day, and call the Sabbath a delight, the holy day of the Lord honorable, and shall honor Him, not doing your own ways, nor finding your own pleasure, nor speaking your own words, then you shall delight yourself in the Lord; and I will cause you to ride on the high hills of the earth, and feed you with the heritage of Jacob your father. The mouth of the Lord has spoken"** (Isaiah 58:13-14).

Regarding the difference between the Sabbath and Sunday, the Sabbath commemorates the completion of creation, while Sunday commemorates the completion of salvation. The first day after the Sabbath (Sunday) is when Christians naturally gathered. Not only the resurrection of Jesus but also the day of Pentecost, when the visible church began on earth, was the first day after the Sabbath. The day when the apostles gathered to worship according to their teachings was also the first day after the Sabbath. The day when the Apostle John received his revelation on the island of Patmos was the Lord's Day, which is the first day after the Sabbath. Therefore, through writings like Calvin's Institutes of the Christian Religion and the Puritans' writings on keeping the Sabbath, I hope we can firmly establish why the New Testament church keeps Sunday as the Lord's Day.[59] Every day belongs to the Lord, but especially Sunday, as the day the Lord has established for His people to worship Him, fellowship with Him, and proclaim that they are His possession. In addition, Dr. Pipa in his book outlines three areas for

---

59 Changwon Shu, "Puritan Theology and Faith," Jipyungseowon, 2013, pages 315 and following.
    Joseph A. Pipa, The Lord's day, Christian Focus, 1997.

how Christians should observe the Lord's Day.[60] First, he advises not to waste time on meaningless activities. Take time to reflect on the preached Word. He also suggests having family worship, spending time with family in praise, prayer, Bible reading, and reading devotional books. It is important to check the spiritual condition of your children and educate them in faith (using catechism teachings). Second, he recommends evangelizing, visiting the sick to comfort them, and fostering intimate spiritual fellowship among believers. One should not waste time on personal matters or entertainment unrelated to spiritual nourishment or devotion. The Puritans' understanding of the Sabbath as a day set apart is still a valuable lesson for modern Christians. Just as the light shines brightest when darkness is deepest, in this spiritually stagnant period and time of crisis in the church, it is time for churches and Christians who walk the path of true Sabbath observance to rise up and shine.

These days, many churchgoers are not tithing. However, if we are Christians, we must live by acknowledging that our lives are entirely due to the Lord's grace. We should not merely confess this with our lips but demonstrate it by giving a portion of our income, earned through lawful means, back to the Lord. Tithing or Sunday offerings are not forcibly collected; all offerings are voluntary. These acts should be the fruits of the love and grace we have received from the Lord. Those who are stingy toward God will experience the truth of the saying, **"You reap what you sow."** **"Let each one give as he purposes in his heart, not grudgingly or of necessity; for God loves a cheerful giver. And God is able to make all grace abound toward you, that you, always having all sufficiency in all things, may have an abundance for every**

---

60 Joseph A. Pipa, ibid, 173ff.

good work" (2 Corinthians 9:7-8). Praise God who is able to make all grace abound! Our dedication, effort, and sacrifice come at a cost. Of course, the believer does not dedicate in order to receive blessings; we participate voluntarily in serving the Lord and building up the church because of the blessings we have already received. However, the Lord who receives our dedication will not send us away empty-handed: **"He who sows to his flesh will of the flesh reap corruption, but he who sows to the Spirit will of the Spirit reap everlasting life. And let us not grow weary while doing good, for in due season we shall reap if we do not lose heart. Therefore, as we have opportunity, let us do good to all, especially to those who are of the household of faith"** (Galatians 6:8-10). This is not all. The writer of Hebrews instills this assurance: **"For God is not unjust to forget your work and labor of love which you have shown toward His name, in that you have ministered to the saints, and do minister"** (Hebrews 6:10). The Lord pours out all grace on those who honor Him as the Lord. The Almighty, who does not forget, ensures that we reap what we have sown.

Not stealing the Lord's possessions means that we value the Lord's possessions. In particular, the author wants to emphasize loving and valuing the Lord's bride, the church. Recently, since the COVID-19 pandemic, there has been a decline in affection for the 'gathered church.' The habit of watching services on YouTube from home has had a big impact. However, the church is the Lord's body and bride, bought with the precious blood of Christ. Modern people are more concerned with body care than ever before. When we add up expenses for fitness training, beauty treatments, and diet management, it consumes not only money but also time and effort, expending considerable energy. As members of the body of Christ, how much effort are we putting into caring for the body of Christ? Does our sweat, in making the church a healthy, beautiful bride, reflect something that the Lord, the owner of the church, will approve of? Is it a church that the Lord is pleased with? A true believer does not dream of being like the foxes that destroy the vineyard. The church is the Lord's vineyard, which He has planted and cared for. We should cherish it and invest our utmost care to bear abundant fruit. It is the Lord's body, and if the body is damaged, it leads to an irrecoverable state. There are many ways to ruin the body: poor diet, accidents, and attacks from enemies, as we have seen before. Knowing this, we should not shy away from the role of a watchman.

In the past, our ancestors truly loved the church. Church was always prioritized over family matters, work, and social life. As a result, the church in Korea grew to an unprecedented size worldwide. But now, we are too busy picking the fruit left by our ancestors, and we fail to prune the branches or plant new seeds to bear the finest fruit. Without fruit, the leaves just grow lush until autumn, when they fall off. The church is on the verge of being cut down and thrown into the fire. The Lord does not wish for His church to be destroyed in this way. As the owner of the church, He will do His part: "**If his children forsake my law and do not walk according to my judgments, if they break my statutes and do not keep my commandments, then I will visit their transgressions with the rod, and their iniquity with stripes. Nevertheless, my lovingkindness I will not utterly take from him, nor allow my faithfulness to fail. My covenant I will not break, nor alter the word that has gone out of my lips. Once I have sworn by my holiness; I will not lie to David. His descendants shall endure forever, and his throne as the sun before me; it shall be established forever like the moon, even like the faithful witness in the sky. Selah**" (Psalm 89:30-37).

God, who came as a descendant of David, came to save sinners and establish the church, which He will never completely destroy. He will certainly leave a remnant, and through them, the church of the Lord will stand firm forever. God, who is merciful and gracious, will not always chide, nor will He keep His anger forever. He does not deal with us according to our sins, nor repay us according to our iniquities... As a father pities his children, so the Lord pities those who fear Him, for He knows our frame; He remembers that we are dust" (Psalm 103:9-14).

What lesson does this teach true Christians? Even if the church seems to be in poor condition, overflowing with faults and failures, and standing on the edge of a cliff, the church of the Lord will last forever. It is the church that the Lord built with His own blood. Therefore, He will not treat us according to the sins we have committed, but in His mercy, He will cleanse us, remove the filthy garments, and clothe us with new fine linen. We should cherish and love the church that is held in the Lord's hands, not the one fallen into the hands of the wicked. That is how we resemble the Lord. Therefore, Apostle Paul said that the concern for the church presses on his heart every day (2 Corinthians 11:28). The psalmist sings: "**How lovely is your dwelling place, O Lord of hosts! My soul longs, yes, even faints for the courts of the Lord; my heart and my flesh cry out for the living God... Blessed are those who dwell in your house; they will still be praising you. Selah**" (Psalm 84:1-4).

The ones who feared leaving this house the most, even though they were captured as captives, prayed three times a day towards Jerusalem, like Daniel, longing for it. David, who had experienced fleeing from Jerusalem, confessed: "**One thing I have desired of the Lord, that will I seek: That I may dwell in the house of the Lord all the days of** my life, to behold the beauty of the Lord, and to inquire in His temple" (Psalm 27:4). Therefore, those who love the Lord's church always pray for its complete establishment.

David, with great certainty, sang: "**Pray for the peace of Jerusalem: 'May they prosper who love you. Peace be within your walls, prosperity within your palaces.'... For the sake of the house of the Lord our God, I will seek your good**" (Psalm 122:6, 9). Just as our Lord loved the church and gave His body for it, we also join in the path of resembling the Lord by loving the church in the same way. Those who cherish what belongs to the Lord and firmly build the church, which the gates of hell will never overcome, are the ones who follow the Lord and become like Him. "**Rejoice with Jerusalem, and be glad with her, all you who love her; rejoice for joy with her, all you who mourn for her. That you may nurse and be satisfied with the consolation of her bosom, that you may drink deeply and be delighted with the abundance of her glory... For behold, I will extend peace to her like a river, and the glory of the nations like a flowing stream; then you shall nurse, you shall be carried on her hips, and be dandled on her knees**" (Isaiah 66:10-12).

Be Like the Gentleness and Humility of Christ

To resemble the Lord cannot be discussed without mentioning His gentleness and humility. Jesus said to those who follow Him: "**Take My yoke upon you and learn from Me, for I am gentle and humble in heart, and you will find rest for your souls. For My yoke is easy and My burden is light**" (Matthew 11:29-30). This passage reveals that the best way to learn gentleness and humility is by taking the Lord's yoke upon ourselves and following Him. Naturally fallen humans cannot expect gentleness and humility on their own. However, gentleness and humility are virtues that go hand in hand. In fact, these traits are refined through suffering. Tribulation trains us, making our rough edges smooth, and the proud become humble through such trials. Originally, the word **"humility"** is known to mean **"low"** or **"miserable."** So why is Moses described as the meekest and most humble of men, resembling Christ? It is because, although Moses grew up as the son of a princess, having been educated in all the wisdom of Egypt, he humbled himself to the position of a servant, willingly suffering with God's people, the Israelites, even though he could have ruled. Christ, too, though equal to God in glory and power, emptied Himself and took on the form of a servant, coming into the world as a man to give His life for those dead in their trespasses and sins. In this sense, the humility of Christ, who came in the flesh to save those who were truly dead in trespasses and sins, those oppressed by the power of death, the poor, the weak, and those vulnerable to exploitation (Amos 2:7, Isaiah 11:14) —who humbled Himself to the point of dying on the cross—serves as an example for all believers to follow. His humility was not simply enduring insults, mockery, and suffering silently. After this suffering, He was exalted with the highest name above all others, and every knee will bow to Him. Thus, Christian humility involves being a servant but being exalted as the Lord, being despised but becoming precious, becoming poor but rich, being attacked by enemies but advancing to glory surrounded by angels.

Generally, people say that husbands and wives resemble each other. Not only do they resemble one another, but the children born to them often look like both the father and the mother. This resemblance is not just in outward appearance but also in their mannerisms, habits, and way of life. In this way, we can understand what it means to be like Jesus. Being baptized into Christ is not just an act of becoming a member of the church with rights and duties. It is spiritually like a marriage with Christ, where we are united with Him, our bridegroom. When we first accept Jesus as our Savior, we are moved by His love and commit ourselves to follow Him forever. This leads us to strive to know Jesus more and walk in His ways. The natural result is that we begin to resemble the Lord. When a man and a woman love each other and marry, they live together, talk together, eat together, sleep together, and go out together. As they do this, they pledge to carry out their responsibilities as husband and wife.

At a wedding, the bride and groom pledge to love, cherish, and respect each other in times of joy or sorrow, health or sickness, promising to faithfully uphold the vows of marriage. The officiant then announces that they are united in marriage and declares that what God has joined, let no one separate. Similarly, when someone is baptized as a believer, they make a vow to walk with the Lord forever. They pledge to live for the Lord Jesus Christ, who gave His life for them, and devote themselves to this path until the end. This vow reminds the believer of their privileges and responsibilities as part of the church. The baptized person, based on this vow, affirms that nothing in this world can separate them from the love of Christ. **"Who shall separate us from the love of Christ? Shall tribulation, or distress, or persecution, or famine, or nakedness, or danger, or sword? ... For I am sure that neither death nor life, nor angels nor rulers, nor things present nor things to come, nor powers, nor height nor depth, nor anything else in all creation, will be able to separate us from the love of God in Christ Jesus our Lord"** (Romans 8:35, 38-39).

Those who have learned and internalized the meekness and humility of the Lord in such confidence will produce miracles. "**A miracle is not a flower blooming on a dead tree. A true miracle is the water you give to your garden every day, even on the day of despair.**"[61] This is because we have hope in the Lord, who gives life even to the dead and enables us to overcome abundantly. The crisis of the church or personal difficulties are always made by ourselves. And it is the privilege of those who love the Lord, who works all things together for good, to turn crises and pain into opportunities for blessing. When we do our best for the body of Christ, His church, until the end, the Lord's hand will be with us, adding strength to help us, and His arm will make us strong.

Because we are united with Christ through an unbreakable love, we can emulate His meekness and humility. We receive all the nourishment we need from Christ. As time passes, the life-giving work of Christ makes us more and more like Him. This is not the result of intentional efforts or a set standard of achievements to check, but the natural outcome of being tied to Him by an unbreakable bond of love. Just as a man who continues to receive female hormones will become feminized, and conversely, a woman who receives male hormones will become masculinized, a believer united with Christ continuously receives life-giving sap from Him. Christ nourishes the church. The entire body receives help through Christ and grows to the full stature of Christ. Therefore, union with Christ is a very natural source of likeness to Him. Let's now look at the biblical lesson that union with Christ teaches.

In fact, union with Christ promotes the sanctification of the believer. We have already been made holy, blameless, and above reproach

---

61   Baek Young-ok, titled "When We Do What We Can," published in the *Chosun Ilbo* on September 28, 2024.

before God through the blood of Christ, but believers must always pursue holiness while living in this world. This is the path of being led by the Holy Spirit, for the Spirit of truth leads us into truth, and that truth sanctifies us (John 17:17). It makes us holy as God is holy. Not pursuing holiness only leaves us with the curse of not being able to see God (Hebrews 12:14). A Christian lives in Christ Jesus, led by the Holy Spirit, and lives as a holy people, just as the Father is holy. This is the process through which the image of Christ is formed in us. This does not happen all at once just by believing in Jesus, but is completed through the process of being trained as citizens of the holy Kingdom of God. The life of a believer who has Christ in their heart is, as Paul confessed, "**I live, but it is not I who live, but Christ who lives in me. And the life I now live in the flesh, I live by faith in the Son of God, who loved me and gave Himself for me**" (Galatians 2:20).

In this way, the path of becoming like Jesus depends on the time spent with Him. The more time we spend with the Lord, the greater His influence on our hearts and minds will grow. The process of gradual sanctification will expand. As mentioned earlier, this is manifested through the killing of sin, self-denial, and joyfully taking up our cross. Being led by the Holy Spirit and rooting ourselves deeply in the truth involves not just dealing with visible sins, but also with the inner sins within us, such as envy, jealousy, pride, malice, hypocrisy, and lust. This is a daily spiritual battle in which we must never put down the full armor of God. This battle does not happen once in a while, but occurs every day, every moment. Therefore, we cannot be satisfied with merely meeting with the Lord once a week, like a weekend couple. Every moment, every day, we must walk with the Lord. Without Him, even breathing becomes difficult. We communicate with Him in prayer, seek His will through meditation on the Word, and live a life that lifts Him up in praise. This is not a task to be performed according to a schedule, but rather the pattern of daily life. We must pray without ceasing in the Spirit, meditate on the Word day and night, nourish our souls with spiritual food daily, and offer praise with thanksgiving according to His grace. This is how each believer, as the bride of the Lord, lives a life that engraves His image within us.

On the other hand, it is through the servants of the Lord, who are entrusted with the Lord's sheep, that the congregation should receive proper pastoral care. Apostle Paul says: **"My children, for whom I am again in the pains of childbirth until Christ is formed in you"** (Galatians 4:19). **"We proclaim Him, admonishing and teaching everyone with all wisdom, so that we may present everyone perfect in Christ. To this end I labor, struggling with all His energy, which so powerfully works in me"** (Colossians 1:28-29). The formation of Christ's image in us does not come from individual testimonies, opinions, or casual stories centered around hobbies or interests of the pastor. Just as the apostle himself did, the truth of Christ's word must be proclaimed and taught.

What the world truly needs is not economic development, scientific progress, or the expansion of social welfare. Even when people lived in thatched houses, human life expectancy was sustained, and when people believed that a rabbit lived on the moon and pounded rice, people still lived on earth. Whether in the age of agricultural life or in this modern era of advanced scientific civilization, one thing remains unchanged: humans are sinners. Since the fall of Adam and Eve, humanity has been dead in transgressions and sins. What humanity needs is the gospel of the cross of Christ Jesus. He preached Jesus Christ. No matter the method of teaching, he used all wisdom to proclaim Jesus.

He did not spare the pains of childbirth until the congregation became perfect in Christ Jesus. So, from the perspective of the congregation, shouldn't we receive the proclaimed word in faith so that it can live and work in us? It must be received not as the word of man, but as the word of God. In other words, just as the apostles' words were implanted in the hearts of the congregation through their open ears, today, through the preacher, the word of the Lord is implanted into the hearts of the congregation. That word transforms the righteousness of believers and produces the fruit of the Holy Spirit. In this sense, the pastoral work of the pastor is the role of deeply engraving the image of Christ into the hearts of each believer. It is to help them become complete in Christ. It is to labor for them to be chosen as a pure bride for Christ. The word "**labor**" carries the meaning of putting forth every effort, as in a sports competition. It is not a vague expectation that the Holy Spirit, who works powerfully within them, will fill in the gaps due to the apostle's incompetence or laziness, but rather it means running as a player striving to win.

The attitude of the congregation toward pastors who serve in this way should not be determined by the pastor's appearance, personal character, or the congregation's own theological views, fickle emotions, or personal preferences. The attitude of the congregation toward a pastor who preaches God's word should be determined by their loyalty to the biblical message the pastor delivers. A pastor must be a shepherd who is willing to serve and sacrifice for the Lord's sheep. A pastor must proclaim and teach only the truth as a worker of the truth. The pastor must love the Lord's sheep with the heart of the Lord. The congregation is not serving because they like the work done in the church, but because they serve all good works with a pure passion for love toward Christ. They give thanks deeply to the Lord for the fulfillment of His will according to the written word.

In this way, becoming like the Lord involves using all means of grace. It is not just His meekness and humility. It involves imitating the qualities and characteristics of the shepherd, who feeds, cares for, protects, and stays with the sheep, sweat and all, to ensure they are safely guarded from thieves and wolves. The task of the pastor is to present Christ as a pure bride to Him, whose joyful voice says, "**My beautiful one, my bride, come with me**" (2 Corinthians 11:2). Therefore, living together includes not only the process of beautifying oneself as the Lord's bride but also becoming perfect in Christ. As a member of Christ's body, we must be careful not to cause harm or dishonor.

A pastor must be ready to die for the sheep. Each believer must put their full effort into adorning themselves as the bride of Christ according to the guidance of the pastor. This will be accomplished through a lifetime of learning and following the Lord. Just as Esther was chosen only after adorning herself according to the royal protocol, those who adorn themselves according to the written word will be chosen as the bride of Christ (Esther 2:15).

In fact, one can adorn themselves without strictly following the prescribed regulations set by the Lord. They may become an object of admiration in the eyes of the world. They may even perform prophetic acts in the name of the Lord, cast out demons, and display great power in His name. However, in the eyes of the Lord, who judges righteously by looking at the heart, all of that may be false. "**I never knew you. Away from me, you evildoers!**" (Matthew 7:23). Binding ourselves to the written word is the safest path to becoming like Christ. Paul declares: "**And we, who with unveiled faces all reflect the Lord's glory, are being transformed into His likeness with ever-increasing glory, which comes from the Lord, who is the Spirit**" (2 Corinthians

3:18).

Those who have intimacy with God experience no conflict. They have no anxiety about belonging. Worries about the future cannot find a place in them. The assurance and boldness of being transformed into the image of Christ is not a privilege for a few, but a privilege for all Christians who are intimate with God. Of course, just because we are close to God, it does not mean we can perfectly see His glory. It is like looking into a mirror. The mirrors in Paul's time were not like the clear, bright mirrors we have today. Ancient mirrors were made of polished metal and provided blurry, faint, and somewhat distorted images. Therefore, Paul said that although we can behold the glory of the Lord on earth, it is still like looking into a blurry mirror, and we cannot yet see it perfectly. However, as we behold His glory, we will gradually be transformed into His image. Though it is not yet, the time will come when we will reach glory after glory, and it will be clearly revealed.

It is not that we shape ourselves into the image of Christ, but that God, who is intimate with His children, shapes us. Just as the Holy Spirit made us born again, He leads us into the path of holy truth and guides us to live in the image of the Son. He will ultimately bring us to glory.

The question, **"How can I change?"** or **"How can they change?"** exists for everyone. As I mentioned earlier, the most remarkable and lasting change depends on intimate fellowship with the Lord. There is nothing as certain as the stream of change brought by the Holy Spirit in the fellowship with the Lord. Even though one has confessed faith in Jesus for a long time, the greatest reason they may not experience change is their failure to have intimate fellowship with the Lord. Even though they may use the means of grace, they remain lazy and lack the zeal to learn from the Lord, getting swallowed by worldly things, thus unable to put their effort into it. This results in avoiding the continuous spiritual warfare. However, as mentioned earlier, when we put on the full armor of God and resist the devil, rather than seeing the bait he throws, we will see the hook behind it. We will see the poison inside the golden cup. Spiritual giants and veterans can see what beginners cannot. While beginners might fall into traps unexpectedly, veterans know how to escape. But beginners might suffocate in those traps. That is why we must follow the Lord closely and never take our eyes off of Him. The devil's tactics and strategies can never overcome the Lord. Therefore, Apostle Paul said, **"we beheld His glory."** Behold! This word does not mean to glance at something casually. It means to look carefully. It means to gaze attentively at the Lord's glory.

We can be transformed by the Lord's glory, but we must pay careful attention to it. There is a huge difference between someone climbing a mountain to find ginseng and someone merely hiking. The hiker cannot shout, **"I found it!"** Only the person who is looking for ginseng can shout that. Similarly, to behold the Lord's glory is to find a treasure that cannot be found in the world. There is a mystery, emotion, and rapture that cannot be fully expressed with words. The glory of being transformed into the image of the Lord will unfold before us. The more we spend time observing the glory of God — the love, righteousness, peace, grace, and holiness — the more we will display the transformation of growth in love, righteousness, peace, grace, and holiness. This is a mystery beyond becoming a skilled assistant from being a beginner. Therefore, when we see someone's appearance resembling that of the Lord, we can assume they have shared a close relationship with Him. When we look into **"God's mirror,"** we often think we are seeing who we are (and in fact, we are), but in reality, we are seeing who we will become. What we will become depends on the knowledge we have of God. If we have a false picture of God, we will see that false image in God's **"mirror"** and be transformed into that same image. This will bring great harm both now and in eternity. Therefore, we must grow in the right knowledge of the Lord.

If we view things through our subjective thoughts, or the false pictures of false teachers, or if we see them as counterfeit, the image of the Son will not be engraved in us, and we will not be able to attend the wedding feast. Instead, we will fall into the pit of weeping and gnashing of teeth in a curse. The Jews who had a false picture of God committed the foolish act of crucifying the Messiah sent by God.

Not everyone who looks in the mirror sees the truth. But the true Christian sees the truth of the Lord through God's mirror. The distorted image of God is restored by faith in Jesus Christ, and through Him, we become blessed participants in the divine nature. A Christian who has received such grace will enjoy the mysterious experience of being transformed into the image of the Lord through intimate fellowship with Him. This transformation is not instantaneous but ongoing. It is from glory to glory. The apostle did not mean that our change is from decline to glory, or from corruption to glory; rather, he is showing us that God's work in our lives is an ongoing process from glory to glory. This transformation does not come by our strength and will but by the Holy Spirit, who comes from the Father and the Son. Therefore, he said, **"it is by the Spirit of the Lord."** This is very important. We cannot achieve or obtain spiritual change just by looking into the Lord's glory in the mirror. Instead, by placing ourselves where the Spirit of the Lord can change us, we will experience the transformation from glory to glory.

Obey Until Death

One of the most difficult aspects of living a life of faith is obedience. Without breaking our will, we cannot obey. We are all like sheep, accustomed to going our own way. We used to act like wild horses, enjoying running rampant. However, once we come to believe in Christ, learn from Him, and follow Him, we marvel at the beauty of obedience. Jesus' obedience blossomed through His emptying of Himself of His rights. He is undoubtedly equal to God in glory, power, wisdom, and knowledge. However, He did not consider equality with God something to be used to His own advantage. He emptied Himself, taking the form of a servant and becoming like a man. But it did not end there. For the salvation of sinners, as decreed by God the Father, He obeyed even to the point of death. He prayed, **"If it is possible, may this cup be taken from Me,"** yet He decisively said, **"Yet not My will, but Yours be done"** (Luke 22:42). To lay down His will, He prayed all night. His sweat became like drops of blood falling to the ground. Despite weeping and crying, the fruit of His prayer was to willingly drink from the cup of death. This is how He accomplished our salvation. This stands in stark contrast to the act of the first Adam.

By the sin of one man, death came to reign through that one man. Adam's disobedience made many people sinners. However, the obedience of one man (Jesus Christ, the second Adam) made many people righteous (Romans 5:17-19). While He was on earth, He never lived according to His own will. Everything He did was in accordance with what the Father entrusted to Him, and He was fulfilling the Father's will. The Apostle Paul followed this example. **"But I consider my life worth nothing to me; my only aim is to finish the race and complete the task the**

Lord Jesus has given me—the task of testifying to the good news of God's grace" (Acts 20:24). Therefore, he said, "**Follow my example, as I follow the example of Christ**" (1 Corinthians 11:1). Reflecting on this, I feel deeply ashamed. When Paul wrote to Timothy, he said, "**Don't let anyone look down on you because you are young, but set an example for the believers in speech, in conduct, in love, in faith, and in purity**" (1 Timothy 4:12). But I fall short of setting such an example in my faith journey and following the path of Apostle Paul.

There are not many who are willing to say what Paul said. Instead, we often use excuses such as the difficulty of practicing true piety or compromising in our lives, and we say, "**Don't look at me, look at Jesus.**" Of course, we must ultimately look to Jesus. However, we must become examples to others of what it means to look to Jesus.

It is wrong to live selfishly and self-centeredly. We must live as citizens of heaven, with a heavenly focus. Our will, desires, and intentions must always be subject to the Word of the Lord so that His will is fulfilled in us and in the situations of our lives. If we can say, "**Follow me as much as you see me following Jesus**," as we see others following Jesus with all their hearts, we would be happy believers.

In the parent-child relationship, it has become the norm to fail to honor or obey parents. Instead of "**Children, obey your parents, for this is right,**" the saying "**There is no parent who can be defeated by their child**" has become a public truth and proverb. Educational theories that prioritize encouragement and praise over correction, arguing that this builds children's confidence, have become more influential than the teachings of the Bible. However, the Bible does not command us to obey and honor our parents because they are superior to others, highly educated, or influential. It simply says, "**Children, obey your parents**" (Ephesians 6:1). Therefore, there are no conditions for obedience.

Just as the Father sent the Son to fulfill His mission even to the point of death, the Apostle Paul also considered his life not precious in order to complete his mission. Similarly, we must obey and honor the parents who gave us life and raised us.

When I was studying abroad, I asked my professor (Clement Graham), who taught practical theology, when it would be appropriate to teach a child to obey. I will never forget his answer: **"Teach them obedience as soon as they are able to understand what it means!"** I always instilled this in my children, and because of this, I have rarely been upset by their disobedience or lack of respect. I am still grateful for my youngest child who obeyed without hesitation when I told her to give up her teaching career in Hawaii and get married first. Now, she lives happily as a pastor's wife, raising children.

When a person becomes a believer, they vow to obey the Bible and the laws of the church. However, in the subsequent life, the Bible is often ignored, and church laws lose their power. No matter how much we emphasize theological positions such as Reformed theology, the reality in the pastoral field is different. The reason why there are so many disputes, lawsuits, and divisions in churches is that people are more focused on their worldly rights than submitting to the authority of the Lord. Churches are governed more by secularism and humanism than by the authority of Scripture and theology. Following the Lord means to give up willingly physical and material benefits for spiritual ones. Only then can Scripture and theology take their proper place. If we realize that the honor and glory of the church, the bride of Christ, are more important than the honor and glory of pastors or individual believers, we will practice the truth that obedience is better than sacrifice. Just as we know the glory that Jesus Christ, the obedient Son, received (Philippians 2), we praise the Lord who exalts His obedient children to high places so that they will not be shamed.

Obedience involves suffering. It is a constant challenge in following the Lord fully. But it is neither something to turn away from nor run away from. **"Christ suffered for you, leaving you an example, that you should follow in His steps"** (1 Peter 2:21). If our obedience to the Bible brings benefit to the church, peace to the home, and harmony in relationships, even if it results in some loss, walking that path will bring glory to God. The world will know that God is the true God and that we are His people.

Forgive

Forgiveness is more effective when done by the stronger rather than the weaker. Jesus, who had no sin, was treated like sinners and was put to death by crucifixion because of our faults and sins. Peter, who was somewhat proud of following the Lord, asked how many times he should forgive a brother who sins and asks for forgiveness. He wondered if forgiving seven times (which, from my perspective, is quite generous) would be sufficient, and Jesus replied, **"Not seven times, but seventy-seven times"** (Luke 17:3-4). However, it is not easy to forgive someone who does not repent. Jesus did not witness Judas Iscariot's repentance (of course, Judas never truly repented and only regretted betraying his teacher). Nevertheless, Jesus did not confront him as a thief or scold him in front of others. He did not warn the other disciples to be cautious of him. Instead, He kept embracing him, repeatedly offering him opportunities to repent. This raises the question: what should we do when someone has never repented? Should we forgive them? Even if we do not reach mutual understanding and the relationship is not restored, we can still choose to forgive from our side and pray, waiting for God to work in their life for the restoration of the relationship.

This is why we are told to pray, **"Forgive us our debts, as we also have forgiven our debtors."** I used to skip this part of the Lord's Prayer for a while because there was someone in my heart whom I couldn't forgive. But now, I pray this part with ease. Jesus did not narrow the scope of forgiveness but rather broadened it. He did not give us reasons to avoid or withhold forgiveness. Jesus prayed for those who crucified Him, asking God to forgive their sins, and the first martyr, Stephen, prayed in the same way (Luke 23:34, Acts 7:60). Therefore, believers who follow Jesus should deeply remember the words, **"Be kind and compassionate to one another, forgiving each other, just as in Christ God forgave you"** (Ephesians 4:32).

Unfortunately, when conflicts arise in the church, it is wrong to become lifelong enemies. We must choose to forgive but abandon condemnation. We should accept others but never participate in their sins. We might doubt the sincerity of someone who repeatedly sins and asks for forgiveness, but Jesus still tells us to forgive and not sever fellowship with them. Joseph, who forgave his brothers for selling him into slavery, prioritized God's will over his personal feelings. He could say, **"Do not be afraid. Am I in the place of God? You intended to harm me, but God intended it for good to accomplish what is now being done, the saving of many lives. Do not be afraid. I will provide for you and your children"** (Genesis 50:20-21). Here, forgiveness does not mean turning your back and cutting off the relationship but continuing to look after and nurture the relationship. The forgiveness we must practice does not only seek peace in our hearts but aims for the restoration of the relationship. This kind of heart comes from having the Lord's heart.

Without the promise of eternal life in heaven, it would be impossible to do. When I was pastoring, I rarely engaged with those who opposed me. I prayed for them, but I refused to engage with them personally. Now, I deeply regret this. If only I had embraced them just one more time and been more open, the relationship might not have deteriorated so badly. Perhaps it is just because I have become more understanding with age. Although I can talk about Jesus' forgiveness, I am still far from applying it to myself.

The root cause of conflicts in the church lies in selfishness, impulsiveness, narrow-mindedness, and emotional factors like pride. Therefore, forgiveness, acceptance, and unity are fundamental elements of the grace covenant. Without forgiveness, we cannot properly serve God or fully experience His grace. Jesus teaches us: **"Therefore, if you are offering your gift at the altar and there remember that your brother or sister has something against you, leave your gift there in front of the altar. First go and be reconciled to them; then come and offer your gift"** (Matthew 5:23-24). If we have been forgiven, we too must forgive. The command to forgive is not just for our inner peace and satisfaction but leads to reconciliation with those who have wronged us.

John Owen said: **"Our forgiving others does not earn us forgiveness. However, our failure to forgive others proves that we have not been forgiven."**[62] These are truly frightening words. If we have a clear assurance of the forgiveness of our sins and believe in eternal life, we should, with the help of the Holy Spirit who dwells within us, eagerly follow the example of the Lord's forgiving and generous love. If we believe that there is no great sin that God cannot forgive, we will not live with the attitude of **"I can never forgive,"** no matter the circum-

---

62 John Owen, *Works of John Owen*, Vol 6, The Banner of Truth Trust, 1981, 497.

stances.

The Way of Serving

Serving has already been discussed in Chapter 1, so I will pass over it briefly here. However, I would like to emphasize one more thing: every believer has the mission to serve in building up the body of Christ. Who should we serve? We should become good neighbors to God's people in the name of the Lord and to those outside the church who are in need of help. In the Old Testament, the teachings on gleaning during harvest (leaving the corners of the fields for the poor, not picking up fallen grains, and not going back for forgotten sheaves) were commands for the benefit of strangers, orphans, and widows. This was the way to receive blessings (Leviticus 19:9-10). While it is important to adopt an attitude of frugality so that not even a single grain of rice is wasted, true loving service will be shown when we willingly and secretly accept discomfort, even if our loss benefits the weak and needy.

Someone said that a religion without gentleness becomes violence, and there is some truth in this. God sent the gospel to the poor, the brokenhearted, the prisoners, and those in captivity (Isaiah 61:1). The psalmist sings: "**He will deliver the needy who cry out, the afflicted who have no one to help. He will take pity on the weak and the needy and save the needy from death. He will rescue them from oppression and violence, for precious is their blood in his sight**" (Psalm 72:12-14).

The reason why Christians must always fulfill good deeds is because faith without works is dead. Job spoke about his good deeds, saying,

"**The foreigner did not sleep in the street; I opened my doors to the traveler**" (Job 31:32). He also made this claim: "**Have I ever denied the desires of the poor or let the eyes of the widow grow weary? Have I ever eaten my food alone, without sharing it with the orphan? From my youth, I have cared for the orphan as a father would, and I have guided the widow from my birth. Have I ever seen anyone perishing for lack of clothing, or the needy without covering? If I did not warm them with the fleece from my sheep, or if I did not pray for them, then may my shoulder fall from its socket, and my arm be broken**" (Job 31:16-22).

The Christ, who deserves to be served, came to serve, washing the feet of His disciples and obediently dying for the salvation of sinners. Like this, we must not ignore the example of service that the Lord has shown us. However, the ultimate purpose of any service is not the satisfaction of the one who serves or the contentment of the one being served, but to bring glory to God, who supplies grace through careful attention and care for all people. Service should not be focused on making oneself stand out, but on making the other person shine. When the purpose of service is self-display or seeking praise from others, it reflects the sinful nature of those who do not know God. "**Religion that God our Father accepts as pure and faultless is this: to look after orphans and widows in their distress and to keep oneself from being polluted by the world**" (James 1:27). These days, it is hard to even find the outward appearance of this, but a true Christian is one who possesses not only the appearance of godliness but the power of godliness. Service is not a transaction for personal gain. It is something we practice because we know that it is more blessed to give than to receive (Acts 20:35). "**Each of you should use whatever gift you have received to serve others, as faithful stewards of God's grace in its various** forms" (1 Peter 4:10). We must be diligent in ensuring that the grace God has given us is not wasted. Blessed is the believer who hears the Lord's praise when standing before Him: **"Well done, good and faithful servant. You have been faithful with a few things; I will put you in charge of many things"** (Matthew 25:23). I hope that each of us will serve sincerely with faithfulness, diligence, and joy according to the grace we have received, walking the path of true faith.

Seek the Things Above

When the Lord was on earth, He never forgot the God above. He always thought of the time when He would return to the place He came from, and He faithfully walked the path to fulfill the mission for which He came. Those who follow Jesus and desire to imitate Him will deeply meditate on the place where He is. The Lord's kingdom is not a kingdom of this world, so we strive to enter the place where the Lord is. Although the world is under His rule, until the time of the resurrection, when the completion of redemption is revealed, the power of the ruler of this world remains strong. Therefore, believers do not cling to this world but set their hearts on the better city. The Apostle Paul teaches this: **"Since then you have been raised with Christ, set your hearts on things above, where Christ is, seated at the right hand of God. Set your minds on things above, not on earthly things. For you died, and your life is now hidden with Christ in God. When Christ, who is your life, appears, then you also will appear with him in glory"** (Colossians 3:1-4).

The starting point for the Christian's practical life is union with the risen Christ. A believer who has been raised with Christ (Colossians 2:12) does not strive to grasp, taste, or touch earthly things. They are citizens of heaven. Therefore, they rejoice above all in the spiritual blessings that belong to heaven. While living on earth, the believer casts off the things of this world and strives to put on the things of heaven (2 Corinthians 5:2). Thus, the goal is not so much to take off, but to put on. This is because they know there is a homeland, an eternal home, awaiting them. They regard life on earth as that of a pilgrim. The Greek word for **"seek"** in **"set your hearts on things above"** indicates a passionate desire or pursuit. To do this, one must set their heart firmly on heaven.

The attitude or mindset of being absorbed in heavenly things must exceed the passion and earnestness with which one once clung to earthly things before believing in Jesus. This is because the things of the earth are like mirages. While they may briefly excite, they ultimately lead to thirst. But the things of heaven are eternal, and thus there is no hunger, thirst, or dryness. They are the living water that will never run dry, and the fountain of eternal life.

Not everything in the world is evil, but the love of money is the root of all evil. It is good to live joyfully, but desiring pleasure is closely linked with evil. Power can benefit many if used wisely, but if abused, it harms many people. Even things that do not seem harmful in themselves (friendship, loyalty, service, etc.) can become obstacles to seeking the things above if they distract from it. Therefore, heavenly wisdom is needed. Heavenly wisdom is **"first of all pure; then peace-loving, considerate, submissive, full of mercy and good fruit, impartial and sincere"** (James 3:17). If these results are produced, then whatever is done is acceptable. In contrast, the wisdom of the earth is full of bitter envy, selfish ambition, boasting, and quarreling. It is **"earthly, unspiritual,**

and demonic" (James 3:15). **"Earthly"** means living according to the values of the world. It means living in accordance with the trends and customs of the world. **"Unspiritual"** refers to living for the satisfaction of animalistic desires and instincts. **"Demonic"** refers to living without regard for God's will, only considering human affairs and thus undermining God's good, pleasing, and perfect will (Matthew 16:23). It is a life deeply rooted in the spirit of this world, which hinders the radiance of the gospel of Christ.

Therefore, a true believer always looks to the Lord who is above, striving to enter His kingdom. One of the greatest examples of this life is Abraham, the father of faith. He **"made his home in the promised land like a stranger in a foreign country; he lived in tents, as did Isaac and Jacob, who were heirs with him of the same promise. For he was looking forward to the city with foundations, whose architect and builder is God"** (Hebrews 11:9-10). Even though Abraham could have built a magnificent palace and enjoyed abundant wealth for generations, he lived in tents, mindful of his life as a pilgrim, knowing that a better city, a city built by God, awaited him. Moses, too, considered the disgrace suffered for the sake of Christ to be of greater value than the treasures of Egypt, for he was looking forward to his reward (Hebrews 11:26). Our Lord did not exchange the power and glory that could be enjoyed on earth for heavenly things. He ascended to the place where God is, seated at the right hand of the Father, and is preparing a place for those who follow Him. As Calvin said, **"We are travelers on the journey to heaven, and we must always keep our eyes on that destination."**[63] This is focusing on our heavenly calling and living for God's

---

63   John Calvin's *Institutes of the Christian Religion*, Book 3, Chapter 9, Section 4, p. 237

glory.

Our true and eternal home is the heavenly kingdom where Jesus is seated at the right hand of the Father, interceding for us. The longing to enter this kingdom intensifies through the trials and sufferings faced on the narrow road. Just as a thirst for health comes through pain, the trials and sufferings of life on earth lead us to yearn for the glory of heaven. This is why suffering is beneficial. It helps us shed the worldly attachment to this life filled with toil and sorrow, and instead, it increases our desire for a better life.

In this sense, Calvin described life on earth as "**life in exile.**" The hope of an exiled life is liberation—the longing to enter the eternal kingdom of the Lord, where there is no more sorrow, pain, death, or separation. Calvin asks, "**If enjoying God's presence is the highest form of happiness, then what is the state of misery if we are without His presence?**"[64] He believes that during our life on earth, we must emulate Christ, who was led to slaughter like a lamb (Romans 8:36), and "**even if the wicked seem to enjoy wealth, honor, and peace on earth, we must lift our heads above all earthly things and look to heaven. Even though we may suffer under the oppression of the wicked, their arrogance, greed, and harshness, we will endure in hope. For when we reach our eternal homeland, the Lord will receive His faithful servants, wipe away every tear, clothe them in garments of glory and joy, feed them with joy beyond words, and invite them into His eternal fellowship.**"[65]

Therefore, seeking the things above is about desiring to live with heavenly things, and in doing so, we can experience the peace, joy, and

---

64 John Calvin, ibid, 237.
65 John Calvin, ibid, 240

satisfaction that come from heaven even while on earth. Though the perfect fulfillment of these promises will come only in the heavenly homeland, the best Christian life on earth comes from a heart fixed on heaven. Believers understand that their lives are now hidden with Christ in God, and because Jesus is seated at the heavenly throne, their thoughts and hearts are also connected to heaven. Heaven is in us, and we are in heaven. In this sense, it would be a blessed thing for a believer to die early and go directly to heaven. Paul also said, **"I desire to depart and be with Christ, which is better by far"** (Philippians 1:23). **"We are confident, I say, and would prefer to be away from the body and at home with the Lord"** (2 Corinthians 5:8). Yet, while we still breathe on earth, we must live by heavenly wisdom, striving to **"please the Lord,"** and whether we live or die, our goal should be to honor Christ in our lives as we journey toward our true homeland. Until that day, we run the race set before us, according to the laws God has established. We fight the good fight of faith, strengthening our faith through the means of grace. Then, we will receive the crown of righteousness.

> Sola Scriptura
> Sola Fide
> Solus Christus
> Sola Gratia
> Soli Deo Gloria

Review of Learning Content

01. What are some ways to resemble Jesus?

02. Why does God command us to love Him with all our heart? (Deuteronomy 6:4-5)

03. What is the most proper way to honor the Lord? (1 Samuel 2:30)
    (1) Why is it that doing God's will does not become our daily bread?

    (2) What are the things that we must honor as belonging to the Lord?
       a. The Lord's Day (Isaiah 58:13-14)
       b. Tithes (2 Corinthians 9:7-8, Malachi 3:8)
       c. The Church: The Body of Christ (Ephesians 1:15-23, 1 Corinthians 12:27), The Bride of Christ (Ephesians 5:31-32)

04. How is true humility attained as a virtue? (Matthew 11:29-30)

05. What are the obstacles to obedience? (Philippians 2:8)

06. Should forgiveness come from me first, or from the other person? (Luke 23:34)

07. Is serving the opposite of being the greatest? (Mark 10:42-45, Galatians 6:9-10)
   * What do I think is the biggest obstacle to serving?

08. What does it mean to seek the things above? (Colossians 3:1-4)

09. Let's share experiences of how we have practiced what we've heard and learned.